3

'If you're a fan of Judith Butler, Hilton Als, Mark Doty, you will love Webb's *Strange Relations*'
Raymond Antrobus, author of *The Perseverance*

'Webb's writing is of a quality rarely seen, and his book returns you to the world slightly changed, equipped with another angle of vision on the quiddity of man'
Diarmuid Hester, author of *Nothing Ever Just Disappears*

'There is palpable urgency to this book as it questions, reimagines and contextualises the link between sexuality, gender and identity; and between fiction and autobiography. I returned to these pages each night in awe and with the feeling that I had encountered something new and necessary and exciting'
Lauren Aimee Curtis, author of *Strangers at the Port*

'Ralf Webb delivers a captivating study of the writers who fought back against the repressive models of post-war masculinity, and dared to imagine a freer, queerer future. A moving and empowering book'
Will Tosh, author of *Straight Acting*

'*Strange Relations* achieves the rare holy trinity for a nonfiction book: its exploration of the mutability of masculinity is rigorously researched, full of humane and original insights, and delivered in the kind of stylish and distinctive prose that could only have been written by an essayist who is also a poet'
Philippa Snow, author of *Trophy Lives*

'A beguiling portrait of the singular artists who have challenged and shaped our ideas of sexuality and masculinity. Impeccably well researched and hugely enjoyable'
Nicole Flattery, author of *Nothing Special*

Ralf Webb is the author of *Rotten Days in Late Summer*, which was shortlisted for the Forward Prize. His poems, essays and short fiction have appeared in *Fantastic Man*, *Granta*, the *Guardian* and the *London Review of Books*. *Strange Relations* is his first non-fiction book.

Strange Relations

*Masculinity, Sexuality and Art
in Mid-Century America*

Ralf Webb

Sceptre

First published in Great Britain in 2024 by Sceptre
An imprint of Hodder & Stoughton Limited
An Hachette UK company

1

A CIP catalogue record for this title is available from the British Library

Hardback ISBN 9781399713214
Trade Paperback ISBN 9781399713221
ebook ISBN 9781399713238

Typeset in Bembo MT by Hewer Text UK Ltd, Edinburgh
Printed and bound in Great Britain by Clays Ltd, Elcograf S.p.A.

Hodder & Stoughton policy is to use papers that are natural, renewable
and recyclable products and made from wood grown in sustainable
forests. The logging and manufacturing processes are expected to
conform to the environmental regulations of the country of origin.

Hodder & Stoughton Limited
Carmelite House
50 Victoria Embankment
London EC4Y 0DZ

www.sceptrebooks.co.uk

For my friends

Contents

Introduction

The moment a muscular, twenty-three-year-old Marlon Brando, costumed in a tight oil-stained t-shirt, appeared on Broadway as the 'sexual terrorist' Stanley Kowalski, theatregoers were confronted with a meteoric vision of male virility never before seen on stage. 'I could hardly hold him within bounds,' Tennessee Williams said of creating Kowalski, the antagonist of his 1947 play, *A Streetcar Named Desire*. It was as though he'd stumbled on some untapped, elemental force, one that the sexually fluid and little-known Brando – the 'best-looking young man' Tennessee had ever seen – was uniquely equipped to manifest. Stanley-Brando represented the eroticised, desiring and desirous male body, an icon of unbridled carnality that stretched the puritanical censorship guidelines which presided over so much post-war American artistic production, and asked new questions about the intersections of sexuality and masculine identity.

Stanley Kowalski is not merely a sex symbol. He is also a tyrant, and his tyranny infects and poisons his relations with the other men in the play, his poker-playing, beer-swilling buddies. Through group failure, these men collectively license Stanley's tragic (implied) rape of the protagonist, Blanche DuBois, and her subsequent sectioning. In many ways, Stanley Kowalski is an embodiment of James Baldwin's belief in the stalled, infantile state of modern masculinity, and *Streetcar's*

I

story an example of the deleterious consequences such masculinity, and malignant relations between men, has on others: women, families, entire communities.

James Baldwin, the novelist, essayist, and one-time collaborator and friend of Tennessee Williams, declared early in his career that 'the great problem is how to be − in the best sense of that kaleidoscopic word − a man'. Baldwin understood that this 'great problem' was more than a personal or individual issue. It cut right to the heart of American society. It may, in fact, be the root cause of so many societal problems. Baldwin identified a failure in American and western life, and a failure of the 'masculine sensibility'. Somewhere, he said, somehow, 'something broke down', and the result is that masculinity is stuck in an immature state, one which promotes violence and cruelty, and leaves its men isolated and unreachable.

The early 1940s through to the mid-1960s − the decades in which the writers in this book produced their most lasting works and became literary celebrities and public figures − was a time of immense cultural and societal upheaval in America, during which conceptions of sexuality and gender were being newly defined by legal and medical discourses, debated in public forums and weaponised for political ends. Tennessee Williams' creation of the magnetic and malevolent Stanley emerged from this upheaval. But *Streetcar* is no dated, mid-century relic. As the theatre critic Ira J. Bilowit remarked, three decades after the play premiered, 'You can't imagine a time when *Streetcar* didn't exist [. . .] when Stanley Kowalski wasn't with us.' Watching Brando as Kowalski today, in *Streetcar*'s 1951 Hollywood film adaptation, his preternatural sexual energy − so much beer foam sprayed over his sweat-slicked torso − is overwhelming, more salacious than much of what passes for the erotic in current mainstream cinema (particularly when it comes to sexualised representations of men). And his rage, meanwhile, all those violent outbursts and wild-eyed death stares, threatens to shatter through our screens.

Tennessee Williams' message of sexual power, infantile masculinity and poisoned male relations, though transmitted from the past, has immediate relevance to our contemporary crisis in masculinity: from the unrelenting tirade of male violence against women to the silent epidemic of men's mental ill-health, loneliness and suicide, and the steep rise in incidents of violent hate crime and discrimination against the LGBTQ+ community. And, just like the mid-century, our present moment is characterised by a colossal cultural shift. Once again, concepts around gender and sexuality are rapidly changing and being fought over, a morass in which the very meaning of masculinity is being critiqued and questioned, and from which it might – can – emerge changed for the better.

In *Streetcar*, masculine identity and the failures of relations between men are depicted by a playwright who had experienced, first-hand, the full effects of such a crisis. But Tennessee Williams' works also offer possibilities for other, stranger, models of masculinity. As do the lives and works of James Baldwin, John Cheever and Carson McCullers, all of whom to a greater or lesser extent knew one another, were influenced by and influenced one another's art. All four writers had relationships and desires that crossed gender lines, and this put them at odds with the dominant gender ideals of their day. They lived and worked at a time when sexuality was widely considered to fall along a homosexual/heterosexual binary, a binary which cost one side everything: heterosexuality was the monolithic norm against which homosexuality was classed abnormal (and, indeed, anything abnormal was classed 'homosexual'). It was a time when to be queer was to be a figurative – sometimes literal – outlaw, when homosexuality was considered a psychological defect, a neurosis, a mental handicap and a moral perversion. But against this domineering, oppressive climate, these writers shared a joint, particular fascination with the idea that sexual identity is fluid, that desire is amorphous, indiscriminate, and resists neat categorisation. And they shared a conviction that such lines of thought, woven through their art, expressed in their lives, might open up new possibilities for understanding masculinity. Might, in fact, transform it.

Tennessee Williams was born in Mississippi in 1911. Though he spent much of his life as a cosmopolite – first as an itinerant, unknown poet, later as a world-famous playwright and celebrity – he always remained transfixed by his homeland. His childhood in Mississippi was 'gracious – full of imaginings', and provided a wellspring of ideas and inspiration throughout his career. The South also intrigued him because he felt 'the war between romanticism' and 'the hostility to it' was particularly sharp there. This war, a battle between those who revere beauty and idealism and those who wish to extinguish it, is a kind of blueprint for understanding his stage plays. It's a battle that plays out time and time again between many of his characters. The dreamer against the hardened realist, the lover against the tyrant, the poet against the world: alternative ways of living, alternative expressions of selfhood, fighting to break free from paternalism, convention and conformism.

The novelist, poet and playwright Carson McCullers also hailed from the South; she was born in Columbus, Georgia, in 1922. For McCullers, writing was a 'wandering, dreaming occupation'. It was a tussle between hard labour and the mysterious workings of the unconscious, from which sprout 'illuminations' that eventually bloom into the finished creative work. Like Tennessee Williams, she sought and found literary success away from her Southern roots. She moved to New

York and published the two novels which established her reputation as a leader of a literary generation before she was twenty-three years old. At that age, she told a close friend: 'I was born a man.'

McCullers enjoyed that her name gave people pause. 'Carson' was frequently taken to be a man's name. Throughout her life, as a means of expressing how she internally felt, McCullers wore men's clothes: baseball caps, dungarees, outsize shirts, slacks, suits. This was also a disruptive act, an act of rebellion; she meant to reorient others' expectations of gender presentation. And in her works McCullers explores the idea that gender and sexuality are unfixed, free-floating signifiers – that everyone is in some sense androgynous in their feelings and desires – and portrays how a dominant, masculinist social order, in order to retain power, goes to absurd lengths to deny this.

With their shared Southern heritage and artistic sensibility, it was perhaps inevitable that Tennessee Williams and Carson McCullers became friends. Theirs was a deep, long-lasting union. Across their careers, they fiercely defended the integrity of each other's artistic vision against critics and naysayers, of which, eventually, there were many. And they advocated for one another's right to portray, through their art, what they called the 'truth': their critiques of intransigent masculinity and the oppressiveness of patriarchal institutions – from the macro to the micro, the military to marriage – that, they knew, sought to delimit and set the terms of love and desire.

Like Carson McCullers, John Cheever – born in Massachusetts in 1912 – also considered writing a kind of sorcery. He wrote in order to 'divine the motives of human conduct'. As well as dozens of short stories and five novels – which chronicle mid-century suburbia, with its parochialism, paranoias and remorseless consumerism – Cheever maintained a private journal for much of his adult life. When excerpts of his journals were first published in book form in 1991, a decade after his death, readers and critics were shocked by what they contained. They held revelations about Cheever's private life that were completely unknown to the public. In prose that alloys asperity and lyric poeticism, Cheever writes about his debilitating alcoholism, his depression, his fantasised and actualised infidelities. He also writes, extensively, about his sexuality.

John Cheever's sexual and romantic interests included both women and men, and he was tortured by this. He felt there was an irreconcilability between his queerness and his masculinity which forced him to live a 'double life', one he found 'loathsome, morbid, and anyhow impossible'. For Cheever, as for many men of his generation, masculinity necessitated heterosexuality. The two were inseparable. Any expression of alternative sexuality or gender was tantamount to surrendering one's manhood. Still, Cheever tried to conjure a more expansive conception of masculine identity, one capacious or fluid enough to permit and even celebrate his queerness. This was a lifelong struggle, and something he returns to time and again in that act of divination and self-examination that was his writing.

John Cheever's fellow Northerner James Baldwin also explored that 'great problem' of masculinity in both his fiction and autobiographical writing. Born in Harlem in 1924, Baldwin cut his teeth in the art of elocution and exhortation as a teenage preacher, before renouncing the ministry to pursue the writing life in New York City's Greenwich Village in the mid-1940s. The Village, a hotbed of radical leftist intellectuals, actors and artists, painters and poets, seemed to promise a route to artistic success. But Baldwin soon learned that this apparent haven for nonconformists was sustained by a set of bewildering social, sexual and racial codes. Its bars were populated by voluntary middle-class exiles play-acting as libertines, its streets plagued by trigger-happy policemen – the

omnipresent face of white, masculinist power – and its subterranean queer scene, he discovered, was a place of danger and
contradiction. This world warped and disfigured his sense of
self, provoking a severe identity crisis. In this context, deci-
phering what it meant to be a man – which necessitated
examining how the forces of class, race and sexuality worked
to construct his own masculinity – was nothing less than a
matter of survival.

These four writers lived and worked during a period of
American history in which homophobia was both virulent and
diffuse. Medical-legal language and laws conspired to promote
a hardened, obstinate version of masculinity whose key characteristic had existed in the cultural imagination for decades, but
hadn't before been so cleanly and clearly articulated: one that
presupposed heterosexuality as the proper mode of desire, and
demanded heterosexuality of its men. A masculinity which –
in order to prove itself – repudiated homosexuality and
anything 'queer' through homophobia.

Homophobia isn't an arbitrary or accidental phenomenon;
rather, it is better thought of as a tool or mechanism of oppression, neatly defined by Baldwin as 'a way of exerting control
over the universe, by terrifying people'. Society, we know, is
organised by male-led institutions, in which men forge relations with one another to establish solidarity and cement
power, enabling – in turn – the oppression of women. Anything
that can affect or set the terms of these power-cementing,
homosocial bonds is therefore, itself, immensely powerful.
This is exactly what homophobia does: when wielded, it
proscribes, restricts or otherwise defines bonds between men.
So inextricable is homophobia from patriarchy that our society, as the pioneering queer theorist Eve Kosofsky Sedgwick

observed, 'could not cease to be homophobic and have its economic and political structures remain unchanged'.

The existence and prevalence of homophobia impacts all men. Sedgwick describes a 'residue of terrorist potential, a blackmailability of western maleness through the leverage of homophobia' that, in essence, contorts and makes paranoid all male relations, regardless of individual sexuality. Simply put, men's relationship to other men, in whatever form that relationship may take – fraternal, platonic, professional, familial, romantic – is haunted by homophobia, the ever-present prospect of being 'accused' of queerness, or being attacked or ostracised in lieu of one's queerness.

Understanding the origins of twentieth-century homophobia helps us grasp the true extent of its impact. The very terms we use today to describe sexuality – indeed, the very concept of a sexual personage – had not yet come into the cultural consciousness prior to the twentieth century. When the historical construct of the 'homosexual' emerged as a category of person, it also described a pathology. Homosexuality was theorised as a sickness, a weakness, an internal flaw: a series of invented, ostracising appellations carried inside one another like Russian dolls. But the societal revulsion towards the 'homosexual' is more textured still. Homophobia is also, necessarily, a form of misogyny. Not only does it govern those power-cementing bonds between men which actively oppress women, but it so often manifests as an essentialist repudiation of the so-called feminine in men. Because we live in a society which relies upon the enforced subordination of one gender beneath another for its very structure, this begins to make a negative, horrible logic. Homosexuality becomes conflated with effeminacy (where effeminacy is metonymic with 'fragility', 'vanity', 'softness', and even – here we begin to sense how dizzying is the waltz between homophobia and misogyny – 'illness'). Both the feminine and the homosexual, therefore, are quashed under the regime of patriarchy, lest they threaten the totality of male power.

The impact of homophobia, the way it poisons and makes paranoid relations between men and men, women and men, the way it impacts society as a whole, was felt everywhere in mid-century America. One of its most obvious and injurious manifestations even made queerness a national security threat. The communist witch-hunt that raged under Senator Joseph McCarthy into the 1950s was accompanied by a parallel witch-hunt of homosexuals, one backed by state police and the FBI, a period in American history since dubbed the 'homosexual panic'. Homosexuality, like communism, became an invisible, omnipresent and insurrectionist threat – a mass illusion of doubles in which one's friend, father, or brother *might not be who they claim to be.* It was a time, as John Cheever remembered, when everyone worried about queerness, and when every man underwent a private, psychic turmoil: 'Is he? Was he? Did they? Am I? Could I?'

Alongside the homosexual panic, America experienced an unprecedented period of economic prosperity following victory in the Second World War. During this so-called 'Golden Age of Capitalism', the nuclear family and household was held as a new societal ideal, and Americans enjoyed unheralded access to consumer goods. To help sustain this ideal – marriage, procreation, and the high quality of life that the sugar-rush of endless consumerism seemed to promise – there was a renewed emphasis on heteronormative masculinity, personified in the image of the breadwinning husband and family man. This was buttressed by a revolution in the psycho-analytic community, where a uniquely American appropriation of Freudian ideas took the nuclear family – and the mandatory heterosexuality it demanded – as the 'norm' to which neurotic patients should be 'adjusted'. Meanwhile, in the Southern US, other, more tangible revolutionary forces were at play. The mid-1950s saw the birth of the civil rights movement, which sought to abolish racial discrimination and segregation. This movement threw fresh light on the history of racist, masculinist violence through which white supremacy operates. The civil rights movement also stoked contentious and revolutionary discourses about the nature of America's very soul. Within these debates, notions of nationhood and futurity – and therefore procreation – loomed large, their shadows inevitably falling over that perilous interpersonal, intra-psychic terrain of masculinity and sexuality.

James Baldwin thought that the 'seismographic shudder' which occurred in the American mind or soul at the mere mention of homosexuality wasn't about a 'fear of sex between men; it's fear of people touching each other'. He knew that an inability or refusal to accept even the existence of sexual inti-macy between men – the all-consuming, totalised terror of queerness – resulted in an inability to accept any kind of affirmative intimacy between men whatsoever. It created a void, a space in between men, which, he argued, had its roots in misogyny. 'When men can no longer love women they also cease to love or respect or trust each other, which makes their isolation complete. Nothing is more dangerous than this isola-tion, for men will commit any crimes whatever rather than endure it.' In this thinking, homophobia is something which enshrouds a spectrum of suppressed or potential affirmative, alternative relationships between men, inclusive and exclusive of the sexual. Each of these four writers sought to celebrate such relationships, to make visible those hinterlands of desire which lie between and outside the supposed sexual binary, and to reveal the consequences of its invisibility.

★　　★　　★

Describing sexuality and desire can be like trying to clasp at smoke, and applying contemporary language to the lived experiences of writers from the past is particularly challenging and treacherous. Language and ideas are products of history, their meanings metamorphose over time. The aim here is not to retroactively assign or ascribe fixed labels of sexual identity, from our ostensibly more progressive era, upon authors who so frequently challenged the notion that there are any stable markers of such identity, authors who believed that desire could not be tallied, rationed, or measured. Nevertheless, contemporary language can help us to speak clearly to one another now.

'Bisexual' is a complex term, often understood to denote a fixed third position between two distinct categories of person, an awkward configuration at risk of reinforcing the very binary that 'bisexual' seeks to evade or disrupt. The term also carries with it a number of stereotypes, the most harmful of which needs defusing before 'bisexual' can be used effectively. This is the homophobic accusation that people who identify as bisexual are really closeted homosexuals, or, conversely, deluded heterosexuals. This stereotype would imply that the only 'valid' bisexual is someone who maintains an even split between their opposite- and same-sex romances; an inauthentic, surely impossible characterisation that reduces desire to arithmetic and the desired to beads on an abacus. The habitual denigration of the term bisexual, however, shouldn't dissuade us from using it. On the contrary, in a culture that casts desire in binary terms there's all the more reason to name, explore and detail bisexuality. In this book, 'bisexuality' will be used to denote and validate a changeable flow of romantic and sexual desire, rather than to describe a static personal identity. In this way it helps us conceptualise and visualise sexual and romantic desire as something which can and docs oscillate, directing itself towards both opposite- and same-sex interests.

And we have more fluid, contemporary terms at our disposal, too. 'Queer', in its original sense, meant odd, peculiar or strange. During the lifetimes of the four writers in this book, it was most often used as a homophobic slur or pejorative, but later reclaimed by the LGBTQ+ community as a positive, celebratory identifier. Since that time, 'queer' has become an elastic umbrella term, signifying a whole set of non-normative actions, attitudes and sexual and gender identities. As a wide, malleable signifier, however, it carries its own potential difficulties. Some suggest the word has ceased to be effective or constructive, that its contemporary usage is too broad, prohibiting it from denoting anything meaningful. Others caution that its current sense leaves it susceptible to co-option by the same social discourses it is used to critique: that any individual or entity, from politicians to the entertainment industry to corporate advertising, can easily appropriate aspects of queer culture perceived as 'fashionable' while disregarding the oppression suffered by those in the community.* 'Queer' remains beneficial, however, describing both the quicksilver of an unconstrained desire, as well as alternative approaches to gender, without erecting boundaries.

Both bisexual and queer, used transhistorically, help us to describe aspects of these writers' lives and works, especially given their own resistance to monolithic configurations of sexual identity. John Cheever, writing in his journals, would often characterise the nature of his own questing desires as his 'sexual iridescence', a wonderful phrase bringing to mind a mysterious rainbow-like play of colour. For McCullers, who was twice married to the same man, and fell in love with several women across her life, love and desire was something messy, sticky and adhesive – like 'jam' – and absolutely could

---

* See, for instance, 'queer heterosexuality,' 'queer baiting' and 'pink-washing'.

not be labelled. Her belief that everyone possessed an inner androgyny was shared by Tennessee Williams. He spent most of his romantic life exclusively with men, but contended that there was no such thing as a precise sexual orientation. Williams believed everyone to be ambiguous sexually, and was reluctant to affix orientation onto his characters, even (or especially) when pressed to do so in interviews. For him, what ultimately triumphed over gender or sexuality was that paradoxically human and celestial trait: love. 'It doesn't make a goddamn bit of difference who you go to bed with,' Tennessee told *Playboy*, in a late-career interview, 'as long as there's love.'

James Baldwin also expressed a fervent dislike and distrust of labels – when it came to sexuality as well as other markers of identity – believing that to label someone was to force them into an 'airless' cell, thereby suffocating some essential truth about their humanity: 'If one's to live at all, one's certainly got to get rid of the labels.' Baldwin, whose romantic relationships primarily, though not exclusively, tended towards men, was occasionally frustrated by the binary view of sexuality, lamenting that for many people 'homosexuality is just the other side of heterosexuality and nobody makes any connections' between them:

Those terms, heterosexual, homosexual, bisexual, are 20th century terms which for me, really have very little meaning. I've never myself, in watching myself and watching other people, been able to discern exactly where the barriers were. Life being what life is, passion being what passion is.

These writers' shared resistance to static notions of sexuality – their willingness to plunge into the vagaries of desire, dredging up revelations of immense consequence to masculinity – is, in part, what makes their stories so special. The many alternative approaches these writers took towards gender norms and conventions are helpfully described as 'queer'; but the term bisexual might specifically denote aspects of their desires and sexualities – and those of their fictive characters – that were non-normative. But we should think of this term as a lens through which to view their sexuality, not as a fixative.

The seeds for this radical reconfiguration of masculinity, however, can be found fifty years before these writers became literary figures. They can be traced back to the life and work of the most influential poet in America's literary history, whose art and ideas were so enchanting that they left an indelible impact on the entire culture: Walt Whitman. In his magnum opus, the poetry collection *Leaves of Grass*, Whitman developed a radical new philosophy of love between men, which sought to promote affirmative male bonds, to celebrate and make visible new kinds of intimacy and communion. He named this philosophy 'adhesiveness'. Whitman's poems suggest something extraordinary: that adhesiveness contains utopian possibilities, and might help usher in a new age, one void of social stratifications and the menace of war.

The canvas upon which Whitman paints this American utopia is suitably visionary: his depictions of adhesiveness occur in a landscape of glistening ponds and rain-slicked pines, a verdant, organic ecosystem that seems to give life to and nourish his bold ideas. In his life and work, Whitman sought to explore the exact same questions that preoccupied McCullers and Williams, Cheever and Baldwin: what is the meaning of masculinity? How should we define it? Why do relations between men so often seem poisoned by cruelty and isolation? What happens – or can't happen – between men, at the crossroads of masculinity and desire?

Poetry is potent. It bleeds in around the edges of things, pigmenting the collective imagination of those who are exposed to it. Towards the end of Whitman's life – just like our current moment, and the mid-century – theories and notions of sexual and gender identity were undergoing a radical, seismic shift. In the midst of this revolution, Whitman's adhesiveness became a volatile, highly charged concept, and had a tangible impact on the twentieth-century frameworks of 'sexuality' which McCullers, Williams, Baldwin and Cheever all worked within and against. *Leaves of Grass* also became a lodestar for countless queer twentieth-century artists and writers. Indeed, for Tennessee Williams, Whitman was a talisman, for Cheever, an enigma, and for Baldwin, a key.

Just as Whitman's story contextualises the mid-century writers at the heart of this book, so, too, can those mid-century writers contextualise our own precarious present. And though artists are not pedagogues – these writers didn't set out to create literal guidelines through the complex terrain of gender and sexuality – their lives and works do cast a light on its deadfalls and quagmires, as well as its unfamiliar, mysterious enclaves, where new, strange and insistent possibilities for masculinity await. Their insights on misogyny, power and violence, on fraternity, paternity and friendship, and their investigations into love, sex, desire and intimacy, help us approach many of the issues men face today from new vantage points: why does masculinity, and the ways men relate to each other, seem so broken? How can we build something transformed and transformative from the ruins?

PART ONE

O Adhesiveness!

The Rebel Soldier Friend

January 1889, Camden, New Jersey

In the dimly lit living room of a modest, two-storey timber-framed house, an enormous grey-bearded man lolls on his rocking chair, a wolfskin draped over the back. Dusk falls. Dry kindling cracks in the fireplace, like joints clicking. Beneath the man's beard, and his flowing mane of white-silver hair, his face glows pale red. He's always prided himself on his rosy complexion, taking it as evidence of manly health, vigour and a strong constitution. But he knows, now, that it counts for little. Because he is ill. Seriously ill.

This is the American poet Walt Whitman, at sixty-nine. A paralytic stroke the previous year has rendered him immobile. His memory – which was always steadfastly reliable – is beginning to fail him. Just this week he sent a runner off to the bank to deposit a cheque, only to be told that he had already had it cashed, more than a year ago . . . He believes this memory loss is a sign that he is approaching the end of his life, what he calls 'the toppling-off place'. But looking around the living room, in this house in Mickle Street – the only house he's ever owned – it's difficult to blame the cheque incident on memory loss alone. The room is a complete mess. The windowsill and tables are cluttered with wax-encrusted candlesticks, empty teacups and heavy tomes, while the floor is carpeted in an ankle-deep litter of 'books, magazines, thrown-down letters and circulars, rejected manuscripts, memoranda, bits of light or strong twine'. Despite attempts from his housekeeper, Mary Davies, to bring order to this visible chaos, Whitman resists, likening this mass of paper to a sea and his room to an old ship's cabin. Whatever is needed from this historic debris, he says, will float to the surface eventually. But he appears less like the captain of a steady ship, and more like a floating swimmer, far out from shore, perilously unaware that he might be pulled under this ocean of paper at any moment.

This mess of printed matter is spawned from a poetic project that has consumed much of Whitman's adult life. One that began many years ago, in his thirties, when he set out to create a book that was alive; a book that could change and develop, decay and regenerate with the passing of time. Inside this living book, he wanted to put a living person: a real individual, a version of himself. Just as the book itself could metamorphose, he imagined, so would this individual shape-shift, shed and adopt a range of personas and attitudes. 'I am large,' reads the familiar quote, 'I contain multitudes.' Through this man inside the book, Whitman aimed to reconcile the individual with the mass. 'This poet celebrates himself,' he wrote of his project, 'and that is the way he celebrates all.' In celebrating the many through one, Whitman believed his poems could imagine – even make manifest – a new vision of America.

The book was *Leaves of Grass*, a collection which won him international renown and became a foundational text in American poetry. *Leaves* went through seven separate editions in Whitman's lifetime, growing from a slim, anonymous volume published in 1855, to a several-hundred-pages-thick 'Deathbed Edition'. It is this final edition which Whitman is now preparing and cogitating on, in 1889, in Mickle Street. He considers its meanings. He wonders if he knows what it means at all. His poetic intentions, which had formerly been so clear, are now confused; he feels that he has lost all control over his book. In this darkened room, the mess of papers, letters and photographs amassed on the floor – that chaotic archive of his life's work – appears as though it wants to physically swallow him up, as if the text really is living, and to keep on living, needs to devour its maker.

By his old age, Whitman has accrued followers and disciples, in both the US and England. Mostly, they are men. Three of them – Thomas Harned, William Douglas O'Connor and Horace Traubel – are with him, now, on this cold January evening, taking care not to crush or step on some precious scrap or missive in the ocean of paper at their feet. These men act as close friends, confidants and caretakers, helping the aged and ailing Whitman with daily tasks. They believe that Whitman is a genius, perhaps even a prophet. 'In his aspect were singularly blended the prophet and the child,' O'Connor wrote of him, 'the child in him inspired love; the prophet, awe.'

Whitman has appointed Harned and Traubel as executors of his literary estate. Realistic about the poet's health, the men understand that the disorder which surrounds them now will soon become a posthumous archive. It will be their task to bring order to and curate that archive. These papers represent the raw clay from which they will soon have the opportunity to build their own version – what they see as the final version – of Walt Whitman, American bard, for posterity.

Horace Traubel, in particular, has a seemingly inexhaustible amount of energy to expend on Whitman and his legacy. A moustachioed, floppy-haired socialist of thirty, Traubel becomes the poet's representative, notetaker, proofreader, accountant and nurse. He painstakingly transcribes countless conversations with Whitman, later creating from these notes nine volumes of journals that chart the poet's final years. Leaning against the warm wolfskin, Whitman rocks pensively back and forth, his firm blue eyes roaming around the room and the men gathered in it, simultaneously appraising and draining. Traubel looks askance at a disordered stack of documents, in a box by the fire. Atop the box, he spies a photograph, and recognises it with a jolt of displeasure. He picks it up. The photograph shows Whitman, in better health, some twenty years ago. He is sitting beside a young man.

Thick, dark locks flow out from beneath the young man's tilted homburg. He and Whitman are not only facing one another, they are – as Traubel will later write – gazing at each other. This is no accident or improvised flourish. Whitman is positioned in the foreground, occupying more space, meaning that the younger man must actively turn and pose in order to meet the poet's eyes. The composition of the photograph is exacting. The photograph's caption, scrawled in Whitman's hand, reads: *Walt Whitman & his rebel soldier friend Peter Doyle.**

Whitman has erroneously dated it as 1865, despite it having been taken several years later. But 1865 will always be enmeshed with Doyle in his memory: it was the year the two men first met. Peter Doyle was a former Confederate soldier paroled in Washington DC, where he worked as a horsecar driver. One evening, Whitman, then forty-five years old, found himself the sole passenger in Doyle's horsecar. Doyle later remembered their first meeting: 'We felt to each other at once [. . .] He was

---

* This photograph, 'Walt Whitman and Peter Doyle by M. P. Rice, *c.*1869', is held at the Bayley Collection, Ohio Wesleyan University. The inscription, on the recto, top margin, reads: 'Washington D.C. 1865 – Walt Whitman & his rebel soldier friend Pete Doyle'. It can be viewed at whitmanarchive.org.

the only passenger, it was a lonely night [. . .] I put my hand on his knee – we understood.'

After that meeting, Peter and Whitman became close, remaining so for many years. They exchanged dozens of letters, which demonstrate their intimacy and comradeship, with Whitman, the older man, so often adopting a paternal role. He proffers advice and mentorship. He refers to Peter as 'my darling boy', 'my young & loving brother'. He signs off: 'Yours for life'. The letters also demonstrate a highly charged physical longing and need for intimacy. In one letter, dated 1869, Whitman writes to Peter that 'my love for you is indestructible, & since that night & morning has returned more than before'. This impassioned feeling was returned by the semi-literate Peter, who, in one note, 'cant Explain the Pleasure i experience from your letters'.

Peter wasn't the only man with whom Whitman had such a close relationship, one that bears the hallmarks of romantic love, without explicitly embodying it. There were others after him – Harry Stafford, Bill Duckett and Warren Fritzinger – men who shared a similar set of characteristics: they were much younger than Whitman; they were labourers or workers; they were marginally literate. The attachments formed between the poet and the men were based, to a greater or lesser degree, on care, whether it was a paternal Whitman mentoring these men or, in his later years, their caretaking of the ailing poet. Fritzinger was especially important to Whitman in that regard, acting as his nurse in the poet's final years. 'I like to look at him,' Whitman remarked to Traubel, 'he is health to look at: young, strong, lithe.'

No author who lived and died in the nineteenth century was photographed more often than Walt Whitman. In this newly

emergent technology, the poet found a means of staging different versions of the self – 'I meet new Walt Whitmans every
day,' he once said, referring to the great variety of self-portraits.
Most of the existing photographs of Whitman are these
portraits, in which he appears alone. He kept hundreds of
copies of his favourites. Although there was ample opportunity
to have them taken, there are no existing photographs of
Whitman with family members. None with his mother,
Louisa, to whom he was close ('How much I owe her! It could
not be put in a scale'), or his younger brother George, who
only survived the civil war by a hair's breadth. Nor are there
any photographs of Whitman alongside those disciples with
whom he spent countless hours in the last days of his life. There
are, however, photographs of Whitman with those younger
men, his proteges-cum-caretakers, in which they stand close to
each other, hands on shoulders, sometimes looking into one
another's eyes. Peter Doyle, the horsecar driver, was the first
person Whitman ever appeared in a photograph with.

Traubel looks at that photograph now. While he finds
Whitman's appearance serene, he is actively repulsed by the
expression on Doyle's face. He finds it 'sickly'. He has seen the
photograph many times before, he confesses, and yet still he
returns to it. The expression on Doyle's face and the gaze he
shares with Whitman must represent a difference in Traubel's
way of relating to the poet, one that allures and repulses him in
equal measure. Traubel then shows the photograph to the
other two men. O'Connor finds it 'silly – idiotic', and Harned's
reaction is more visceral still; not only does he mimic the
'sickly' expression on Doyle's face, he suggests that 'Doyle
should be a girl.'

The photograph is placed back down, part once again of the
room's disarray. During this exchange, something profound has
been sensed in the photograph. It captures an intimacy, one

that Harned can only imagine being appropriate if it were shared between a man and a woman. The fact that this intimacy is shared between men disturbs the disciples. Perhaps they feel threatened, not because the photograph depicts something radically different from or unrecognisable to their own way of relating to Whitman, but because it is only minimally different. After all, they also care for him, they are devoted to him, they desire to be in his company. Their affection exists in the same province as Doyle's. This similarity may be the source of their discomfort; that the feelings they have towards their poet-prophet might be misconstrued as overly intimate, inappropriate, effeminate.

In response to his disciples' mockery, Whitman, seated in his rocking chair, extols Doyle's masculinity. He was a 'rare man', Whitman says, 'a little too fond maybe of his beer, now and then, and of the women: maybe, maybe . . .' If the photographic depiction of male intimacy has perturbed the disciples, such that they can only address it through denigration, then Whitman's rebuttal reads as an attempt to affirm Doyle's machismo, and therefore, presumably, his own. There are few tactics more effective at achieving this than exaggerated claims of traditional virility, and thus, in a defensive move, Whitman extols Peter's fondness of women.

In this room, approaching the turn of the century, nearing the end of Whitman's life, the word 'homosexual' does not yet exist in English. Nor the words 'bisexual' or 'heterosexual'. The very notion of sexual identity – that combination of desires, acts, behaviours and feelings which today is one of, if not the, defining markers of personality – has not been articulated. Instead, the established nomenclature for same-sex acts between men is 'sodomy'. Sodomy is prohibited, socially and legally: it is sinful, immoral, abject. And even this nomenclature doesn't exclusively denominate same-sex male behaviours: sodomy is also used to describe non-procreative sex acts between men and women, as well as rape.

But in Europe over the past two decades – the 1870s and 1880s – there has been increasing incidence in the scientific community of a new, medical-legal language that seeks not only to describe sex acts between men, but to categorise such acts as indicative of a whole new personage, whose psychology, possibly even physiology, is congenitally abnormal. In the scientific and educated classes, the notion of a non-normative sexual identity is being theorised, classified and pathologised. As Foucault famously observed: 'homosexuality appeared as one of the forms of sexuality when it was transposed from the practice of sodomy onto a kind of interior androgyny, a hermaphrodism of the soul. The sodomite had been a temporary aberration; the homosexual was now a species.' This 'interior androgyny' refers to the emerging medical hypothesis that homosexuality resulted from an inversion of one's masculine and feminine sensibilities. But the notion of homosexuality-as-species is central: for the first time, it was theorised that no part of one's individuality was unaffected by one's sexuality, that one's self and sexuality were inseparable. Sexuality is not something one does, it is something one *is*.

In his work, Whitman crafted a poetic language and philosophy which sought to make visible a spectrum of desire between men, ranging from friendship and comradeship to emotional and physical intimacy, a need to be close to one another, a need for bonds and relationships that are not characterised by mistrust and exploitation. He believed this 'superb friendship, exalté, previously unknown' has always existed, that it 'waits, has always been waiting, latent in all men'. He referred to it as 'adhesiveness' and throughout his life argued passionately for its importance. His experiences as a nurse during the civil war, when he tended to legions of sick and dying soldiers, strengthened his conviction in its redemptive power. In adhesiveness, Whitman saw the potential for a utopia.

But now, nearing that 'toppling-off place', nearing the end of his life, Whitman's poetry is being set against this new, rapidly solidifying sexual lexicon, this new sexual, pathologised personage. Letters are arriving from Europe. Another disciple, an Englishman, is asking questions: what is the true meaning of adhesiveness? Do you, Walt Whitman, endorse sexual love between men? Whitman is caught between the future and the past. Around him, illuminated by the glow of the fire, the probing, shifting eyes of his disciples. The sight of Harned mocking Peter, his rebel friend and erstwhile love. Strewn about his feet, the letters from Europe, demanding answers. And the text, the poetry, his life's work: it's gone – going – feral, growing out of control, taking on a life and meanings of its own.

An Orgy in Arcadia

Have you ever seen tree roots bubbling up from beneath concrete, or flowers bursting through cracks in the pavement? The jolt of recognition, that beneath the drab mundanity of the everyday the organic is all around us, striving to break through, up from the earth and into the light? In its design, the first edition of *Leaves of Grass* creates a similar feeling. Everything about it indicates organicism, spontaneous and natural growth. Everything about it seems alive.

By 1855, the year the first edition of *Leaves* is published, Whitman has spent years working for a smattering of small New York newspapers as an editor, freelance journalist, typesetter and compositor. The printed word is his wheelhouse. He channels all this specialist knowledge into the material composition and promotion of *Leaves*: he designs the book, self-publishes, self-promotes and sets type for some of its pages. The title itself evokes images of rolling plains, or lush green fields, blanketed with spear-shaped grass stems. Its pun – where 'leaves' also refers to the pages of a book – suggests that this grass is literally contained inside the book's covers: that you are holding in your hands a portable landscape. The title is printed on the forest-green leather cover in gold embossed lettering, surrounded by patterns of tendrils, vines, stems and tufts, as though living matter is literally bursting out through the material. No author name is given on the cover, spine, or title page.

The book appears to have sprouted into existence of its own accord, an earthy treatise spat out from a crack in the road. But its aliveness goes beyond this.

'It was also his objective,' Peter Doyle remarked, after Whitman's death, 'to get a real human being into a book. This had never been done before.'

In the first edition of *Leaves*, the frontispiece – an illustration facing the title page – features a miniature portrait of the poet, an engraving of a now-lost daguerreotype. Like the front cover, it has no name attached to it. The unusually small portrait depicts a man from the knees up. Around his waist there is a pool of shadow, giving a startlingly effective illusion of depth and dimension. This makes it seem as if this miniature man is literally springing out of a hole or a fold in the paper, from some interstices or otherworld between ink and imagination, to inhabit the pages.

The man depicted is in his late thirties. One hand placed on his hip, the other shoved casually into the pocket of his coarse worker's trousers. Atop his head, a black hat tipped at a devil-may-care angle. His eyes are set within a rugged face, framed by a close-trimmed beard. The man's facial expression gives off the impression of hard-won, worldly experience. It came to be known as the Carpenter portrait, the first of Whitman's poet-guises. It is the poet dressed in the costume of the everyman, the labourer, the vagrant. The Carpenter isn't *humble* in this everyday outfit: he looks confrontational, cocky, even comely. It's the poet as a celebration of masculinity; and the poet as sex symbol.

The Carpenter portrait exemplifies all the qualities and characteristics that Whitman believed, throughout his life, made a 'superb' man. It projects vigour, appetite and physical beauty. It shows a man of 'reckless health, his body perfect [. . .] a good feeder, never once using medicine', a man with a 'face of undying friendship and indulgence toward men and women'. This description appeared in a review of the first edition of *Leaves of Grass*, a review that Whitman wrote himself and published anonymously. It was one of several reviews that he published of his own work, always unnamed, though the hagiographical tone hints at the true authorship. Such self-authored puff pieces are suggestive of a writer with a confidence in his own work matched only by a fear that it would go unnoticed by an indifferent public. But these reviews also demonstrate the extent to which Whitman wanted to emphasise a preferred reading of the Carpenter portrait, a preferred reading of the poet, and thus the poems themselves. As he explains in another anonymous self-review, *Leaves* is the attempt 'of a live, naive, masculine, tenderly affectionate, rowdyish, contemplative, sensual, moral, susceptible and imperious person, to cast into literature not only his own grit and arrogance, but his own flesh and form'.

And this preferred reading not only focuses on the Carpenter's athleticism, and impossibly perfect health, but on his face. On the gaze – not one of mere friendship, but one of indulgence, of pleasure-taking – that he turns on both women and men. After the frontispiece, the first edition of *Leaves* opens with a pages-long preface, written in prose, which establishes a theory of poetry the subsequent poems hope to enact. It closes with a famous proposition: 'The proof of a poet is that his country absorbs him as affectionately as he has absorbed it.' Absorption is essential: the idea or image of a symbiosis, an exchange, between the poet and the reader, the man and the nation, the individual and the mass. Absorption is accentuated elsewhere in the preface, too, in a startling imperative for the reader to 'read these leaves in the open air every season of every year of your life'. If you do so, 'your very flesh shall be a great poem'.

This implied transmutation – that the flesh, the body, will become poetry – carries with it echoes of transubstantiation, the changing of the blood and body of Christ into wine and bread. It's a knowing overlap between the Carpenter and Christ, between poet and prophet (also emphasised in the shared – if in Whitman's case, costumed – trade of both men). More astounding is the implication that the book *itself* has this power – that it constitutes a strange ecology, one capable of propagating the very flesh of the reader with 'leaves of grass' that will cover and grow across their body. To read the text is to be altered by it, not in terms of contagion, but something more like cross-pollination.

After the lengthy preface-treatise, we arrive at the poems themselves. From the very first line of the opening poem – which would later be titled 'Song of Myself' – the promise of bodily symbiosis offered by the preface is redoubled. The first word of the poem announces a poetic 'I', Whitman's poet-persona, the voice of the Carpenter, one that celebrates an individual self of such largesse and expanse that it is able to become collective and absorptive:

I celebrate myself,
And what I assume you shall assume,
For every atom belonging to me as good belongs to you

The poet, the man inside the text, will bind himself to the anonymous reader, exchanging and sharing the foundational substance of himself, the atoms that constitute his body, with them. It's a tremendous, braggadocious act of poetic imagina-tion, one that carries more than a hint of carnality about it. The poem then commences with a scene of departure: the poet floats or drifts from a room in a house, out to the bank of a river in a wood. Ellipses are freely sprinkled throughout the lines, like stones skipped over water, demarcating undulations, ripples, peaceable developments and evanescences of thought. Until, by the bank, the poet becomes 'undisguised and naked'. Here, he takes blatant, orgiastic pleasure in the sights, scents and sounds that surround him – 'the sniff of green leaves' – as well as in his own body. The poet's euphemistic descriptions of his own genitalia and seminal fluid – the 'loveroot, silkthread, crotch and vine' – might sound salacious even to today's ear.

And so we have been carried, through the gold and tendril-covered lettering of the cover, through the indulgent, confrontational gaze of the Carpenter, through the promise of textual transmutation, finally, into the poems. Poems which establish a scene of rich, potent, earthy eroticism, and which we are – by the very virtue of reading this cross-pollinating text – absolutely embroiled in. The reader-poet relationship that Whitman has created is one of intoxication and flirtation, denudation and spectatorship, friendship and indulgence. These ingredients – the organic, the erotic, the male, the virile – constitute, in large part, the matrix of Whitman's poetic project, from which his manifold social, sexual and political ideas will emerge.

'Song of Myself' is astronomical in scope. Written in free verse, utilising variable line lengths, this sprawling poem is both a celebration of the individual and a metaphysical sermon, in which the poet declares himself both 'the poet of the body' and 'the poet of the soul'. It is also a kind of journalistic brico-lage, at times resembling an itemised catalogue of everything Whitman believes constitutes the makeup of the nation. The 'good feeder' that Whitman insisted was evident in the Carpenter here manifests as a nominative greediness, the poet urgently and indiscriminately naming all that he sees, always hungry for more. Lengthy, breathless lists are unleashed in a nervous torrent, rapidly denoting flora and fauna, peoples and professions, from birds and bees to canal boys and opium eaters, coalmen and congressmen, lexicographers and chemists, prostitutes and presidents.

This listing is first a mechanism of taking, of possessing – the more that the poet-persona names, the more he accumulates and absorbs and the bigger he becomes. But because of the opening promise that 'every atom belonging to me as good belongs to you', this enlargement is meant to be experienced by the reader, too. 'The bodies of men and women engirth me, and I engirth them'; an enlargement that also seeks to bestow sexual potency. But in the midst of his fevered, hungry hoarding of persons and things, the poet alights on a calm, pastoral scene. It is here that *Leaves* embarks on its first mysterious exploration of gender and sexuality.

We are by the waterside. Twenty-eight young men are bathing together, next to the shore. Nothing distinguishes these men from one another. They are all 'so friendly'. All bearded, all with long hair, glistening in the sun. They are a homogenised group, an impression of idealised masculinity painted in broad strokes: the virile man bathing, presumably, in the nude. These young men are first seen through the eyes of a young woman. A voyeur. She lives in a 'fine house' nearby, and watches the men from behind the blinds of a window. The poet asks us to watch with her. He even asks us to speculate: 'Which of the young men does she like the best?' Then, true to the promise of absorption, the poet shape-shifts, and subsumes himself into this woman's imagination: 'Where are you off to, lady? for I see you, / You splash in the water there, yet stay stock still in your room.'

He is looking through her mind's eye, inhabiting her fantasy – her gaze becomes his. He is also the voyeur, peeking through the blinds. After this merging of selves, the young woman is described laughing and dancing along the beach, carefree and joyous, to become 'the twenty-ninth bather'. She sees the glistening, bearded young men. She joins them, 'and loved them'.

And yet, her gaze is not returned. The men do not see her. Instead, an 'unseen hand' passes over their bodies:

It descended tremblingly from their temples and ribs.

The young men float on their backs, their white bellies
    swell to the sun . . .
they do not ask who seizes fast to them,

They do not know who puffs and declines with pendant
    and bending arch,
They do not think whom they souse with spray.

The scene comes to a close, the unseen hand having moved across their torsos, down beneath the water, to seize their genitals and bring them to climax. It's a bold, luscious sex scene set within a pastoral vision of harmony with nature, an Arcadia. It is, in fact, an orgy; the exact number of young men is drummed into us, and yet their idiosyncrasies aren't in focus. There's instead a mass effect: bellies, beards, temples, ribs. Hair and flesh and fluid, and a lot of it. But the erotics of this group sex scene are difficult to pin down. There's something disinterested or off-kilter about it. Whose erotic fantasy actually is this?

It doesn't belong to the young men. They receive this sexual caress passively and silently. They neither know, nor think, nor ask. They have no active desire for the person doing the caressing: they don't even know that she's there. The men merely float, lackadaisical in all their male beauty, until they are brought ambivalently to orgasm. The erotic fantasy seemed, at first, to belong to the young woman: she was the voyeur who lusted, from the confines of her home – a space of apparently cloying domesticity – after the group of men. And yet, it is not clear that she finds any pleasure, herself, in the implied profusion of sex acts that might have slaked her thirst. Whitman does not do anything more to describe her desire. Moreover, at some point on her carefree run between the house and the bathing men, she seems not only to have lost her desire, but also to have shed or shrugged off her gender. The hand is 'unseen'. From the perspective of the young men, the hand belongs to no one, man or woman. It is a disembodied force moving across them, invisibly. The person it belongs to is never known – we cannot actually be sure that this twenty-ninth bather is the young woman at all. In the moment of entering the male space – in becoming the twenty-ninth bather – the young woman loses her identity. But the hand itself is eroticised: it trembles with anticipation at what it is about to seize. So, to whom does it belong?

The only player left is the poet, who slipped into and inhabited the young woman's gaze, and who, in doing so, shared or embodied this lusting over the young men. The young woman is fused with Whitman in a joint, perhaps androgynous persona. By embodying the woman's lust, Whitman finds the means to route his own – or his poet-persona's – erotic desire. It is only through her sight that Whitman can first depict and then project a version of himself onto a scenario with the bathers. Just as O'Connor and the disciples, years later, will only be able to parse the loving look of Doyle and Whitman by saying that Peter should be a 'girl', so the poet, in this first edition of his opus, makes visible same-sex desire by routing it through the eyes of a woman. In both these instances, the 'feminine' is subordinated to the 'masculine': Doyle the girl is silly, but Whitman the man is serious. The bathing men reach mutual climax, but the lady is not permitted sexual satisfaction.

35

In this bathing scene, this anonymous orgy in Arcadia, Whitman experiments with his poetic self, pushing it into inchoate, murky waters. It occupies a position of anonymity and androgyny, where it can indulge in or seize fast to the homogenous male body. It seems that the poet is trying to find a way of depicting and talking about sex, eroticism, yearning, that has a scope wide enough to include a heretofore prohibited expression of desire between men; an experiment which, in this case, exploits the gaze of a fictive woman to make visible male desire.

Clap a Crown on Top of a Skull

July 1849, New York City, New York

In 1849, in the middle of Lower Manhattan, in the depths of a sticky New York summer, Walt Whitman, a young man of thirty, stands in the entrance hall of a large brick building. He is being watched, looked at by the dead. Animal skulls are mounted on the walls, from far-flung places. The protruding feline maws of tigers and hyenas. There are death masks, too, and paintings of the deceased. But what pulls Whitman's attention, what attracts him like a magnet to this peculiar display, are the shelves upon which rest dozens of inanimate, beige-white porcelain and plaster heads, with pupil-less eyes. Some of these busts are bisected with thick black lines, in odd, seemingly arbitrary patterns, like the contours of a map, or the fictive borders of an inner, cerebral country.

Whitman isn't confused by them – unlike some of the other visitors to this display, who might gawp in hushed silence – because he knows exactly what they represent. These lines are said to show the locations of the 'organs' of the brain. Each organ corresponds to a different mental faculty or function, and their size – which demarcates the degree to which that facility is 'developed' – is perceptible in raised bumps, on the surface of the skull. The poet has come to here, to Clinton Hall, a cabinet of curiosities-cum-lecture theatre, a publishing house-cum-examination room, with three dollars in his pocket. He has come to pay to have his skull read by phrenologists.

The person doing the examination is a quiet, big-eyed man with slicked-back white hair: Lorenzo Fowler. Lorenzo's older brother, Orson, is somewhere around, possibly hidden away in a back office, scribbling in a cashbook. Orson is a slimmer man with sunken cheeks and piercing eyes. Together, the brothers – assisted by their younger sister Charlotte and her husband Samuel Roberts Wells – have spent years establishing a phreno-logical business empire, and are largely responsible for the popularity of this pseudoscience in antebellum America.

At the heart of their business headquarters in Clinton Hall is the Phrenological Cabinet. It's a public display of skulls, busts and other esoterica. The Cabinet has become a Manhattan hotspot, attracting hordes of sightseers. The young Whitman visits regularly. He has been interested in phrenology for several years, having reviewed phrenological publications for the *Brooklyn Eagle*, where he mentioned the Fowlers' work admir-ingly. He finds the idea of phrenology 'funny': not in the comedic sense, but in a sense of strangeness. It holds, for him, 'mystery and power'.

That sense must be palpable, now, as Lorenzo Fowler runs his fingers over Whitman's head, at a slow, leisurely pace, across the territory of his 'brain organs', to ascertain the size of each corresponding bump. Stepping into Clinton Hall from the street is like passing through a portal, from the quotidian busy-ness of a New York summer's day, into a realm of phantasm and fantasy, lorded over by Lorenzo. A man who claims to have seized from the chaos of the world a form of order and classi-fication, a man who claims to have found, in the skulls of white men and the skulls of indigenous peoples (many of which were stolen, or acquired through nefarious means) evidence of the superior intelligence of his own race. As is well documented, phrenology promoted bogus but readily believed racist arguments for white supremacy, and the Fowlers' system was no different. A man filled with a grotesque and invented medical authority, Lorenzo promises to reveal who, exactly, you are. And he promises to tell you how, exactly, you can improve your life.

The Fowlers' particular brand of phrenology wasn't merely diagnostic, but ameliorative. If you lacked in one of the forty-one separate mental faculties that the Fowlers claimed to have discovered, they argued that, through cultivating particular habits, you could develop and improve that faculty. On the contrary, if a faculty was in 'excess', you could cultivate habits to depress it. Theirs was a practical pseudoscience. It promised that anything is possible: that you can become a better person, a better individual.

The reading that Lorenzo Fowler gives Whitman changes the poet's life. It shows, supposedly, a man of a distinctly rare, near-perfect character. Lorenzo's diagnosis, written out as a chart, opens by surmising that Whitman 'has a grand physical constitution, and power to live to a good old age. He is undoubtedly descended from the soundest and hardiest of stock. Size of head large. Leading traits of character appear to be Friendship, Sympathy, Sublimity and Self-Esteem.' The chart goes on to list the forty-one organs of the brain, measuring Whitman's according to 'degrees of development' ranging from one to seven. The higher the number, the more developed the organ. Whitman's chart is flush with sixes and sevens. None of his brain organs measures below a three: none of them is 'small'. The chart proves, to him, that he is of excellent physique, genealogy, virility, and holds exceptional moral and intellectual characteristics. And he is immensely proud of this reading, later joking about the large size of his 'aquativeness' organ, which was said to lead to a fondness of 'liquids; desire to drink; love of water, washing, bathing, swimming'.

Whitman receives his phrenological examination during what he would later call the 'formative stage' of the development of the first edition of *Leaves*. Lorenzo Fowler's analysis plays a central – if not *the* central – role in the development of Whitman's expansive, absorptive poetic-persona: the common overlaps of largesse, bodily health and magnanimity are immediately clear. The preface of *Leaves* even reads like a trumped-up version of his phrenological chart: 'extreme caution or prudence, the soundest organic health, large hope and comparison and fondness for women and children, large alimentiveness [. . .] with a perfect sense of the oneness of nature and the propriety of the same spirit applied to human affairs [. . .] these are called up of the float of the brain of the world to be parts of the greatest poet'. It's a convenient closed circle: Walt Whitman's traits align precisely with those of 'the greatest poet'.

But the leading trait that Fowler highlighted was 'Friendship'. In phrenological language, the quality of friendship belongs in the mental faculty called 'adhesiveness'. Adhesiveness denotes a social feeling, a desire to congregate and form attachments with others, a desire to indulge in friendships. In phrenology, this is not the same as sexual love or attraction. A separate mental faculty, 'amativeness', describes that, denoting an attachment to the opposite sex only, and the desire to love and be loved by the opposite sex.

Although it doesn't denote sexual attraction, adhesiveness does describe a kind of same-sex desire: a desire for closeness, physical and emotional intimacy, proximity to one's friend, who might, of course, be of the same sex. This word, this idea, burrows into Whitman's mind. In adhesiveness, the pseudoscience has presented Whitman with a new vocabulary, a protolanguage, laying the lexical foundations upon which he will soon build an entire poetic-philosophy of love between men.

After his visit to Lorenzo, Whitman strikes up a friendship with the Fowlers. Six years after his skull reading, almost to the day, the first self-funded, self-published edition of *Leaves* goes on sale at three bookshops in America, including the Phrenological Cabinet at Fowler and Wells, where it sits along-side an assortment of other radical and esoteric publications (among them, books on free love and the water cure). So *Leaves* begins its public life as a gilded curio, an object of fasci-nation and fancy, surrounded by dead-eyed busts and stolen skulls.

Nevertheless, it finds its way into the hands of one of America's most influential writers and philosophers, the tran-scendentalist Ralph Waldo Emerson. The transcendentalist movement, which peaked in the mid-nineteenth century, promoted self-cultivation and self-reliance, emphasised the importance of direct experience above logic and believed these tenets crucial for achieving a spiritual unity with others and with nature. An appreciation of nature's goodness was essential to the transcendentalists: nature represents the divinity of crea-tion and ever-changing interconnectedness of all living things. 'Nature,' wrote Emerson, 'is not fixed but fluid.'

After reading *Leaves*, Emerson sent Whitman a private letter, stating that the collection was 'the most extraordinary piece of wit and wisdom that America has yet contributed'. Emerson's work was an enormous influence on Whitman, and so such esteemed praise helped his confidence in his poetic project soar. The following year, in 1856, he published a second, modified and expanded edition of *Leaves*, still utilising the Carpenter portrait, and still in cahoots with the Fowlers as booksellers and distributors. True to his eternal self-promotion

– and much to Emerson's ire – Whitman published that private letter, in full, in the second edition. He even excised one of its quotes – Emerson's salutation that 'I greet you at the beginning of a great career' – and printed it on the book's spine, without the transcendentalist's authorisation.

But this confidence is short-lived. Despite such an endorsement, the second edition is a failure. It sells terribly. Of the few reviews it garners, some amount to outright hit pieces. 'So, then, these rank *Leaves* have sprouted afresh,' reads a review in the *Christian Examiner*. 'We hoped that they had dropped.' The rankness is said to be found in the poems' open deification of the bodily organs, senses, and appetites. The *Long Islander* – where Whitman used to work – is harsher, aiming to deflate the poet's outsize ego with this cutting barb: 'It will become a "Household Book of Poetry" just about as soon as [the first edition,] of which we read in advertisements, but never see in any household.' To make matters worse, the Fowlers begin to distance themselves from the book. After some spiky correspondence, Whitman and the phrenologists part ways.

By the late 1850s Whitman's project is in a state of uncertainty. The man he had put inside the book – the Carpenter, with his brash confidence, his working man's get-up – is dissipating. Whitman himself begins to change. He adopts the role of a metropolitan dandy: clad in pinstripes, he spends evenings drinking in Pfaff's beer hall, a frenetic hub of Manhattan literary bohemia, where he likes to simply 'see, talk little, absorb' rather than engage in the boozy, literary gossip. For cash, he scrapes together a living as a writer-editor for the *Brooklyn Daily Times*. He takes on additional hack work, too, including a column writing gig for the *New York Atlas*. The column, which he writes across 1859, is penned under the pseudonym Mose Velsor (Velsor was Whitman's mother's maiden name). It is titled 'Manly Health and Training'.

'Manly Health' is a bizarre, somewhat campy, repetitive and hastily written self-help guide for men. It covers everything from diet, fashion and exercise to work, sex and masturbation, aiming to guide the reader along 'the great highway of manly health, on which all may travel, and must travel'. And certainly, it is for men, and only men. Mose Velsor has little to say about women. They are either depicted as corrupting objects of sexual desire, or, conversely, as inadequate mothers. The 'healthy manly virility' of modern men, Velsor writes, seems to have 'given place to a morbid, almost insane, pursuit of women, especially the lower ranges of them'. It is also a sad truth, writes Velsor, that most modern mothers are unaware of the 'best conditions of treatment' that lay the foundation for their sons' 'future manliness and fine physique'.

That 'fine physique' is the unifying thread of 'Manly Health'. The overwhelming impression this self-help guide gives is a veneration and idealisation of the male body. And Velsor holds up, as the ideal, the apparently pliant, nimble, muscular men and youths of ancient Greece. In the nineteenth century, particularly among the European educated classes, there was a renewed fascination with classical antiquity, which was so often represented by images of muscular, lithe and nude men. This Victorian 'cult' of ancient Greece, Sedgwick writes, 'positioned male flesh and muscle as indicative instances of "the" body, of a body whose surfaces, features, and abilities might be the subject or object of unphobic enjoyment'.

Such enjoyment is evident in Velsor's descriptions of the imagined Grecian man. One cannot talk about exercise, Velsor writes, 'without the thoughts irresistibly turning back to ancient Greece'. The 'regular swimming' of the Greeks, he argues, gave them the 'round and full form' so noticeable in their statues. The Grecian manly games are given special attention: they served to create a 'very hardy and handsome-bodied race'. Wrestling, he says, was a 'great physical art' and he imagines the wrestlers would have been 'naked, and had their bodies anointed with oil'.

How much of Whitman is in Velsor? How much of the poet is in the hack? 'Song of Myself' and 'Manly Health' both celebrate an impossibly perfect male constitution. Where Velsor argues that the most desirable thing for a man is to become 'strong, alert, vigorous [. . .] with a perfect body, perfect blood – no morbid humors, no weakness', Whitman describes his own Carpenter portrait as indicative of 'reckless health, his body perfect'. But Whitman-as-poet venerates the male body for different reasons to Velsor-as-hack. The Carpenter, in all his tumescent maleness, acts as the vector through which the poet portrays an expansive, interrelated, absorptive selfhood: the celebration of all through the celebration of one. Velsor's muscular man, however, is deployed towards less metaphysical and certainly more sinister ends.

Like a distorting mirror held up to the image of the Carpenter, the idealised male body in 'Manly Health' is often sublimated into a eugenicist argument for 'the development of a superb race of men'. And this *is* eugenics: Velsor openly muses on 'the science, it might be called, of breeding superb men and women', and asks, 'what can be more momentous than the growth of a perfect race of men?' The male body, for Velsor, is perfectible, and it is through the perfection of the collective male body that the 'physical perfection of the race, here in the United States' is attainable.

These eugenicist postulations may feel particularly hacky when they come embedded in column entries such as 'The Great American Evil – Indigestion', but they nevertheless reveal an easy slippage inherent in Whitman's formation of the male poet-persona in 'Song of Myself'. With a trick of the light, the Carpenter – that supposedly expansive self, the vessel through which the poem hopes to embody and celebrate a democratic nation of many – shape-shifts into the exemplar of a 'superior' race of white, able-bodied men.

There is another theme threaded through 'Manly Health', however, that speaks to something more complex than bodily veneration – and less repugnant than the 'perfection' of the race. It is a quiet, but very present, appeal for the male reader to cultivate new ways of relating to other men: to grow and take pride in friendships and affections. Mose Velsor encourages the reader to 'pass forth, in business or occupation, among men, *without distrusting them*, but with a *friendly feeling toward all*, and finding the same feeling returned to you'. It sounds a lot like the phrenological faculty of adhesiveness.

In these inter-edition years, Whitman the boozy bohemian, the hack writer, considers giving up poetry altogether. A man of contradictions, he continues to write reams of new poems nonetheless. Just as he adopts the pseudonym Mose Velsor to churn out his bizarre column, he is also penning the poems that will soon fill a third edition of *Leaves*. His poetic project is coming back into focus. And what will give it a new driving force, a new cohesion, is precisely this appeal for new relations between men.

Calamus-Leaves and Women-Love

The third edition of *Leaves of Grass* appears, with a new publisher, in the summer of 1860. It scarcely resembles the two earlier editions. The Carpenter frontispiece is gone, replaced with a stipple engraving of an older, hirsute but manicured and close-trimmed Whitman. He does not confront the reader with a fierce, confident gaze, but looks somewhat melancholically out of frame. No longer clad in working man's garb, this Whitman has transformed again, wearing a loose black suit and cravat. He is fuller, larger in stature, too. In parallel, *Leaves* has become larger. An additional 146 poems have been added and separated, along with the existing poems, into clusters. The third edition is printed at a higher run. It sells well and receives largely positive critical attention. Whitman's life work is becoming a success.

Whitman refers to his project in this thick, heavy book as 'The Great Construction of the New Bible'. The opening poem, 'Proto-Leaf', clearly states the aims of this quasi-religious text. It will be 'Free, fresh, savage'. It will contain 'chants inclusive – wide reverberating chants / Chants of the many in One'. 'Proto-Leaf' ends with an exclamation, a cry for a new kind of society:

O to be relieved of distinctions! to make as much
   of vices as virtues!
O to level occupations and the sexes! O to bring
   all to common ground! O adhesiveness!

O the pensive aching to be together – you know not
why, and I know not why.

That repeated, yawning 'O' reads like a wail, a grief-stricken
ululation. In a way, it is: the poet is yearning and longing for
an ideal, grieving something which doesn't yet – and might
not – exist, a nostalgia for an imagined future. The 'O' is also
like a portal, a gateway into a vision of communion, a dream
of a universal common ground, in which divisions of class and
sex are erased. Central to this dream, caught in the crosshairs
of that 'O', is that pseudoscientific, phrenological mental
faculty: adhesiveness.

But Whitman's poetic adhesiveness is much transformed
from the Fowlerian rubric. He takes the idea of adhesiveness as
a 'social feeling' – as the Fowlers described it – and on the one
hand restricts it, using it in his poetry to refer only to relations
between men. On the other hand, he liberates it, such that it
becomes 'limitless, unloosened'. Adhesiveness is the sense that
the poet finds 'profoundly affecting in large masses of men'.
Adhesiveness is 'to be loved by strangers'. It is a pensive aching
for another, without knowing why. It is a profusion of images
of male intimacy: touching, gazing, bonding, kissing, embracing, fraternising, yearning. Whitman's adhesiveness expresses a
spectrum of affirmative relations between men: a mélange of
friendship, care, comradeship and physical intimacy.

In the third edition of Leaves, and each later edition published
in America throughout Whitman's life, he explores adhesiveness in a cluster of poems titled 'Calamus'. It is one of two
clusters in which Whitman explicitly engages with relations
between the sexes. The other is 'Enfans d'Adam' (later retitled
'Children of Adam'), which Whitman hoped would be 'the
same to the passion of Woman-Love' as 'the Calamus-Leaves
are to adhesiveness, manly love'.

'Calamus' is not a treatise. It is poetry, after all, not politics. Its logic is a dream-logic, a stream of associations, images and ideas, which catch the light then dim again, like damselflies darting above a brook in leaf-shade. In 'Calamus', the poet wades into the waters of imagination and asks us to follow. Whitman wants us to speculate with him: what are the consequences – for the individual and the collective – if we imagine, and even enact, this new spectrum of affirmative relations between men?

Calamus is the name of a grass (commonly known as sweet grass) which flourishes by the ponds, marshes and riverbanks of the north and Midwestern US. For Whitman, calamus represents 'the biggest and hardiest kind of spears of grass' and he admires the 'fresh, aquatic, pungent bouquet'. *Big* and *hard*, those familiar Whitmanic adjectives, accurately describe the calamus grass's inflorescence: it is distinctly, almost comically, phallic in shape. Incidentally, the root also has mildly psycho-active properties, of which Whitman may have been aware ('My brain it shall be your occult convolutions! / Root of wash'd sweet-flag!').

But calamus has another meaning. The name was used in an ancient epic poem, the *Dionysiaca*, written by the fifth-century Greco-Roman poet Nonnus. The *Dionysiaca* includes a tragic story of two youths, named Calamos and Carpos. These boys are 'playfellows'. They are beautiful, athletic, vigorous – that idealised Grecian male body that so preoccupies Whitman, and his former hack-self, Mose Velsor. The two boys take part in a swimming contest. Calamos opts to let his lover swim ahead and win the race. But a sudden wave rises up, water rushes into Carpos' mouth, and he drowns. Calamos cries – 'Who has quenched the light of love?' – and, in grief, drowns himself. In this way, he joins Carpos in annihilation. But there is regenera-tion, too. Having drowned, Calamos 'thus gave his form to the reeds which took his name and like substance'.

There is no explicit reference to the *Dionysiaca* in Whitman's writings. But the story of a relationship between two boys, playfellows – possibly lovers – mirrors the theme of adhesiveness, 'manly love', so closely that it seems unlikely he wouldn't have had it in mind when composing 'Calamus'. The myth's aquatic setting is also mirrored in the 'Calamus' poems. As with that orgy in Arcadia – where the gender and corporeality of the twenty-ninth bather dissolve away, like sediment scrubbed from an artefact, to reveal a tableau of nude men in a homogenous climax – water features heavily in these poems, becoming a screen onto which adhesive relations between men are projected, and a screen which can give cover to his expressions of same-sex desire.

It is down by the water, in the woods, where 'Calamus' begins. In a secluded spot, 'in paths untrodden / in the growth by margins of pond waters', the poet feels glad to be 'away from the clank of the world' and declares his intention to sing songs of 'manly attachment'. He will 'tell the secrets' of his 'days and nights' and do nothing else but 'celebrate the need of comrades'. By the pond, the poet is 'no longer abashed' because the secluded spot allows him to say things that he 'would not dare elsewhere'. Whitman is declaring his intent to sing and celebrate adhesiveness. He is also coyly indicating that there is something expressed by adhesiveness that has heretofore been illicit or clandestine, which he will now wrench from the shadows and spill over the printed page.

What follows in the cluster's second poem is a hallucinogenic dream sequence, painted in pink and lilac, flush with wildflowers and vines and cloaked in the scents of earth and cedar. We are still by the pond. The poet wades into the waters. There, he is met by a procession – 'a silent troop' – of men who appear ostensibly from nothing. They have been translated into being through this matrix of water, lilac and earth, this other-worldly combination of 'tomb-leaves' and 'body-leaves'. The men are not fully corporeal. Instead, they are the 'spirits of friends, dead or alive – thicker / they come, a great crowd, and I in the middle'.

The poet begins to gift these spirits whatever organic matter he can find: a branch of pine, laurel leaves, a handful of sage, moss produced from his pocket. He is trying to communicate something, via these plants and flowers, to these ghostly, amassing men: he is looking for language in living matter. The moss pulled from his pocket like stuffing hints at evisceration: he is giving the men a part of his body, the innards of himself, in an effort to connect. It recalls the transmutative formula introduced in the first edition, where the poems are of flesh, and to read the book is to have your own flesh transformed into poetry.

The poet then draws from the water the calamus root. In this pungent, phallic plant, the poet at last finds signification, declaring that it 'shall henceforth be the token of comrades'. Through this sensory, phantasmagorical scene, the idea of communion between men, dead and alive, unashamed, unabashed – the idea of adhesiveness – begins to find expression. There is the tantalising possibility that the calamus root also signifies a state of drugged consciousness: a disinhibition, a loosening of fixed and learned behaviours that makes possible new ways of relating with others. (This might be wishful thinking, however; despite the decidedly trippy tenor of the poems there is no concrete evidence that Whitman was savvy to the plant's psychotropic properties, which in any case can only be experienced by consuming an inordinate amount of the dried root.)

Later in 'Calamus', he declares his intent to actively cultivate adhesiveness across the nation. The poet becomes a nurseryman, or latter-day Johnny Appleseed, who will 'plant companionship thick as trees along all the rivers of America'. Such

metaphorical landscape alteration has a corresponding impact
on social relations:

> It shall be customary in all directions, in the houses
> and streets, to see manly affection,
> The departing brother or friend shall salute the remaining
> brother or friend with a kiss.

Adhesiveness transforms the customs that structure or
govern both public and private space, the houses and streets.
To put it another way: adhesiveness effects an entire alternative
model of social organisation. Whitman wishes to create
'Without edifices or rules or trustees or any argument, / The
institution of the dear love of comrades'. This institution of
love between men will not be governed according to typical
power structures. It will not be governed at all. Whitman's
poetry now fits, remarkably, into the fantastical genre of world-
building. From a dream within a dream, the poet sees a 'new
City of Friends':

> Nothing was greater there than the quality of robust love
> – it led the rest,
> It was seen every hour in the actions of the men of that city,
> And in all their looks and works.

This City of Friends, an anti-institution, an ungoverned
anarchy of adhesiveness in which love between men is the only
organising factor, would be a city, he writes, 'invincible to the
attacks of the whole of the rest of the earth'.

Not all of 'Calamus', however, is about these grand visions
and group male relations. In the third edition of *Leaves*, there are
moments of concertina-like compression from the general to
the specific, from the mass back to the individual. The ninth

poem of 'Calamus', for instance, appears to recount an erstwhile relationship with another man, evoking confessional experiences of loss and pain. It reads like the end of a romance. All the tale-tell signs are there – sleeplessness, loneliness, even jealousy – 'hours discouraged, distracted – for the one I cannot / content myself without, soon I saw him content / himself without me'. The poet then wonders if there are others like him, other men who have 'out of the like feelings?' He is desperate to know if any other man has felt and experienced this, 'his / friend, his lover, lost to him?' The ninth poem is the moment in which the language of romantic love, with its obsessions and jealousies, its disastrous and discombobulating fallout, becomes most closely wedded to the language of adhesiveness. It is also the passage in 'Calamus' where the line between poet-persona and Walt Whitman the man feels most thin, most confessional.

The ninth poem was struck from subsequent editions. Does this show Whitman's reluctance to attach himself to such an apparent heartbreak, a reticence to reduce the distance between real-self and poet-self, or is it evidence of a trepidation around the way this poem reroutes the language of romantic love to describe a relationship between men? Is this the real 'secret' of his nights and days? Then again, there is nothing furtive or encoded about the ways that manly attraction and same-sex desire are expressed elsewhere in 'Calamus' – hand holding, embracing, 'fluid' and 'affectionate' longing looks, bed sharing, and kissing – though such intimacies, here, are described in positive terms. Perhaps this hints at an answer: if adhesiveness is a bonding, aggregative force, the glue that holds together Whitman's dream of a common ground, there may be no room for heartbreak and jealousy; for reality to intrude upon the fantasy of an endless, reciprocated love between men.

Two years after Whitman wrote and published 'Calamus', his belief in the necessity of adhesiveness as an idealised force would become even greater. Following decades of mounting political tension centred on the issue of slavery, Abraham Lincoln, the anti-slavery Republican, is elected president. And in 1861, after several Southern states secede from the Union, the American Civil War breaks out. During these war years, Whitman eschews his bohemian leanings and transforms yet again. He becomes a nurse, 'a friend visiting hospitals occasionally to cheer the wounded and sick', primarily in Washington, DC. He records his thoughts and observations, his hastily sketched narratives of the lives of these befriended, dying soldiers, in dozens of notebooks. These notebooks gradually become stained with the men's blood – a more literal overlap between text and flesh, books and bodies.

Whitman's descriptions of the wounded soldiers he attends to sometimes resemble that accumulative, torrential cataloguing in 'Song of Myself': their ailments, characteristics, attitudes and personalities are described, listed and logged. But his war writings can also be read as a textbook demonstrating adhesiveness in action. Whitman becomes a caretaker, father and brother to the men. He reads to the sick – passages from the Bible, but also passages from *Leaves*. He sits with those suffering from typhoid and diarrhoea. He holds their hands. He brings them water, cooks them rice pudding, gifts them pipe tobacco, helps them to dress, writes letters to their relatives, all without a moment's thought that he is putting himself in harm's way.

Whitman also venerates the soldiers. One soldier, named Tom, is 'a fine specimen of youthful physical manliness'. Though Tom has been shot through the lung, pumped full of stimulants and is barely conscious of his surrounds, Whitman nevertheless finds him 'handsome, athletic, with profuse beautiful shining hair', lamenting that Tom will never know 'the heart of the stranger that hovered near'. Whitman is gazing at Tom, just as he is nursing him: a mix of care and covetousness that would pattern his relationship with Peter and those young men who came after him. Given the circumstances, such veneration might be read as exceptionally touching (a beatification of the innocent dead) or uncomfortably leery (a nurse ogling his patients). Regardless, it is as though the beleaguered sick and dying, in their absence of health, merely reinforce Whitman's belief in the importance of perfect health – characteristics he claimed were exemplified in his own Carpenter portrait when he published the first edition of *Leaves*, and which he extolled as the hack Mose Velsor. In one scene of sobering war reportage, Whitman sees 'at the foot of the tree, within ten yards of the front of the house [. . .], a heap of amputated feet, legs, arms, hands, &c, a full load for a one-horse cart'. Set against such sights, the unreality of the venerated male body trumps, or at least allows him to endure, the reality of sickness, death and disfigurement.

And what effect would such sights – piles of male limbs, amputated by male surgeons, from wounds inflicted by other men in a war orchestrated and executed by other men – have on his concept of nationhood, let alone on the ways that men relate to each other within society? Adhesiveness as an affirmative, bonding force becomes newly vital in this context. In *Democratic Vistas*, a dense and knotty prose work published in 1871, Whitman sought to diagnose the problems of the American body politic in the wake of the war. He writes of 'adhesiveness or love as that which fuses, ties, aggregates, making the races comrades, fraternizing all'. Adhesiveness as a peacemaking force is here reified in plain language.

'Calamus' is included in each later edition of *Leaves* published after the war. From those shaded, cedar-scented and pink-tinged pond waters, its poet suggests something truly radical: that to action adhesiveness might create a heretofore unimagined society. One in which distinctions of gender, class and possibly even race are removed. We might say, in contemporary language, that his poems suggest that to make visible and celebrate a spectrum of intimate, affirmative desire between men is to denude the patriarchy of a central source of power, and that this creates space for wider equality. The City of Friends, the reflection of a dream on rippling pond water, is a utopia.

But what if the light shifts, ever so slightly, and we look at the reflection from another angle; the primacy given to male bonds, the emphasis on health and vitality, forces the question. Does this utopian vision, this city of friends, have space for anyone who is not a handsome, able-bodied man, and does its coherence as a vision depend on the exclusion of the 'female'? In essence: where are all the women?

Somewhere nestled among that sea of paper, in the room in Mickle Street, lost among the hundreds of copies of self-portraits, the letters and manuscripts, there is one exceptional photograph. An outlier. The only extant image of Walt Whitman in which he appears with an adult woman. She is Mary Williams, the wife of Frank Howard Williams, a Philadelphia-based poet and playwright. Whitman was a regular guest in their home. He was fond of the Williamses, grateful for their hospitality, and doted on their young children. In this photograph, taken in the late 1880s, an aged Whitman is captured sitting among the children, cane at his side, his arm around the youngest daughter, Aubrey. The eldest child, Marguerite, stands behind, against a backdrop of palm-sized leaves that overspill a picket fence, and the son, Churchill, sits cross-legged on the grass, a rifle in his lap. To Whitman's left, in a flowing white dress, hands peaceably cupped, sits Mary. It's a tranquil scene, a kind of family portrait in which Whitman adopts a grandfatherly role.*

But an explosion of violence has been introduced into the photograph. Mary's face has been scratched away, leaving an eerie white void. Some Whitman scholars speculate that the poet did this himself, that he took a sharp object and consciously scraped away the face of the only adult woman that he is known to have been photographed with. Mary hasn't been removed from the photograph entirely: her body remains. The body of a woman and mother, without a face. The scholar Ed Folsom argues that this act of photographic effacement can be interpreted as Whitman's urge to situate himself in the 'transgressively blended role of father/mother', enacting in photographic representation that absorptive, expansive, egalitarian poet-self presented throughout *Leaves*, a self capable of both fathering *and* mothering the children of the nation. This generous interpretation would seem to raise further questions: why, then, leave Mary's body in the photograph, why not excise her entirely? It also encourages us to pay closer attention to Whitman's treatment of women within the poems.

In 'Children of Adam', the companion cluster to 'Calamus', Whitman becomes a 'chanter of Adamic songs' and walks through 'the new garden' where he hopes to be 'surrounded by beautiful, curious, breathing, laughing flesh'. On the surface, these poems argue for a return to a prelapsarian innocence, where sex between men and women can be celebrated without shame. 'Sex contains all,' he writes, 'bodies, souls, meanings, proofs.' Through a sheer deluge of sexual imagery, Whitman aims to drive a wedge

---

* This photograph, 'Walt Whitman and the Family of Francis Williams, 1888', is held in the Library of Congress. The inscription, on the verso, reads: 'Family of Francis Williams, ca. 1888', though it is not known who inscribed it. The photograph can be viewed at whitmanarchive.org.

between that ecclesiastical conjoining of sex and sinfulness: 'Without shame the man I like knows and avows the delicious-ness of his sex, / Without shame the woman I like knows and avows hers.' Crucially, though, there is one thing he can't – or won't – decouple: Whitman's heterosexual love-making is almost always enacted or lusted after for the purposes of procreation, rather than mutual pleasure or passion. In this formula of his, women are almost always, and only, potential mothers.

It is into 'you women' that the poet will 'press with slow rude muscle', and 'dare not withdraw till I deposit what has so long accumulated within me'. It is through women that he will 'drain the pent up rivers of myself', demanding 'perfect men and women out of my love-spendings' – a sentiment that explicitly recalls the eugenicist contemplations of 'Manly Health and Training'. At times, these sexual images are so hammy they read like satire, as with the eminently silly metaphor of a 'hairy wild-bee' that 'gripes the full-grown lady-flower' and 'takes / his will of her, and holds himself tremulous and / tight upon her till he is satisfied'. They also seem to suggest an inability on behalf of the poet to imagine penetrative sex between men and women as anything beyond male ejaculate, and, maybe later, some babies: sex as an expression of the male lust for progeny.

But is this really lust, or is it a kind of anxiety, questing towards a seemingly maternal reproductive power that, as a man, Whitman feels unable to harness? For a poet so obsessed with absorption and growth, perhaps his inability to imagina-tively occupy motherhood was creatively aggravating, resulting in these scattershot metaphors that suggest women are no more than repositories for men's 'love-spendings'. More abstractly, many feminist thinkers have theorised that there is a primal fear of the maternal in men; that the pregnant woman, under-going a state of indomitable bodily transformation forever inaccessible to men, repulses, fascinates and terrifies all at once.

Then again, perhaps Whitman's persistent overtures to procreation are a way of evading something that, true to the sexist medical discourse of the day, he might find inherently mysterious, and even in poor taste: namely, women's sexual pleasure.

There are more ambiguous erotic moments sprinkled throughout this cluster, however, which complicate its seemingly anxious erotics of progeny. Although Whitman begins these poems as an Adamic, hyper-masculine impregnator of women, the 'I' sometimes relinquishes such a fixed, gendered subject position. This is most clearly (or unclearly) rendered in another dream sequence, situated, yet again, in an Arcadian setting – 'the wet of woods through the early hours' – perfumed with the scents of apples, mint, crushed sage and birch.

In this wet woodland, two sleepers at night lie close together. An arm tantalisingly slants 'down across and below the waist of the other'. One of these sleepers is a young man. With a 'glow and pressure', this youth seems to address the poet – 'he confides to me what he was dreaming' – and yet remains caught between wakefulness and sleep, roiling around in 'the mystic amorous night' with 'strange half-welcome pangs, visions, sweats'. Then, much the same as that anonymous orgy in Arcadia, a hand appears. Presumably, it belongs to that second sleeper, though the lack of precise referent enables it to simultaneously function as the 'poet's' hand. The hand roams across the youth's body, ratcheting-up his half-lucid, fevered anticipation of sexual release to a point of 'painful' torment. He 'flushes and flushes', and then – for the first time in this scene – a brief moment of female sexual desire is depicted: a young woman suddenly appears, who likewise 'flushes and flushes'.

Is this young woman the second sleeper, or is she in the boy's dream, a figment of his imagination? The answer doesn't arrive. Rather, the young man now fully awakens to the 'trembling, encircling fingers' of that roaming hand. The tension is ready to be released – or, in Whitman's language, the 'limped liquid within the young man', 'the vexed corrosion', the 'irritable tide' – and in the scene's final stroke, Whitman's 'I' makes an astonishing reappearance: 'The souse upon me of my lover the sea, as I lie willing and naked.'

In this scene, Whitman commits to portraying a confusion of identities, and we are left wondering whether the poet is equating himself with the second sleeper, or the young woman, or both; we are left wondering whether it is Whitman or the woman who lies willing and naked, or indeed if they are one and the same. The youth's strange visions raise similar questions: does he dream of sex with a woman while being caressed by a man, or does he confide his desires to a man in a dream, while being caressed by a woman? Perhaps this mystic amorous night is another iteration of 'The Bathers', where Whitman can only express, or begin to express, sex acts between men – souse and all – when routed through the implied presence of a woman, here smuggled inside a cluster of poems that are, in the main, a paean to progeny. Immediately after the two sleepers scene, the poem shutter-clicks to an image of 'twin-babes that crawl over the grass in the sun'. Watching over these children, there is a woman: another mother. But any question of sexuality or desire is displaced; she is only there as a guardian. Perhaps these are the only roles that women can occupy in Whitman's utopia: they are either there to triangulate male desire, or else act as mothers.

There's a different interpretation of this sequence, however. Its power might lie in the fact that there are no answers as to who is who. The gender ambiguities, dream-logic and untethered 'I' raise the possibility that – beneath the excessive cladding of all the procreative, phallocentric imagery – there is a different, even more democratic, erotics at work in this cluster of poems: a lambent sexuality in which gender is liberated from a binary position, becoming an object of free play.

Diseased, Feverish,
Disproportionate Adhesiveness

Whitman is sitting in his rocking chair, looking out of the dirty window of his living room in Mickle Street and lamenting his lack of mobility. He feels like a shut-in. Nevertheless, he's submitting work. That's a way of getting out, at least. Tomorrow, he'll mail some pieces for publication – a couple of 'throws against oblivion', as he calls them. It's funny, he thinks, how poets believe their work should last forever. A man makes a pair of shoes, and knows they will wear out eventually. Why should a poem be any different? Poems wear out, too.

Traubel, the dutiful caretaker and literary executor, stands by Whitman's side. He is 'systematically collecting W. W. data' for his archive – though systematic is a stretch. The rules of the Whitman archive go like this: stand around, like a crazed botanist with a butterfly net, and wait until the poet flings some scrap of paper into the air for you to catch. 'I'll be handing you stuff from time to time,' Whitman remarks, 'for yourself – for use – perhaps for history.'

Today, a spring afternoon in late April, Whitman and Traubel are discussing the matter of another disciple. The Englishman. A man named John Addington Symonds. He has been corresponding with Whitman, via letter, for over sixteen years. Whitman tells Traubel that Symonds is always asking questions in his letters. Always driving at him, urgently, persistently. He is like a man standing in a road, Whitman says, refusing to move, until he gets an answer: he needs to know the true meaning of the 'Calamus' poems.

John Addington Symonds is a prominent biographer, man of letters and penner of poems that trace the history of male love through the ages. Many of these poems he literally locked away, subsequently hurling the key into the brown waters of the River Avon. Self-censorship is a necessity: Symonds is a supporter of romantic love between men, and spent much of his career writing about it, whether indirectly or explicitly. If his writings fell into the wrong hands, they could have seen him prosecuted, or worse. Symonds was tormented, in his personal life, by his own sexual desires, and not only because they were legally and socially condemned. He was also tormented by a lack of language: a deficit of objective or affirmative terminology with which to discuss, express, or merely denominate his sexuality. 'I can hardly find a name which will not seem to soil this paper,' he wrote, in a privately printed essay. 'The accomplished languages of Europe in the nineteenth century supply no term for this persistent feature of human psychology, without importuning some implication of disgust, disgrace, vituperation.' But where the accomplished languages of Europe failed to describe this sexuality in unprejudiced terms, Symonds believes that a new American language might have succeeded: the poetry of Walt Whitman.

After first reading 'Calamus' – in particular, that ninth poem which was struck from later editions – *Leaves of Grass* became for Symonds 'a sort of Bible'. He remembered in his memoirs that his 'desires grew manlier, more defined, more direct, more daring by contact with Calamus'. What Symonds called his 'abnormal inclinations' had been 'modified by Whitman's idealism', bringing him 'into close and profitable sympathy with human beings even while I sinned against law and conventional morality'.

Symonds didn't publish his memoirs in his lifetime. They remained under lock and key for many decades after his death. 'It would hardly be fair to my posterity,' he wrote, 'to yield up my vile soul to the psychological investigators.' Nevertheless, he believed that a study of 'the evolution of a character somewhat strangely constituted' would not be without its 'utility', indicating a painful tension between self-recrimination and a belief that an essential part of himself, an essential part of his life, required elucidation.

But in 'Calamus', Symonds thinks he has found a means of alleviating that self-recrimination, and clarifying this part of himself. His reading of 'Calamus' provides him with an affirmative expression of his sexuality, one free of disgust or disgrace. Through such emancipation – the liberation from shame – he felt it possible to achieve a greater communion not just with other men, but with all human beings. But he needs to know. He needs to hear it from the horse's mouth. He needs Whitman to close the gap between persona and poet, reality and dream, and confirm that his poetic intent is, in fact, to express and describe such a sexuality. And the Englishman's appeals for clarity are contained in an envelope, which Whitman now thrusts into Traubel's hand.

'You will be writing something about Calamus some day,' Whitman says to his disciple, 'and this letter, and what I say, may help clear your ideas.'

Symonds writes from his father's house in Clifton, Bristol, while gazing out at the trees, docks and churches, a labyrinth of spires and rooftops. After setting the scene, and offering some words of flattery and adulation, he gets down to business. For many years, Symonds says, he has been attempting to explain 'the forms of what [. . .] you call adhesiveness'. When Symonds first read *Leaves*, he writes, he came to feel 'that the Comradeship which I conceived as on a par with the sexual feeling for depth and strength and purity and capability of all good, was *real* – not a delusion of distorted passions [. . .] but a strong and vital bond of man to man'. Then comes the question: 'I have pored for continuous hours over the pages of Calamus [. . .] longing to hear you speak, burning for a revelation of more developed meaning, panting to ask – is this what you would indicate?'

Traubel reads the letter. Whitman, watching him, asks: 'Well, what do you think of that? Could that be answered?'

But Traubel is unmoved. He finds the letter 'quiet' and somewhat harmless, replying that 'it only asks questions, and asks the questions mildly enough'. His eyes must skim over the words 'burning', 'panting' – he doesn't recognise or sense Symonds' urgency, as Whitman does.

'I often say to myself about Calamus,' Whitman relents, 'perhaps it means more or less than what I thought myself, means different – perhaps I don't know what it all means – perhaps never did know.'

But two years later, Whitman is no longer so equivocal. The cat-and-mouse correspondence between himself and Symonds reaches fever pitch. In yet another letter, Symonds all but demands an answer to his question: in conceiving of adhesiveness, in writing 'Calamus', has Whitman contemplated the 'possible intrusion of those semi-sexual emotions and actions which no doubt do occur between men?'.

He is saying: your poems hint at it, they say it in a thousand other indirect ways, now speak it plainly. Whitman's reply is unambiguous. The fact his 'Calamus' poems could have even given rise to such a reading, he replies, was 'terrible'. He refers to Symonds' mention of semi-sexual emotions and actions between men as 'morbid inferences, which are disavowed by me and seem damnable'. In postscript, he even claims paternity over six children, fathered out of wedlock. It's a desperate boast, one which misreads its audience: Symonds, himself a father of four, understood first-hand that being a married father and having same-sex desires aren't mutually exclusive. It may be that Symonds read this rebuttal as a character assassination – that his feelings of abnormality were redoubled by it – but there is a resoluteness in his reply to Whitman.

'You must not think that the "morbid inferences", which to you "seem damnable", are quite "gratuitous" or outside the range of possibility,' Symonds writes in reply. Almost as castigation, he reminds the poet of the importance, the essential novelty, of his own work: 'Frankly speaking, the emotional language of Calamus is such as hitherto has not been used in the modern world about the relation between friends.'

Whether you like it or not, Symonds says, whether you want to disavow it or not, the poems do mean something. They express something. In the uncertain, shifting, fluid sexual lexicon of the latter nineteenth century, in that terminological struggle in which categories of sexual identity are rapidly taking shape, 'Calamus' expresses and denotes a whole spectrum of desire between men. And this has the capacity to affect and change individual men for the better, to bring men closer to one another, and that might modify those morals society deems 'conventional': but only if that spectrum can also include the sexual. It is as though Symonds is saying that the entire concept of adhesiveness, with all its transformative potential, won't have any efficacy at all unless it also ratifies and acknowledges physical and sexual intimacy. To condemn that, to shun that, is to render the entire philosophy inconsequential.

How should we read Whitman's late-in-the-day rejection of what he calls 'morbid inferences'; does he dread that his poems will be seen as endorsing sodomy? Does he sense the eyes of his disciples roaming around the mess of papers at Mickle Street, sickened by the Doyle photograph, ready to judge him? Or perhaps he is resisting the fixity of Symonds' question, convinced that the meanings of his work are, and should remain, inherently mysterious, fluid and uncertain. 'I maybe do not know all my own meanings,' Whitman had said to Traubel. 'I say to myself: "You, too, go away, come back, study your own book – an alien or stranger, study your own book, see what it amounts to."'

Although Walt Whitman and the English disciple never met in person, they were captured together in a photograph. Dated 1889, and taken in Mickle Street, the poet is photographed sitting in profile, sharply in focus. To his left, leaning against a wall, blurred but in perfect parallel, can be seen a portrait of John Addington Symonds, one which he posted to Whitman in his correspondence. The portrait's eyes seem fixed on the poet, who looks out of frame. Two men, close yet estranged, one confrontational, the other avoidant. It's a photographic irony that Symonds, who sought fixity and certainty from Whitman, should be blurred, and Whitman, who remained elusive and slippery, is in crystalline focus.*

Whitman's rebuttal to Symonds prompted biographers, in the early twentieth century, to hunt through the poet's papers for evidence of a definitive love affair he may have had with a woman. Such evidence might give credence to Whitman's claim of paternity, and so, in their narrow view, protect Whitman's legacy from 'accusations' of homosexuality. One of his early biographers, a man named Henry Bryan Binns, looked

---

* This photograph was taken by the photographic firm Kuebler Photography, and dated *c*. 1889. It is held in the Library of Congress, and can be viewed at whitmanarchive.org.

to the poems themselves for such evidence. In the 'Children of Adam' cluster, he alighted on a particular poem, titled 'Once I Pass'd Through a Populous City', in which the poet appears to recall a romance with a woman: 'Day by day and night by night we were together [. . .] I remember I say only that woman who passionately clung to me.' Binns, treating this poem as an autobiographical confession, speculated that Whitman, in his real life, had an affair with a lady of higher social standing while he travelled through New Orleans as a younger man, the titular 'populous city'. Binns went as far as to suggest that this mysterious New Orleanian lady was, very likely, the mother to Whitman's six spectral children. But when the original manuscript for this poem was later discovered, such speculation would lose any claim to validity. In Whitman's initial draft of the poem, the genders were reversed. The poem was not about a woman, but about a man. This edit might well support the notion that the poet, in his art, felt impelled to unfasten masculinity and femininity from their fixed positions. Alternating between a 'male' and 'female' lover, with a few pencil marks, doesn't seem to stress a stratification of gender so much as underline its ultimate irrelevance or fungibility.

There's another gender-switching incident in the poet's papers. In a distressingly impassioned, self-chastising notebook entry, made in 1870 at the apex of his relationship with Peter Doyle, Whitman penned, complete with capitalisation, 'GIVE UP ABSOLUTELY & for good, for this present hour, this FEVERISH, FLUCTUATING, useless undignified pursuit of 164'. The number, here, is accepted as basic alphanumerical code, where 16 is 'P', and 4 is 'D': Doyle's initials. The note continues: 'Avoid seeing her, or meeting her, or any talk or explanations – or ANY MEETING WHATEVER, FROM

THIS HOUR FORTH, FOR LIFE'. But Whitman has written over the original pronoun 'her'. It initially said 'him'. This valuable bit of 'W. W. data' shows that Whitman consciously sought to edit, rewrite and encrypt the on-page portrayal of his personal masculine and sexual identity. If Whitman the poet felt impelled to loosen the lines of gender, Whitman the man, it seems, needed to erase any indication that his lived desires deviated from his masculinity. Hence, Doyle once again becomes a 'girl'.

In a following notebook entry, Whitman reprimands himself to 'Depress the adhesive nature / It is in excess – making life a torment / All this diseased, feverish, disproportionate adhesiveness'. These private jottings offer a brief glimpse into Whitman's personal struggles and torments, in which his poetic conception of adhesiveness, that relentlessly affirmative, inflated, spiritual philosophy, is suddenly made small again, described in Fowlerian phrenological language as a mere 'faculty' in excess. What's more, he calls it 'diseased': an attempt to dispel very real and meaningful desires, desires that clearly caused him great distress, through pathology. The language bears a close relationship to John Addington Symonds' own self-recrimination. Whitman's admonishment of the English disciple was perhaps born of similitude rather than difference: a rejection of something he recognised in himself, something that conventional morals and laws – the vituperation of the 'sodomite', the emergence of the congenitally 'abnormal' homosexual – caused him to shun.

Whitman's final, declarative rebuttal of Symonds' 'morbid inferences', if nothing else, signals just how charged a concept adhesiveness had become by the end of his life. And that the journey of adhesiveness should be so peculiar, so perilous

– from the American eugenics movement, to idolatry of exclusively able-bodied men, to invocations of all-male utopias – is testament to how volatile a concept it remains today. But its more alluring, more hopeful aspects are worth holding on to. Whitman's efforts to walk 'paths untrodden' and pull from the murky pond waters a vision of celebratory, intimate, affirmative bonds between men – his lifelong quest to project this vision through ever-changing, cryptic verse – rippled outwards, inflecting early theoretical frameworks of gender and sexuality and influencing countless queer artists. And his commanding instinct that, between men, at the nexus of masculinity and desire, there lies some mysterious, unwieldy force, one with enormous, transformative consequences for society, would take on new meaning in America several decades later, in the mid-twentieth century.

PART TWO

A Feeling of Estrangement

Sea-Summer

Tennessee Williams is dying. He's standing on a pier on Nantucket Island, eyeing the overcast sky, exhausted and beset with anxieties. The past few weeks have taken their toll on him. He's never had 'such a freakish run of bad luck' in his life. His initial summer plans – a vacation in Taos, New Mexico, with his boyfriend Pancho – had to be abandoned. He'd started driving there, in a second- or third-hand Packard convertible roadster. But the car broke down, its bearings burnt out, in Alvo, Oklahoma, of all places. At the very same time, his body broke down, too. There was an emergency operation on his appendix, conducted by a group of amateur doctors, fresh out of the army. Then, barely recovered, a fiery incident with Pancho. This young, rakish Mexican American is an angel of goodness, Tennessee thinks, except when he's drinking. The problem is, he's always drinking. One evening, apropos of nothing, Pancho tore up all Tennessee's clothes and smashed his typewriter. Though, strangely, he left his manuscripts intact. Perhaps he sensed that to destroy them might destroy the man.

Against his better judgement, and from a desperate need to avoid loneliness, Tennessee has 'permitted' Pancho to join him on this vacation in Nantucket. The two men have rented accommodation for the summer: 31 Pine Street, a grey, lopsided frame house, equidistant from the cemetery and the shore. But the run of bad luck has followed Tennessee here. The elements are conspiring against him. Two days ago, a storm rolled in, bringing violent winds that shattered all the glass windows. The weather's been dismal since. Nothing but cold rain and cold air. To make matters worse, a stray, pregnant cat crawled through one of the broken windows and gave birth to a litter of kittens in the downstairs guest bedroom.

Nantucket's not an entirely arbitrary choice of location. Tennessee has a connection to the island. His father's side of the family, which carries the name Coffin, 'flourished' here a couple of generations ago. There's a neat irony in the idea of a family of flourishing Coffins; and the notion that Tennessee should return to such a place while convinced of his imminent death makes a twisted, Southern kind of sense. He's been experiencing severe heart pain, palpitations and cold sweats for weeks now. 'The physical machine,' Tennessee writes to a friend, is 'in a state of collapse, and what may politely be called the spiritual element is crouching in the corner with both hands clasped to its eyes'. The palpitations themselves are nothing new. The strong black coffee he drinks every morning before turning like a 'blast furnace' to his typewriter, a necessary antecedent to 'getting the creative juices flowing', certainly doesn't help. But this time his heart feels different. This time it feels serious. It keeps him up at night. It surely signals some terminal condition, the approach of the end of his life.

Now, he and Pancho wait on the pier, bracing themselves for yet another roadblock to their restorative summer getaway. But this one is self-inflicted. Tennessee has invited a guest to join them for a few days. Someone, he believes, to be the greatest living writer in America, if not the world: the young Southern novelist, Carson McCullers. A few weeks ago, in the midst of that run of bad luck, he'd been kept awake all night, chain-smoking cigarettes and wiping away tears. This insomniac turn wasn't caused by his heart pains, but by Carson's new novel, *The Member of the Wedding*. He'd first read her debut, *The Heart Is a Lonely Hunter*, some years before, writing to a friend that it is 'so extraordinary it makes me ashamed of anything I might do [. . .] What a play she could write!' Disturbed and touched by *Member*, he hastily penned a fan letter – the first he'd ever written – sending the adulatory missive off to Carson the following morning. On discovering that they had friends in common, he felt inspired to invite her to join him and Pancho in Nantucket. He should like to spend some time with the world's greatest living writer, he said, before he gave up the ghost. Flattered, McCullers accepted.

The two men scrutinise the ferry's departing passengers. They don't know who, exactly, they're looking for, but expect to spot an austere, sophisticated literary type, a glamorous young woman, standing out in the crowd. But she's not there. It appears everyone has left. Did she even board the ferry? Just as they head up to see if anyone remains, a tall, *tall* girl comes down the gangplank, carrying two worse-for-wear suitcases, clad in a man's shirt, a baseball cap and slacks, and wearing a radiant, crooked grin.

'Are you Tennessee and Pancho?' Carson asks.

Tennessee Williams and Carson McCullers are both Southern writers. Tennessee hails from Columbus, Mississippi, Carson from Columbus, Georgia. In their work there is a shared tension between a nostalgic yearning for and fondness of the Southern landscape, its people and customs, and a frustration with its stifling social mores, political conservatism and racist heritage. But it isn't their shared Southern roots alone that unites them. Their work also shares a unique, profound fluency in matters of the human heart, individual loneliness and desire, and the possibilities and failures of love.

Love and desire, for Tennessee and Carson, aren't forces that can be neatly categorised. They do not fit into boxes. They are wild and fluid, encompassing everything from the spiritual to the base, the erotic to the platonic, the triumphant to the disastrous – and they are experienced by and between all of us, indiscriminate of sexual orientation, gender, class or race. For both writers, this is an essential truth in their work. It's also an essential truth in their lives: they are both queer, and live openly as such. From his mid-twenties onwards, all Tennessee's romantic relationships are with men, yet he will attest in interviews that his desires include both men and women;* Carson, who married Reeves McCullers in 1937, divorced him in 1942, and remarried him several years later, also fell in love with and romantically pursued women. We might say that they both had a bisexual sensibility, and that they both vouched for and intended to make visible the double-direction, changeability and putative contradictions of love and desire. And both writers routinely, and self-consciously, synthesised real life into their art. To express this essential truth in their works – the fierce, untamed democracy of rangy desire – they critique the forces that seek to obscure it: compulsory heterosexuality and the incoherent, contradictory codes that give structure to gender, particularly masculinity. And they were doing this at a time of intense cultural and societal change, in which the very

---

* Making this point in a late-career interview, in the context of a wider discussion around his sexuality, Tennessee was told his thinking was full of contradictions, to which he replied, 'I am contradictory, baby'; a sentiment that echoes one of Whitman's most famous lines: 'Do I contradict myself? / Very well then I contradict myself, / (I am large, I contain multitudes.)'

meanings of sexuality and masculinity were being warred over and newly defined, and an intense, state-sanctioned atmosphere of homophobia and misogyny deliberately implemented.

Carson, at twenty-nine, is six years younger than Tennessee. When she and the playwright first meet in Nantucket, she is in the middle of a tremendous decade of creative endeavour, during which she will write all her major works. Carson has been hailed a genius. A prodigy. An *enfant terrible*. Or, as one contemporary referred to her, sensing something doomed about her aura (or simply acknowledging her excessive alcohol consumption), a *fleur du mal*. Indeed, when it comes to her health, it has often seemed that Carson really is doomed. She is the 'victim of a conspiracy of troubles', susceptible to pneumonia, viruses and sheer bad luck besides (in 1942, a dentist accidentally broke her jaw bone during a routine molar extraction, which became infected). And this summer in Nantucket is the last she'll enjoy of relatively fair health, before she is struck with a cerebral stroke in the winter of 1946. Her later years will be tragically beset with rheumatic heart disease, breast cancer and a broken hip, necessitating use of a wheelchair; the resulting nerve damage from these ailments will render her incapable of typing, except by using a single finger, hitting one key at a time.

The book that first earned Carson notoriety was her debut novel, *The Heart Is a Lonely Hunter*, written when she was twenty-two and published a year later, in 1940. It bestowed on her the kind of overnight literary fame that seems almost mythical. In many ways, the publication of *Hunter* did for Carson's creative career what the staging of *The Glass Menagerie* did for Tennessee Williams'. When this play, his Broadway debut, appeared in 1944, it flung him to national and international fame. But Tennessee's success wasn't so sudden. Thirty-three years old at the time of *Menagerie*, Tennessee had spent years in obscurity, vagabonding around the urban wildernesses of America, penning poems, filling up diaries, doggedly pursuing his art but being met with failure after failure, wondering if he'd ever 'make it' at all.

Now, in Nantucket, these artists meet as creative equals. Carson has since published two more novels – *Reflections in a Golden Eye* and *The Member of the Wedding* – and has twice been awarded the prestigious Guggenheim Fellowship. Tennessee, still radiant from the success of *Menagerie*, is working on several more scripts, sensing – correctly – that his best work lies ahead of him. One of these, currently a few sketchy ideas tentatively titled *The Poker Night*, will next year become his most famous stage play, *A Streetcar Named Desire*, and cement his reputation as America's greatest living playwright.

A shame, then, that he should now be dying.

But with Carson's arrival, he soon begins to forget all about his heart palpitations. The first afternoon on Nantucket passes in a haze of easy intimacy and excitement. At the pier, the trio embrace. Within minutes of meeting, Tennessee and Carson discover a mutual love for the poetry of Hart Crane, something that helps Tennessee form an instant and instinctive attachment to Carson. Crane – a poet whose tragic fate was suicide by drowning, possibly instigated after he was assaulted in a homophobic attack – is one of Tennessee's most beloved writers, in whose work he takes solace and inspiration. 'My personal trinity let me think of them,' he listed in an early poem, 'Whitman the brawler, the cosmic-voyager Crane, / and soft-spoken Chekhov on evenings of wind and rain.'

When they return to 31 Pine Street, Carson adores the house. She isn't bothered by the clutter and mess – the broken windows, the litter of newly born kittens curled up on her guest bed. Perhaps this atmosphere of 'southern degeneracy', as Tennessee described it, which he felt had 'completely triumphed over the brisk New England climate', made her feel more at home. With Carson's presence, the house is transformed. She brings an atmosphere of warmth and light. In fact, she appears to have literally brought the sun with her. Almost from the moment of her arrival, the weather improves, and the seawater becomes warm and calm enough for swimming. The trio form a rough routine, heading out to the beach each afternoon, where Tennessee swims so far out that Carson thinks he might actually drown. Later, by candlelight, they fatten up on canned pea soup and diced weenies, or 'Spuds Carson', a culinary innovation of hers consisting of potatoes mashed with onions, butter and cheese. Role-playing as cook is a deviation for Carson. In her former home life, before her rise to fame, it would often be her husband, Reeves, who'd take care of the cooking and cleaning while she worked on her writing. After candlelit dinner, cocktails and conversation, Carson plays songs on the piano, or Tennessee reaches for a book of Hart Crane's poetry – stolen from the St. Louis Library some time ago – and begins to orate, wise to the parallels between Crane's suicide by drowning and his own reckless swimming escapades.

And then there's the work. Tennessee has an evergreen, irresistible pull towards work. It's like an internal motor that propels him through waking life, and he carries Carson into this restless slipstream. The two writers spend mornings sitting at opposite ends of the long dining-room table, working at typewriters, smoking and occasionally passing a bottle of bourbon back and forth. Tennessee encourages Carson to adapt *The Member of the Wedding* into a stage play, though he doesn't see himself as her mentor, feeling that he has little by way of creative advice to offer the greatest writer in the world ('Carson didn't need me,' he would later remark, 'except as a catalyst for herself'). Meanwhile, he's trying to work out the problems of his next play, *Summer and Smoke*. It is the only time that Tennessee has felt able to work in the presence of someone else. It is the first time that Carson writes for the stage.

Naturally, such a creative union excludes Pancho, who begins to feel that Carson is competing for Tennessee's affections. At first, he even thinks that Carson is vying to marry him, though, as the summer progresses, this concern will show itself to be wildly unfounded. Carson *is* nursing a crush, but not for Tennessee. There's a small social scene on the island, and the three attend parties together. At one, Carson meets a glamorous baroness, and quickly becomes infatuated. According to Tennessee, Carson would sit up half the night, slowly working her way through a bottle of Johnnie Walker and fantasising about the would-be romance. This particular infatuation occupied Carson's mind until the baroness visited 31 Pine Street. She had brought her pet dogs with her, and one of the bloodthirsty mutts mauled and killed one of Carson's adopted kittens. That was the end of that.

The days roll into weeks. Far from exhausting itself in a fire of mutual overzealousness, the relationship between these two writers blossoms. It begins to resemble what Carson, in *The Member of the Wedding*, might describe as a 'We of Me' relationship: a private club, a perfect intermingling of one self and another, an individual coddled into a collective, in a mutually sustaining communion. For Tennessee, the discovery of his and Carson's friendship seems nothing short of miraculous. He feels that Carson possesses an immediate and intuitive 'understanding of another vulnerable being', which enables her to give 'affectionate compassion' more freely than almost anyone else he's ever known. Their summer together forms the foundation of a deep and lasting relationship, one that the two writers seemed almost destined to make.

Portrait of a Girl

Summer 1940, New York City, New York

Carson McCullers is looking at herself in the window of a Fifth Avenue bookshop. There's a blow-up, black-and-white portrait of her in the display. It's a promotional photograph, in which she is sitting at a table, signing a stack of hardbacks – copies of her debut novel, *The Heart Is a Lonely Hunter*. The advance accolades, printed on the dust jacket, are predictably enthusiastic. 'A strange and powerful book,' one reads. 'I can't understand how a twenty-two year old girl can know so much of love and loneliness,' reads another. The *New Yorker's* chief literary critic, Clifton Fadiman, will soon sound a similar note of perplexity, labelling Carson a 'round-faced, Dutch-bobbed girl' able to deal 'familiarly with matters no nice twenty-two year old girl is supposed to be an authority on'.

At first glance it might seem that Carson has actively goaded her critics into such an infantalising, gendered response to her work. In the photograph, she is not dressed as a 'nice young girl'. She's instead clad in menswear: an oversized men's shirt with a sharp, fang-like collar, and a men's corduroy jacket. But Carson hasn't only adopted this style of dress for the promotional shot. She's always instinctively understood the inseparability of dress and gender codes, and has always felt an urge to tweak and manipulate the former to readjust her relationship to the latter. As a child, her tendency to wear beat-up, scruffy tennis shoes to school, as opposed to the neat pumps worn by other girls, would incentivise cliques of her classmates to hurl rocks at her, along with epithets such as 'weird' and 'queer'.

This alternative form of public presentation isn't something Carson McCullers will relinquish after her ascent to literary fame. On the contrary, her preference for outsized men's shirts, undersized boys' jackets, short-cropped hair, baseball and cyclist caps, men's slacks and dungarees will be noted by many of her literary peers. Carson's commitment to reorienting her relationship to gender through dress – a proclivity described by Hilton Als as 'androgyne', and by Sarah Shulman as a 'lesbian persona' – affects others, too. When Anaïs Nin, that writer so fluent in erotic love between men and women, meets Carson in 1943, she will first mistake her for a boy.

In the author photograph, the shirt Carson wears is borrowed from her husband, Reeves, with whom she's now ambling along Fifth Avenue. Reeves McCullers, four years Carson's senior, is a former soldier: clean-cut, angular and the 'best looking man' she's ever seen. His eyes possess a unique, mysterious quality. They seem to shift colour depending on his mood, an iridescent display of blue, grey and green, like the tones of the tree-shaded creek he and Carson – in their early, happier years – liked to swim and skinny-dip in. But lately, his eyes have taken on a steely quality. For Reeves, seeing his wife in the bookshop window is jarring. It's not the gender ambiguity that distresses him. It's the name. His name, *McCullers*. Reeves feels that it should be *him* in the window, celebrated as a rising literary star. He is also a writer, although by all accounts a writer who doesn't write. Carson has never seen a word of his work. Reeves' inability to find time to dedicate to his practice is apparently down to his hard-won, salaried job at the Retail Credit Corporation, the first steady job he'd found in some years. This disparity – the putative breadwinner versus the artist, the would-be writer versus the actual writer – has ratcheted up an emotional tension in their marriage, so that their relationship seems set to fray.

The young, eternally cash-strapped couple had been living in small towns in the South since their informal engagement in 1937. For the past eight months it was Fayetteville, North Carolina. There, Reeves would work while Carson would write. She was on a quest: prospecting for the illuminations, the seeds of vibrating and pulsating ideas that she felt were the essence of the creative process. The previous year, she'd entered an outline of *The Heart Is a Lonely Hunter* into a national writing competition, run by the publisher Houghton Mifflin. Though she didn't win, she was placed second, and awarded a book contract and a $500 advance. From that point on, Carson became almost single-mindedly dedicated, committing herself morally, ethically and with all her strength to the completion of the novel.

But as the months flew by she found herself stuck, unable to pull the amorphous, mysterious, half-sketched world of *Hunter* into a cohesive structure. Until she was struck by an illumination: the invention of the central character, a deaf mute named John Singer. Suddenly, the pieces fell into place. Carson found that she'd unleashed a great creative force, and the illuminations kept coming, in their thousands. On completing the manuscript of *Hunter*, she immediately set about writing a second novel – originally titled *Army Post*, later renamed to *Reflections in a Golden Eye* – a process she found as pleasurable as eating candy. Before her twenty-third birthday, before she enjoyed any reputation as an author whatsoever, living and working in complete obscurity, Carson McCullers had created two major works of twentieth-century American fiction.

On receipt of the second half of her advance, paid to her on publication of *Hunter*, Carson and Reeves ship all their belongings to New York, and follow on the next day. They board an overnight train to the city – and a modest fifth-floor rented apartment in the Village – and vow never to live in the South again. Or, perhaps, never to live *together* in the South again. Though they both understand this moment marks a new life, a new start, neither can predict the rapidity with which their world and relationship will change in the wake of Carson's literary debut. Her rise to fame, during which she 'blossomed like a sunflower on the literary scene', occurs too quickly for Carson to make any sense of it ('I was a bit of a holy terror,' she later recalled). Within weeks, Carson will situate herself in New York's socialite circles. She will be invited to a small, exclusive get-together hosted by Klaus Mann – son of the German novelist Thomas Mann – his daughter Erika, and her spouse-of-convenience, whom she married to obtain a passport, the queer British poet W. H. Auden. One of the Manns' long-standing friends (and Erika's former lover besides) will be there, too, having herself just arrived in New York. Her name is Annemarie Schwarzenbach, a thirty-two-year-old Swiss heiress, writer, photo-journalist, morphine addict and anti-fascist.

Annemarie, described by a friend as looking like 'the Archangel Gabriel', is androgynous in both physique and dress, sharing Carson's inclination towards alternative forms of gender representation through attire. On meeting Annemarie at that little party, Carson becomes instantly enamoured with her. Annemarie is, Carson thinks, 'bodily resplendent' with a 'face that will haunt me to the end of my life'. Her burgeoning infatuation flares into an impassioned, all-consuming love that will provide Carson with a wellspring of energy, inspiration and despair for months. Hers and Annemarie's relationship will also further destabilise her marriage, but perhaps not in the way one would expect. Reeves is not outwardly perturbed by the romantic frisson between them as women. He is amicable with Annemarie. But he uses his own friendship with her against Carson, stoking her jealousy, claiming that Annemarie confides secrets to him: in particular, that Annemarie, supposedly, believes Carson is seriously unwell.

This new, triangular dynamic in Carson and Reeves' marriage, in which love and infatuation with a third person provoke jealousy and competitiveness between them, will become a pattern. Eerily, Carson has already explored triangular romance, its jealousies and power imbalances, in *Reflections*, which she will dedicate to Annemarie. The part-coincidental, part-choreographed overlap between her real and fictional worlds is a legend she'll later promote, claiming that everything significant in her fiction has actually happened to her, 'or it will happen, eventually'.

But all this is yet to come. Now, standing on Fifth Avenue, she gazes at the image of herself in the bookshop window. Carson McCullers looking at Carson McCullers, author of that strange novel, *The Heart Is a Lonely Hunter*. A girl, or something like it, growing into the role of 'wunderkind' sketched out for her by the literary establishment, remaining tethered to her envious husband just as she remains tethered to the past, the South and everything there that has shaped her.

Love and Estrangement

The setting of *The Heart Is a Lonely Hunter* is typical of McCullers' fiction – a small community in the Deep South, tainted by an atmosphere of latent hostility, division and suspicion. The seasons are violent and richly described, with burning hot summers and short, sharp winters, autumns where the foliage glows like fire. Overhead, the Southern skies are vast, glassy and often empty, pure azure which clarifies, in the dusk hours, into deep violet. Carson's writing, as Richard Wright characterised it in an early review of *Hunter*, is like 'a projected mood, a state of mind poetically objectified in words', one which has a 'sheen of weird tenderness'. The characters that drift through this murky world are each physically and spiritually isolated. Men and women, teenagers, doctors, soldiers and labourers, all driven by a need and desire to communicate, but tragically failing to translate this into communion with others. In her work, this failure is shown not to be solely an individual fault. Rather, it is the result of impenetrable barriers, structures and social mores, often drawn along the lines of sexuality and gender.

The characters in *Hunter* – among them, a tomboyish girl, Mick Kelly, and a recently widowed café owner, Biff Brannon – find temporary and illusory relief from their isolation in the company of John Singer, a deaf mute who works in the town as an engraver. Ever-present, and receptive to their company, John Singer sits and listens as these characters try to communicate 'the words in their heart' that 'do not let them rest'. But Singer is largely unresponsive. He is like a blank screen onto which they project a fantasy version of a man – he becomes 'whoever [they] wished he would be'. Such is the power of their fantasy, and the myopia of their individual loneliness, that they fail to recognise Singer's own painful solitude. For Singer is desperately alone. His partner, Antonapoulos, with whom he had once lived and shared his entire life, has been taken from him.

Singer and Antonapoulos, we are told in the novel's very first sentence, 'were always together'. Yet 'these two friends were very different', linked only, it seems, by their shared deafness. Singer is tall, immaculate, soberly dressed and 'quick', whereas Antonapoulos is uncleanly, sloppily clothed, overweight and 'dreamy'. From the outset, their coupling seems unlikely. Very early on in the novel, Antonapoulos develops unexplained violent and kleptomaniac tendencies, and is hastily sent away by his cousin – for whom he works, at a fruit store, and about whom Singer has fostered a 'strange feeling' – to the state insane asylum.

'*You cannot do this*,' Singer pens on the little pad he carries in his pocket, '*Antonapoulos must stay with me.*' But it's no use. The cousin merely repeats, utilising the little English in his possession, that it's 'none of your business'. Singer is thrust into complete solitude: 'he had been left in an alien land. Alone.' In an effort to dispel his solitude, he writes letters to Antonapoulos.

> The only thing I can imagine is when I will be with you again [. . .] The way I need you is a loneliness I can not bear [. . .] I am not meant to be alone and without you.

But he does not send these letters, preferring instead to surrender himself 'wholly to thoughts of his friend'. As the duration of their separation extends, Singer experiences a 'submerged communion' with his beloved. He thinks of him with 'awe and self-abasement, sometimes with pride – always with love unchecked by criticism'. When Singer travels by train to visit Antonapoulos in the asylum, he gazes out at the fleeting landscape, at the gnarled roots, tree moss and water flowers blossoming in the gloom. In this 'kaleidoscopic variety of scene, this abundance of growth and color', Singer finds his feelings for his beloved reflected. The lush, dripping, organic growth expresses his 'bliss' at their imminent reunion, a bliss so potent as to be deathly: it 'almost stifled him'.

Singer's desire for Antonapoulos, however, is wholly one-sided. During his first visit to the asylum, Singer brings extravagant gifts: a fruit basket, a miniature flicker film projector. Antonapoulos merely tears off the wrapping paper, and turns, disinterested in the presents, to his supper. Clothed in the luxuriant pyjamas that Singer had earlier sent him – another love-offering – Antonapoulos is aloof, mysterious, looking at Singer with drowsy eyes. The 'placid composure of his face was so profound', in fact, 'that he seemed to be hardly aware that Singer was with him'. This is the key, organising principle of the relationship between the two men: it is one of hopeless, impassioned and unrequited love.

Singer's desire is fuelled by its lack of reciprocation: he doesn't send the letters; he prefers the unreal 'submerged' communion, the fantasy rather than the reality. He doesn't notice his beloved's disinterest. Rather, his eyes fill with tears of happiness at merely being in the same room as him. Nevertheless, Singer's love does depend on the existence of the love object. On learning of Antonapoulos' death, towards the end of the novel, he shoots himself through the chest. That is, through the heart. And nobody in the town knows why.

What does it mean that the central relationship in McCullers' debut novel is one in which a man is unrequitedly in love with another? The two characters have sometimes been read as coded archetypes of gay tragedy, with their respective fates (madness and suicide) a phobic comment on the absolute otherness of same-sex desire: the only 'natural' outcome of homosexuality being madness or suicide. Such a reading ignores the coldly transactional manner in which Antonapoulos was first despatched to the asylum. The tragic fates of both men are set in motion by another man – Antonapoulos's cousin – who considered their relationship *unbusinesslike*, brutally ignored Singer's appeals, and terminated their union.

Singer and Antonapoulos's relationship could also be considered in the context of the unrequited love tradition that wends its way throughout the whole of the western canon: a tradition that is most frequently about a man's love for a woman. In Goethe's *The Sorrows of Young Werther*, for instance, the titular Werther not only communicates the desperate longing of his love for Charlotte through letter writing, his fate is precisely the same as Singer's. Accepting that his love is and will always be unrequited, he shoots himself. Thought of this way, McCullers' creation of Singer and Antonapoulos might be a 'queering' of the canon of unrequited love. Through them, we come to understand that the ability to love and be loved, the roles of the desired and desirer, exist independently of one's sex or sexuality. Singer's indecipherable, inexplicable longing for the disinterested Antonapoulos is such because the source and motives of love and desire are, themselves, indecipherable. Carson McCullers has simply chosen to show these forces occurring between two men. In the opening pages of her debut novel, she has set about dethroning the supremacy of heterosexual love. It is *not* the default sexuality from which other kinds of sexuality vary. There is no default.

In the minor, somewhat unassuming character of Biff Brannon, McCullers expands her exploration of fluid desire and its incompatibility with the social construct of masculinity. Central to *Hunter's mise en scène* is the New York Café, an all-night eatery-cum-bar, which remains illuminated with harsh electric light even as the streets become dark and deserted, casting a 'sharp, yellow rectangle' on the sidewalk. Much like the diner in Edward Hopper's famous painting *Nighthawks* (1943), the illuminated interior of the New York Café is not indicative of warmth and respite. Rather, it serves to expose the loneliness of its denizens. In the café, there is 'no noise or conversation, for each person seemed to be alone'. At the dawn hour, the café is suffused with ambient hostility, generated by its male customers, day and night labourers, whose 'mutual distrust' gives 'everyone a feeling of estrangement'.

Biff Brannon is the café's all-seeing eye. Standing at watch behind the till, he regularly works fourteen-hour shifts, noting the comings and goings of the town's residents. He has, he believes, an almost preternatural ability to identify in others the 'special physical part' they keep 'always guarded'. In Mick Kelly, it is 'the new, tender nipples beginning to come out on her breast' – an observation which signals his growing obsession with her. Biff, over the course of the novel, becomes hopelessly infatuated with Mick. He watches her, thinks about her, blushes in her company. But only while she remains in the quasi-androgynous state of the adolescent tomboy.

Biff's desire for Mick is most acute when he recognises that she looks 'as much like an overgrown boy as a girl', and, conversely, dampens at the end of the novel, when Mick is forced to capitulate to traditional, normative, womanhood. Mick, who begins *Hunter* as a kid dressed in boys' clothes, fostering dreams of international travel and a career as a concert pianist, ends the novel a shift worker at a department store, bejewelled with green, dangling, uncomfortable earrings. At the store, with a horrible irony emphasising the absurd performance inherent in her newly 'feminised' role, she is tasked with selling costume jewellery.

Biff, meanwhile, locates in Mick's adolescent androgyny proof of his privately held conviction that 'by nature all people are of both sexes', enabling him to conclude 'that marriage and the bed is not *all* by any means': sexuality and gender cannot be accounted for by the rules and customs of matrimony alone. His desire for Mick, while tethered to her physical body, doesn't reach towards consummation. It may be sexual or psychosexual, but he doesn't want to sleep with her. Rather, he wants to parent and nurture her, to give her things, 'not only a sundae or something sweet to eat – but something real. That was all he wanted for himself – to give to her.' And in this parental role he doesn't see himself as the father: he sees himself as Mick's 'mother'. Biff is a man whose attraction to a thirteen-year-old girl is predicated on her gender ambiguity; whose attraction to her reifies his belief in a universal, innate androgyny; and whose final object of desire is not the girl herself, but to become, himself, her mother.

On recognising that all he wants to do is 'give' to Mick, he suddenly feels 'a strange guilt . . . the dark guilt in all men, unreckoned and without a name'. This strange guilt is surely the guilt of a predator – Mick is, after all, thirteen years old – but is it so simple? Is it not also the guilt of a heretic, belonging to a man who wishes to 'betray' the rigid codes of his given sex and gender? After all, Biff's entire world, his entire life, is the New York Café, that environment of male hostility so potent that it makes everyone feel alone. His desire for Mick, his desire to be her mother, is at least in part a desire for emancipation from this masculinist world in which relations between men are defined by distrust. If Singer and Antonapoulos's relationship is a challenge to the assumed supremacy of a fixed, monolithic heterosexuality from which anything else is deviant, then Biff's desire for transexual transgression is a bold challenge to the notion that one's gender, and possibly biological sex, is a given, a certainty, a foregone conclusion.

But what of this dark, nameless guilt that McCullers' narrator tells us is in *all* men? Not long after publication of her debut novel, McCullers explained to the anti-segregationist journalist Ralph McGill that she believed Southerners, in particular, share a special 'consciousness of guilt'. It is one not fully 'knowable or communicable', and it results in an intense spiritual loneliness. She sought to capture this sense of estrangement, she told McGill, in the themes of *The Heart Is a Lonely Hunter*. McCullers explained that this guilt originates from the fact that Southerners had 'lived for so long in an artificial social system that we insisted was natural and right and just – when all along we knew it wasn't'. She was referring, in part, to the segregation laws and secular liturgy that undergirded life in the South, strictures whose very existence proved 'how little we believed our own deceits'. The essence of this argument, however, McCullers knew to be universal. Life under the rubric of any contrived hierarchy, any set of enforced, stifling strictures, results in individual estrangement. This is something she tried to avoid and fight against in her personal life and relationships, and something she continued to expose and critique in her work.

The Invert

Summer 1941, Yaddo, Saratoga Springs, New York

Gin. Cigarette smoke. Tall trees. Days and days spent dreaming at the typewriter, awaiting illuminations, drafting letters to friends and lovers. It's summer in Saratoga Springs, and the light is pellucid. A year after the publication of *Hunter*, and several months after the publication of *Reflections in a Golden Eye*, Carson McCullers spends a season at Yaddo, the renowned artists' retreat and colony. This sprawling estate, flush with thousands of conifers and pines, is centred around a grand mansion built in the Queen Anne Revival style, a hodgepodge of timber, turrets, stone and spires. Its fêted residents span the art forms, from literature to music, painting to dance. For Carson, Yaddo will become a place of solace and retreat, a place of community, and she will return many times over the next decade. Now, she is at work on a new story, *The Ballad of the Sad Café*. It's a fairy-tale novella about an unlikely love triangle between a hunchback, an industrious, masculine woman and her no-good delinquent ex-husband.

Despite the space and time afforded to work, however, Carson, at twenty-four, is feeling utterly alone. Annemarie, who returned to Europe earlier this year, is always on her mind. So, too, is Reeves, who has been distant and irregular in his correspondence. Their marriage is reaching crisis point. The

91

couple, now situated in their triangular relationship with David Diamond, are again battling the familiar forces of jealousy and possessiveness. Diamond, a twenty-five-year-old, dewy-eyed ballet composer with a moon-like face, met Carson and Reeves two months ago, back in New York, while attending a party hosted by one of the Manns' avant-garde set. David is also an artist on the ascent, and formed an instant, electric attachment to Carson, whom he privately described as a 'child-woman'. So mesmeric, so peculiar was the effect of Carson on Diamond that the composer felt impelled to gift her a ring that he was wearing, and which she had admired. 'I gave Carson my ring,' he recorded in his diary, 'and with it went my adolescent suffering.' It was as though Carson's mere presence had – temporarily – extracted from Diamond the pain of his queer youth like poison from a wound.

Across the next forty-eight hours, however, Diamond's attachment also grew to include the downhearted Reeves. In impassioned diary entries, Diamond recorded the meetings the trio had together over the following days. This included his bearing witness to the married couple's fiery and occasionally violent arguments. Would his desire for these two nourish him, he wondered, or destroy him? So intense were Diamond's feelings that only a week after their first meeting he wrote that 'it is a strange love we three feel for each other'.

Carson now writes a long letter to David from Yaddo, attempting to express her feelings about love and sexuality. She speaks about her desires for other women, and her attachment to Annemarie. She tells David that she has recently read a book, by a man named Havelock Ellis, that has helped her to understand her own sexuality, and to make sense of her complex marriage to Reeves. In the letter, she refers to herself as an 'invert'. Later that summer, she will tell a friend at Yaddo that she believes, quite seriously, that she was born a man.

These sentiments reflect the once-pioneering theory of sexual inversion, a theory that dominated scientific sexual discourse in America and Britain from the late nineteenth century until the early-middle twentieth century. Constructed around a binary view of gender and sex, inversion theory posits that one's biological sex aligns with an 'inner self': a man is a man internally (mentally) and externally (physically). A sexual invert is a person whose external and internal selves do not align. An invert has 'a woman's soul trapped in a man's body', or vice versa. This is how inversion theory sought to account for same-sex desire. A man who sexually desires another man is actually, internally, a woman. A woman who sexually desires another woman is actually, internally, a man.

One of the key architects of inversion theory was an English physician, social reformer (and staunch eugenicist), the aforementioned Havelock Ellis, whose works Carson had been reading at Yaddo. To explain the existence of sexual inversion – why it might occur in a given individual – Ellis stressed that it was a congenital or possibly hereditary phenomenon. He argued that one's sexuality (whether inverted or not) is an essential, innate, fixed trait, quite separate from social or environmental influence. In turn, he used the argument of congeniality to call for greater social tolerance of 'homosexuality'. An invert, Ellis claimed, cannot help being an invert. Inversion is not a pathogen to be cured; it is instead 'one of those strange things which happened when God was not looking' and therefore the invert should not be treated as a 'degenerate'.

Ellis first published his ideas in a book titled *Sexual Inversion* (1897) – which was summarily banned in Britain for obscene libel – and later expanded on them in the seven-volume *Studies in the Psychology of Sex* (1900–36), a vastly influential and comprehensive theoretical account of sexual physiology and behaviour. But Ellis didn't build these theories alone. He collaborated with another man on *Sexual Inversion*, somebody whose work and contributions were crucial to the evolution of his ideas. This man supplied Ellis with his own privately printed research into the history of male same-sex desire in ancient Greek culture. He supplied Ellis, too, with a number of real-life case studies of 'sexual inverts'. This man had a personal interest in the development of inversion theory, having dedicated much of his life to trying to understand his own same-sex desires. He was the English poet, historian and Whitman disciple, John Addington Symonds.

Symonds doubted the ahistorical approach of other sexologists and was eager that Ellis consider the social and cultural history of same-sex desire, which Symonds had examined in scholarly, privately printed essays on ancient Greek sexual customs, from male concubinage to pederasty and martialism. Symonds was concerned, too, that unless he collaborated with 'somebody of medical importance' his ideas would be received as those of 'a mere eccentric'. But Ellis struggled to imagine that same-sex desire and love between men (let alone women) could be anything other than an 'anomaly' at any point in history, and was dubious that such cultural studies could provide any enlightenment to sexual inversion. This would require 'a very strong impetus to go against this compact social force which on every side constrains the individual into the paths of heterosexual love'. Symonds passed away before *Sexual Inversion* was published. Despite his contributions, Ellis would later play down their significance in the shaping of his theory. He didn't ascribe authorship to Symonds for the case studies that he had supplied. And though Ellis chose to include some of Symonds' historic essays in the first edition of *Sexual Inversion*, he dropped many in subsequent editions, or else played the part of editorial butcher, hacking away huge chunks of Symonds' writing, leaving his intended historical-cultural arguments mutilated. It was as though, Wayne Koestenbaum argues, Ellis had performed a 'symbolic castration on his dead collaborator'.

At a time when same-sex desire was being culturally transferred from the realm of sinful acts and behaviours to that of personal identity, Ellis's work is notable for its calls for greater social tolerance of inversion. Nevertheless, his theories held heterosexuality as the constant, unshifting, rigid norm from which inversion differs. So megalithic is this view that, in the words of Sedgwick, sexual inversion theory sought to preserve 'an essential heterosexuality *within* desire itself [. . .] desire, in this view, by definition subsists in the current that runs between one male self and one female self, in whatever sex of bodies these selves may be manifested'.

Ellis's writings and interest in theories of sexuality had personal relevance, too. His marriage to Edith Lees, the women's rights advocate, might today be termed an 'open marriage'. Lees was herself, in Ellis's eyes, an 'invert', though a troubling case: her desires were for both men and women. Ellis's autobiography, titled *My Life*, considers Lees' so-called inversion, her mental breakdown and his caretaking of her (wherein he projects a kind of inversion onto himself, imagining that he is Lees' mother) and his attempts to understand the complexities and complications of their marriage in light of this. Published in America in 1939, *My Life*, along with Ellis's other publications, was often kept hidden in libraries, only available on request. Nevertheless, it found its way into Carson's hands that summer in Yaddo, who found her own sexually complex marriage mirrored in its story. Unbeknownst to her, in private her husband had sought similar elucidation in Ellis's works. Some years earlier, when he was a soldier, Reeves had spent time in the camp's library, consigned to a tiny back room where he could read Ellis's supposedly scandalous texts on inverted sexuality in secret.

Carson's assertion of 'inversion', her choice of masculine attire and her declaration that she was born a man has led some contemporary writers to argue that, born today, she might be living as a transgender man, and that her life – possessing 'an identity that history had not yet discovered', in Sarah Schulman's view – is what enabled her to inhabit her sexually and gender-fluid characters like Biff Brannon with such ease and empathy. It's a curious speculation, one that risks reducing McCullers' life and art, her dissection of the incongruities of sex and gender, to a historical naivety, inadvertently implying that it emerged from tortured bewilderment rather than from a confident, active desire to experiment with the constraints of proscribed self-identity.

Nevertheless, McCullers certainly possessed a particularly acute empathy when it came to others who were caught in the vice-like grip of gender norms. Her ability – like Biff – to recognise in others those hidden, secret parts was evidenced later in her life, when she met and forged a long-lasting friendship with Dawn Langley Simmons, neé Hall, a prolific biographer and novelist. On first meeting Dawn in 1964, who was assigned male at birth and lived as Gordon Langley Hall for the first decades of her life, Carson immediately recognised that Gordon was, in fact, a transgender woman ('You're really a little girl,' Carson said to her). The two maintained a correspondence – exchanging gifts, providing mutual advice and creative encouragement – for five years, up until Carson's death in 1967. Dawn Simmons had gender-affirming surgery in 1968, and would later credit McCullers with giving her the confidence to become who she really was. Whether Carson's empathy towards Dawn was born from sharing a trans identity cannot be known, but it certainly speaks to a compassion based on shared humanity, a reflection of Carson's favourite, oft-repeated quotation of the Roman playwright Terence: 'nothing human is alien to me'.

It's telling that Carson looked to Ellis's works and life story at a time when her own marriage was undergoing a crisis instigated, in no small part, by the queerness of its members. But despite Carson's many sexually fluid or ambiguous characters, it isn't the case that she simply mapped inversion theory onto her fiction. Her artistry was more complex and mysterious than this, not to say radical. McCullers' critique of modern masculinity, and the masculinist social orders which seek to destroy or eradicate fluid, queer desire, is far-reaching and profound. Nowhere in Carson's fiction is this critique more severe than *Reflections in a Golden Eye*.

A Healthy Body and Patriotism

Reflections in a Golden Eye, McCullers' short second novel, was written in just two months, almost immediately after she finished drafting *Hunter*. She found the process fun – to her, it was 'play-writing', writing for the sheer joy of language and ideas – but there is nothing especially fun about its story. Tennessee Williams, writing an introduction to the novel on the occasion of its reprint in 1950, described it as a distilled tragedy, cooled by a 'Grecian purity'. Crisp, terse and succinct in structure and language – 'cut like a jewel', in Tennessee's reckoning – *Reflections* centres on Penderton, a middle-aged captain in the US Army, stationed at a peace-time fort in the South, who shares a quandary not dissimilar to Biff's in *Hunter*. He is a man at odds with, yet completely governed by, the masculinist rules that constitute his world, an environment which ultimately forces his queer desires into violent ends.

An army fort in peacetime, we are told, in the novel's opening line, is a dull place. 'Things happen, but then they happen over and over again.' The fort is inert, muscular, linear – huge concrete barracks, neat rows of officers' homes – 'all is designed according to a certain rigid pattern'. It is the fort's failure to remain rigid and patterned, however, that sets the story in motion. 'There is a fort in the South,' the story begins, 'where a few years ago a murder was committed.'

98

Captain Penderton is unhappily married to Leonora, a woman who fears 'neither man, beast, nor the devil', and whose sexual potency, which gives her body 'a subtle quality of vibration', disgusts him. Like Biff, Penderton has a dual, inner sexual nature. He 'obtained within himself a delicate balance between the male and female elements, with the susceptibilities of both the sexes and the active powers of neither'. This neutered duality may imply sexual impotence, but certainly not an impotent desire. On the contrary, Penderton has 'a sad penchant for becoming enamoured with his wife's lovers'. Leonora's latest lover is Major Morris Langdon, a man who only cares about two things, 'a healthy body and patriotism'. Certainly, Langdon doesn't care for his own wife, the bedridden Alison, who is still grief-stricken over the death of their infant child several years before, and only able to find comfort in the presence of her carer, Anacleto, whom Langdon resents. Penderton has come to feel 'an emotional regard' for Langdon that is the 'nearest thing to love he had ever known'. Like a child, he wishes to distinguish himself in the eyes of the major, his superior. This keeps the love triangle in a curious equilibrium, enabling Penderton to carry 'his cuckoldry with a cynical good grace that was respected on the post'.

But there is another love triangle at work in the plot, one that functions like a photo negative to the open secret, and thus socially sanctioned, cuckolding of the captain by a superior officer. Another man has become obsessed with Leonora. A private, by the name of Ellgee Williams. Slim, angular, muscular, with full lips and strong hands, Private Williams is the platonic ideal of a young male soldier – he is Major Langdon's 'healthy body', or the muscular man of Mose Velsor's *Manly Health* – though he doesn't represent the patriotic spirit of either. Private Williams is different. He is 'something of a

mystery to the other men', spending his leisure time in solitude, risking court martial by riding a horse to an isolated spot
in the woods, stripping, and idling naked among the virgin
pines and wildflowers.

One evening, Private Williams catches sight of a nude
Leonora through the Pendertons' window. A change comes
over him, and he can think of nothing else. He returns to spy
on her every night, quickly learning the habits of the household and growing confident enough to break in and 'reconnoiter' through the captain's quarters to Leonora's bedroom
(while the captain is, most often, interred in his study, half-
drunk or dosed on sleeping pills). There, Williams crouches,
and watches her sleep. Again and again, night after night. His
motivation isn't mere lust. It seems born of a bored indifference towards the governing rules and structures of the army
camp, combined with a fascination, laced with contempt, with
Leonora's body.

She is, after all, the first naked woman that Williams has ever
seen: a destabilising encounter for the young soldier, who was
raised in an intensely misogynistic, all-male, religious household, where he was taught that women 'carried in them a
deadly and catching disease which made men blind'. As a teenager, Williams displaced maternal-sexual longing onto the
body of a cow: he would press his head against the animal's
warm flank, and milk her while talking in 'soft, urgent whispers'. Through this nonhuman erotics, Williams attempts to
recuperate lost maternal desire – an act of bovine breastfeeding
– while also creating a kind of grim hierarchy in which women
are less deserving of affection than animals. That Williams
should feel this animal 'clean' enough to warrant intimacy,
whereas all women are 'contaminated', is a fantastic, horrific
detail demonstrating the extent of his misogyny. In some
respects, these are the only organic overlaps between the

transgressive, irreverent Williams and the regimented world of the army post: both reject women and denigrate the feminine, both champion the healthy male body over what they see as weak, infirm or 'diseased'. Private Williams' unique upbringing also gives new dimension to his obsessive need to watch Leonora: Williams can only action his fascination with the feminine at a remove, a secret, sterile distance, one in which he retains control and power and thus hopes to avoid the feminine 'infection'.

As Private Williams becomes increasingly obsessed with Leonora's body, so Captain Penderton becomes feverishly obsessed with Williams, though he knows nothing, at least consciously, of the private's nightly voyeurism. The captain's contact with the soldier began accidentally. Some months ago, Private Williams had carelessly spilt coffee over Penderton's trousers, staining the heavy expensive silk: a symbolic ejaculation if there ever was one. True to a stain, or spillage, Williams remained in the captain's mind. Soon, he notices him everywhere in the camp. His annoyance grows to hate, and his hatred tilts, perilously, into obsession. This tipping point occurs one afternoon, when the captain takes Leonora's prized horse, Firebird, out for a ride. A nervy, inelegant rider – earning him the nickname Captain 'Flap-fanny' among the troops – Penderton loses control of the horse. It bolts, galloping wildly into the woods, and the captain, relinquishing all control over the animal, possibly relinquishing his hold on life, experiences a moment of intense, rare freedom that brings him close to rapture. The world rushes past in kaleidoscopic vision – white flowers, pine cones, fiery shafts of light – and he is reminded of the 'miracle of [his] blood, muscle, nerves, and bone'.

This orgiastic moment of pure freedom is unbearable for the captain, generating a kind of beautiful agony that he can only index through violence. Once the horse stops, he brutally beats

Firebird, thrashing the animal to the point of exhaustion. Collapsed, lying on the earth, the captain looks up to see the naked Private Williams watching him with 'vague, impersonal eyes'. It is as though Penderton, in relinquishing all control, all claims of status and authority, has undergone some rite of passage that leads him into Williams' domain: a glade, an apparent Arcadia, with a nude young man in the model of classical statu- ary, awaiting him. But if this space was once an idyll, the captain's explosion of violence has blemished it. He is unable to speak, to break beyond shock at the sight of the naked Williams. Without a word, the soldier then takes the beaten horse, disappearing with it into the woods. Williams is like a sentinel; stewarding away the horse, the private punishes his superior for his act of violence, as though to suggest he is undeserving of the freedom and liberation facilitated by the animal. And in removing himself from the idyll, Williams withholds his body from Penderton, only frustrating and exacerbating the captain's desire.

This encounter, unacknowledged between the two men, seals their respective fates. From then on, the captain does little else but devour sleeping pills, think about Private Williams and follow him around the camp. His desire for Williams becomes as sustaining as it is debilitating. He is 'conscious only of the irresistible yearning to break down the barrier between them'. He daydreams about relinquishing his rank as captain and being an enlisted man again, envisaging an idealised version of the barracks where relations between men are solely affirmative, the 'hubbub of young male voices' and 'the irresistible shenani- gans of camaraderie'. Meanwhile, in the shallow-lit, subterra- nean realm of the captain's unconscious, there are half-guessed possibilities, fragmented memories of shadows and noises in the night.

How can such a dynamic end? The captain eventually becomes aware of the soldier's trespass. One night, unable to sleep despite having taken several pills, he catches Williams in the act of breaking into his home. With clinical efficiency, Penderton arms himself with a pistol, moves through the house and finds Williams crouching over Leonora's bed. Immediately, he fires two shots into the private's chest. The gunfire wakes Leonora, who can't comprehend what she is seeing: these men, she thinks, are unreal. They appear to be actors in a play. Penderton slumps against the wall like a 'broken and dissipated monk', while Williams, though dead, retains the look of 'warm, animal comfort', the look of life. In destroying the object of his desire, the captain destroys himself.

Once a man enters the army, McCullers' narrator tells us in the opening page, 'he is expected only to follow the heels ahead of him'. It is a patriarchal institution structured by a dogged hierarchy. Deviation or transgression is not tolerated. The first love triangle between the major, Leonora and Penderton can exist peaceably in the camp because it correlates with the chain of command: no transgression of power occurs, owing to the relative rank of each man. Leonora, meanwhile, though she takes personal comfort and sustenance from the romance, is for Penderton a bartering chip, something inert that he has effectively 'given' to the major. That bargain helps him stay close to the major. It may, even, encourage the major to look favourably upon him. Although Penderton's same-sex desire for Major Langdon is itself transgressive, it can be sublimated into this transactional exchange, where a woman is the commodity: a 'harmless' wish to be distinguished in his superior's eyes, which doesn't upset the hierarchal order of the army camp but is instead in concert with it.

But Private Williams is something different. He is a link in the chain that's slipped. He floats freely. He roams. For Captain Penderton, he represents the tremendous force of his own same-sex desire, which cannot be avoided, negotiated with, or sublimated. To admit this desire – to break down the barrier between himself and the private – would be to go against the whole institution, his entire world, something unimaginable. Of course, the private is also transgressing, trespassing on the captain's literal property, and, in this masculinist world, figurative property: Leonora. Captain Penderton's final murder of Private Williams seems the only option available to him. It sustains his performance as 'husband' and his rank as 'captain', while eliminating the object of his desire, a penetration of the soldier's body that is also, necessarily, an obliteration: two slugs of lead in the heart. As with the relationship between Antonapoulos and Singer in *Hunter*, this violent ending doesn't show that death or tragedy are the de facto outcomes of same-sex desire between men: it shows how a masculinist, patriarchal order seeks to stifle such desire, and forces it into such outcomes, in which both men and women suffer.

Is it curious that Carson should have likened the writing of this tragic tale to 'eating candy'? Not when we consider how effectively the novel reveals the patent absurdity of the masculinist structures under critique. There's a kind of campiness to the writing, at times, as though Carson is relishing her exposure of the military industrial complex's ridiculous, willed ignorance to the ways that all-male spaces, however tightly regulated, will engender or sustain the conditions for same-sex desire. This is made clear when Major Langdon recalls the first time he and Leonora fucked, outside, in a blackberry bush, within two hours of meeting. What did it feel like? It was just like being on 'manoeuvres', outdoors in the rain and sun, watching 'the fine looking soldiers' making coffee over campfires. A wonderful feeling, the major recalls, 'the best in the world!'

★   ★   ★

Reflections in a Golden Eye was published at the precise moment when the American military, a masculinist regime governed by harmful and ultimately fickle structures, set about reinforcing those very structures. *Reflections* was first printed in two instalments, in *Harper's Bazaar*, in October and November 1940, before being published in book form that winter. By this time, Germany, under Hitler's Nazi Party, had conquered France and was embarking on a full-scale bombing of Britain. In this climate, the American public were perhaps not primed for a tale in which an army captain murders a private whom he obsessively desires. Its publication in *Harper's* resulted in a number of cancelled subscriptions – including, allegedly, that of the wife of 'Old Blood and Guts' General Patton, the cigar-chomping icon of the US military.

Mere weeks before the magazine publication of *Reflections*, President Roosevelt signed the Selective Training and Service Act: the draft. For the first time in the nation's history, conscription was implemented during peacetime. With the signing of this act, an independent body was reinstated, the Selective Service, which was tasked with identifying men suitable for military training. A medical directive was created which listed psychiatric 'categories of handicap' and 'deviations' that should disqualify men from being drafted. Bringing such psychiatric exemptions into the draft had never been done before. The argument was economic: weed out 'inferior' soldiers now, soldiers who would be likely to suffer mental trauma through combat, and avoid spending money caring for such psychiatric casualties later. In May 1941 – three months after *Reflections* appeared in book form – a revised, final version of this directive was issued to thousands of doctors at draft boards (most of whom had no psychiatric training). Among the listed deviations were two words: 'homosexual proclivities'.

This directive, argues historian Jonathan Ned Katz, amounts to the very first state-sponsored, federal institutionalisation of

the term 'homosexual' in the US. And without even mention-
ing 'heterosexuality', the directive implicitly sanctioned it as
the norm, the ideal of health from which unfit men, inferior
men, deviate. Two years later, in 1943 – by which time the US
military was fully engaged in the war and had extended its
mandatory conscription liability to include boys as young as
eighteen – the power of this directive would be underscored.
A new section was added to US Army Mobilization recom-
mendations, titled 'Sexual Perversion'.

Penned by a psychiatrist named Lawrence Kubie, the Sexual
Perversion amendment explained how army doctors could
effectively distinguish between a 'homosexual' man and what
they called a 'normal' man. Where the latter has 'a conventional attitude toward sexual problems' and a 'masculine body',
the homosexual, so the directive now claimed, has a 'feminine'
body, exhibits 'effeminacy in dress and manner', and might
have an expanded rectum from passive anal sex (notably, the
focus here is on the passive: there is no mention of the man
who might be doing the penetration, nor of other kinds of
non-penetrative sex between men). Fearing that 'normal' men
would pretend to be homosexuals to escape the draft, military
officials argued that maintaining diffuse, widespread revulsion
towards homosexuality was necessary, both inside and outside
the military, to deter such 'malingerers'. Likewise, this elevated,
intensified homophobia was designed to disincentivise patriotic queer men – 'reverse malingerers', in awkward military
lingo – who sought to hide their sexuality from medical exam-
iners in order to serve in combat.

The essence of the Sexual Perversion passage is clear: the
state not only equates homosexuality with the abnormal, but
'homosexual' becomes inseparable from 'effeminacy'. Misogyny
and homophobia are twinned within a state institution. And
the conflation between queerness in men and effeminacy in

men is circular: homosexuals are more likely to have feminine characteristics, effeminate or 'sissy' men are more likely to be homosexuals. Both homosexuality and effeminacy come to be considered, within the military, as pathogens. A man who exhibits either, it was thought, would be like a rotten apple in the barrel, endangering or disturbing group morale because he would inevitably become the subject of ridicule and distract other men from their military duties.

The military was thus left in a contorted position that, even today, characterises many all-male environments. Because fear and revulsion of the 'homosexual' is, in part, fear and revulsion of the so-called feminine in men, to prove that one is not feminine one must celebrate and champion the masculine, the 'healthy' male body. But, as Carson shows us with Major Langdon, the difference between celebrating – or relishing – the masculine and *desire for* the masculine is so slim as to be almost nonexistent. Sex with Leonora is only good because it *reminds* Langdon of the company of men. What, after all, is the difference between a man's man and a man who desires and wishes to be desired by other men?

Carson's *Reflections in a Golden Eye* doesn't merely mirror the national psychosexual climate leading up to America's involvement in the war. The novel actively critiques the absurdities of a one-size-fits-all approach to desire. It challenges the masculinist social orders which set the terms of desire along a homophobic, misogynistic binary where there is a 'normal' sexuality against which anything else is deviant and defective. Towards the end of the novel, Captain Penderton – momentarily disinterested in ingratiating himself to Major Langdon – lays bare these absurdities. Langdon, Penderton, and Leonora are sitting around a table, playing cards. Langdon is lamenting the effeminate characteristics of his wife's former carer, Anacleto, mournfully wishing that he could have enlisted

him in the army ('it might have made a man out of him') even
though, he concedes, Anacleto would have been miserable as a
soldier. Penderton's response is suddenly clear and definite.
'You mean,' he replies,

> 'that any fulfilment obtained at the expense of normalcy is
> wrong, and should not be allowed to bring happiness. In
> short, it is better, because it is morally honorable, for the
> square peg to keep scraping about the round hole rather than
> to discover and use the unorthodox square that would fit it?'
>
> 'Why, you put it exactly right,' the Major said. 'Don't you
> agree with me?'
>
> 'No,' said the Captain, after a short pause.

In her letter to David Diamond, which Carson wrote at
Yaddo in the summer of 1941, Carson echoed her fictional
captain's sentiments. Love, she told Diamond, cannot be made
neat, it cannot fit into neat categories and classifications. One
of the categories that Carson felt her love and desire could not
fit into or be contained by was marriage. Having deliberated
over it for some time, she resolves to divorce Reeves, a separation that will set the wheels in motion for his own return to
the army. In September, Carson packs up her belongings, and
boards a train to New York, where she asks her lawyer to initi-
ate the divorce proceedings.

This won't be the end of Carson and Reeves' coupling,
however. Throughout Reeves' military service – which will
conclude after he sustains a serious wrist injury storming the
beaches at Normandy – the two will write to each other as
much as possible, and subsequently remarry in a civil ceremony
in New York, in 1945. They will then live with each other on
and off in New York and the South, before leaving the country
for France, where they set up home in a Paris suburb. But

theirs will be a perilous reunion, one which will ultimately end in death: in 1954, Reeves will commit suicide by overdosing on barbiturates.

Carson and Reeves were ensnared in a relationship characterised by love, resentment, toxicity, perilous necessity and an extreme, mutual dependence on alcohol – 'cool spring water', as Reeves saw it. But it seemed clear, to many of Carson's friends and relatives, that the couple's problems were connected to their queer sexualities and the way that Reeves felt at odds with his masculinity. In the analysis of Carson's biographer, Virginia Spencer Carr, Reeves had viewed his remarriage to Carson, which coincided with his compulsory discharge from the army, as a kind of capitulation: the coming to light of his fear that 'he could not always be a leader of men, a professional soldier, the head of a household, a man's man'. Considered this way, *Reflections*, which is, at heart, about a military man who destroys himself because his ingrained notions of masculinity are misaligned with his desires, eerily prefigures Reeves' demise. It almost lends substance to Carson's claim that her fiction functioned as clairvoyance, and that all the significant events she depicted would 'eventually' happen to her in real life.

Critics were largely baffled by *Reflections*. The gendered condescension that had been levelled at Carson with *Hunter* in the form of praise (no normal, nice young girl should be capable of writing such a dark, brilliant debut) was now used as a line of attack. One critic felt her 'infant-terrible insight' was detrimentally 'unmellowed and unhallowed', while another prescribed homework, suggesting she brush up on her Mark Twain and Chekhov. Still another critic, writing in the *New York Herald Tribune*, was 'offended' by the novel's 'arrogant and pitiless fearlessness, which, besides giving an unpleasant effect, betrays her youth'. Almost every negative or lukewarm review also shared a distaste and dislike for what they perceived as McCullers' undue attention to the 'abnormal', lamenting the vividness and centrality she gave to the characters' 'inversions' and 'perversions'. One critic claimed this prohibited the reader from identifying with anyone in the book, which rendered it heartless. Another, writing for the *Atlantic*, had more pragmatic concerns: 'if this is a fair sample of army life, and if the country is soon to pour itself into the army, then God Save the Union!'

It wasn't only the literary establishment, however, that took issue with *Reflections*. Its publication also caused Carson's family a deal of distress. In a demonstration of the barely repressed conservative violence typical of the South that Carson so hated, the McCullers family home, back in Columbus, Georgia, received a threatening phone call. Somebody claiming to be a Ku Klux Klansman spat vitriol down the receiver, calling Carson a 'fairy', and threatened to attack their home. The book also caused a stir with the neighbours and townsfolk, who were convinced that Carson had based the novel on actual people living and serving at Fort Benning, a nearby army post where Reeves had once been stationed. 'Everyone accused me of writing about everybody else,' she later remembered. But this gossipy, small-town paranoia – the townsfolk's firm belief that the cast of *Reflections* was based on real people – merely demonstrated to Carson how likely it was that illicit desire, infidelities and violence really were fomenting behind Fort Benning's walls. 'I must say I didn't realise,' she quipped, tongue in cheek, 'the morals of the Post were that corrupt.'

Almost two decades after the publication of *Reflections*, Carson reflected on her creative process in an essay, 'The Flowering Dream', published in *Esquire*. 'When I write about a thief, I become one,' McCullers wrote of crafting characters. 'When I write about Captain Penderton, I become a homosexual man.' McCullers was a precise and exacting writer. Her material rarely arrived in torrents, but emerged with the slow, alchemic inevitability of a developing photograph: a latent image gradually appearing through the gloom. And so her words here aren't offhand, but carefully weighted and considered. McCullers even burnt several drafts of this essay, deeming them too personal, but retained this line. The statement is both immensely bold – to literally claim the status of 'homosexual man' in print, in 1959 – and metaphysically alluring. It attests to the seriousness with which she believed in the slipperiness of sexuality and gender: the notion that transfiguration can occur through imagination, that one can be brought to occupy, through the portal of writing, the gendered subject position of another.

Down and Out in New Orleans

September 1941, New Orleans, Louisiana

'We ought to be exterminated,' a young man says, 'for the good of society.'

Fifteen hundred miles away from Yaddo, where Carson is now packing her bags, two down-and-out artists are sitting in Macks, a raucous New Orleans bar: Oliver Evans, a twenty-six-year-old poet, and the penniless playwright-cum-vagabond, Tennessee Williams. In a few years' time, Tennessee will be carried to the same celebrated artistic heights that Carson is currently enjoying (and, years later, Oliver will become Carson's first biographer). Now, however, the literal and figurative distance between these two obscure men, drinking in Macks, and the lush literary utopia of Yaddo couldn't be greater. But their current contemplations – the relationship between sexuality, gender norms, society, art and the truth of the human heart – carry more than a few echoes of Carson's work and considerations over her transitional summer.

'We are the rotten apple in the barrel,' Oliver goes on.

Tennessee sits opposite his new friend, feeling bleak and anxious. His heart palpitations are strong. This 'cardiac neurosis' has haunted him for a long time. It was particularly acute in the summer of 1935, six years ago, when he was living at his grandparents' house in Memphis, a couple of blocks from

Southwestern University. He was Tom, then: this was before he adopted the nom de plume 'Tennessee', frequently shortened to Tenn or simply 10. That season – that age, at twenty-four – was marked by three concurrent realisations. It was the summer he knew he was unquestionably a playwright. He spent afternoons at the university's library, reading the short stories of Anton Chekhov, and became involved in a local dramatic theatre club, the Garden Players, for whom he co-wrote a one-act melodrama titled *Cairo, Shanghai, Bombay!*. Staged on the great sloping back lawn of one of the Garden Players' houses, Tennessee was enchanted by the genuine, loud laughter that his writing had provoked in the audience. 'Then and there the theatre and I found each other, for better or worse,' he would later recall.

It was also the summer that his erotic and romantic attraction to other men became concrete. He befriended two men, a pair of young Southwestern University students. He didn't realise at the time that they were lovers. They took him out to a swimming beach by a lake, where he became infatuated with one of them, the 'shining blond'. Later, over beers with the blond, the heart palpations came upon him all at once. They snowballed into a full-blown panic attack, necessitating a trip to the doctor. Here was the third realisation of that summer, one that would become as central a concern in his life as his work and sexuality: what he called the 'delicacy' of his physical nature. 'You must do everything carefully and slowly,' that doctor had told him after the panic attack. Naturally, the young playwright didn't listen. There was nothing slow about his twenties, and there will be nothing slow about the rest of his life.

Tennessee Williams is a man restlessly, fervently driven by work. Work, work, work. Writing for Tennessee is tantamount to breathing, and the typewriter almost a mechanical extension of his body ('Dilapidation of my typewriter,' he jotted in his diary, 'which is in almost as collapsed a state as myself, is a considerable handicap'). He works without respite. And – as he recently experienced – without reward. His debut as a serious playwright, last winter in 1940, was a flop. *Battle of Angels* centred on a young would-be artist-poet named Val who, bedecked in a snakeskin jacket, possesses a 'fresh and primitive quality, a virile grace'. On its opening night in Boston, the production was beset with technical issues so dire many audience members walked out before the final curtain. Critics also found the play 'putrid' and smutty, and deemed the dialogue overstuffed with double entendres. *Battle* closed after just two weeks, without a hope in hell of ever making Broadway.*

While there was perhaps something catalysing in creative failure, such a silver lining could not easily be found in the other setback Tennessee suffered in 1940: heartbreak. Tennessee had fallen in love with a young ballet dancer from Canada, Kip Kiernan, 'a great bronze statue of antique Greece come to life, but with the face of a little boy'. The two men began an affair. 'I love you,' Tennessee wrote to Kip, 'with robust manly love, as Whitman would call it.' But his invocation of that affirmative, fluid adhesiveness between men didn't stick. Days, at most weeks, after their relationship had begun, it ended.

Kip was warned by a friend that Tennessee was trying to turn him into a 'homosexual', and Kip felt he'd 'seen enough of the world' to know he ought to resist this apparent transformation. As Tennessee remembered it, Kip said he didn't want his 'being' to be 'violated' in this way. The effect on the thirty-year-old playwright was devastating. 'I shall have to go through

---

* Tennessee would later rework the play into 1957's *Orpheus Descending*, and the subsequent screen adaption, *The Fugitive Kind* (1960), would star Marlon Brando as Val.

the world giving myself to people until somebody will take me,' he noted in his diary, in the aftermath. He hurled a shoe at Kip's friend, and fled. He went to New York, to Mexico, to Florida, all the while feeling desolate and 'utterly alone, alone', running out of funds, cruising and having casual sex. Throughout, he carted a typewriter with him and a few treasured books (among them, *Leaves of Grass*). And his itinerancy has led him here, to New Orleans, where he's secured a cheap room and intends to 'hover like a bright angel over the troubled waters of homosociety' while seeking retreat and sanctuary in the city.

And the waters, tonight, certainly are troubled. Tennessee looks at his glum, dispirited friend, Oliver. It's long past midnight. He'd rather be in bed reading until his heart feels 'stuffy', but he senses that he might be able to pull Oliver out of his spiralling thoughts.

'We ought to be exterminated at the age of twenty-five,' Oliver continues.

If that happened, Tennessee says, society would lose some of its most 'humanitarian members'.

'A *healthy* society does not need artists,' Oliver replies.

'What is healthy about a society with no spiritual values?' says Tennessee.

'Then you think spiritual values are identical with *us*?'

'No,' Tennessee admits, 'but we have made some unique contributions because of our unique position.'

It's no use. Oliver repeats that he is rotten, and that his rottenness prevents him from doing what he should do: isolating himself from others, shutting himself away from society.

Oliver's self-hating rhetoric is sadly unsurprising at a cultural moment in which young men across the country are being drafted for the war effort, for the ostensible patriotic good of the nation, but rejected if they are deemed unfit for service, if they are 'homosexual'. Tennessee sleeps off the conversation. The next morning, he plans to set out on a cycle trip to a nearby lake, where he hopes a swim will 'provide something more clarifying than last night'. He wonders how many people feel this way, the same way as Oliver: an intense, intolerable burden of guilt. It's only natural, inevitable, he thinks, that we will *all* feel some degree of sorrow and humiliation at times. But to carry such guilt around . . . He doesn't want to live this way. He won't live this way.

For Tennessee, it is his 'deviation', he feels, that helps him to recognise need in others. More than this, he believes it is what helps him to 'express the human heart' – its desires, its truth – through his art. He is currently working on the short story 'Portrait of a Girl in Glass', which in 1944 will become his first Broadway success as *The Glass Menagerie*. And just two years after that triumph, he will write *A Streetcar Named Desire*, a meteoric vision of sex, desire and broken masculinity which will hit Broadway with such power as to change American culture forever.

Meat!

Marlon Brando, clad in blue denim work clothes and a form-fitting t-shirt, hurls a 'red stained package' across the stage and pitches the one-syllable line – 'Meat!' – as though it's a bomb going off. In this moment, the eroticised male in modern American culture is invented. In the assessment of novelist, public intellectual and self-identified bisexual Gore Vidal, before the little-known Brando (whose own sexual orientation, incidentally, was fluid) burst onto Broadway in *A Streetcar Named Desire*, male actors and film stars may have been handsome, but never before have they been *sexed*. Never before have they been erotic. Brando – the most beautiful man Tennessee has ever seen bar 'one or two exceptions' – changes all this in his performance as Stanley. Roaming around the stage, he is, in the words of Arthur Miller, a 'tiger on the loose, a sexual terrorist' uniquely able to 'roar out Williams' celebratory terror of sex, its awful truthfulness and its inexorable judgements' with an authority that remade American theatre. The image of this erotic modern man – buff arms and biceps on display, undershirt soaked in beer and sweat – will sear itself onto the retinas of millions of Americans when the play is adapted for Hollywood in 1951, with Brando reprising the role.

The sexed-up Stanley was created by an artist reportedly unable to write anything unless 'there is one character in it for whom I have physical desire'. For Tennessee, creativity and sexual expression, or release, have always gone hand in hand. To his friend Donald Windham, he once compared writing to 'jack[ing] off on a page', and elsewhere described completing a creative work as like completing a 'love affair'. To an interviewer, Jim Gaines, he said that 'the power of a writer is very closely related to sexuality, to sexual power', and to Carson McCullers he once claimed that the trinity of his life was work, sex and alcohol, describing the inability to work as creative impotence. In the eyes of Vidal, Tennessee's entire artistic practice can be understood as an attempt to close the circle of desire: Tennessee would translate real, personal, unfulfilled desire into the fictional characters of his theatre, so that the living flesh of actors and performers, curated by the playwright, could express and satiate it. The scale and scope of stagecraft were necessary to achieve this, because desire is a force, in Tennessee's own words, 'made to occupy a larger space than that which is afforded by the individual being'.

Desire is also, as he has Blanche read in *Streetcar*, 'the opposite of death'. That is, they are two sides of the same coin, they run on twin tracks: a notion foreshadowed by the heroine's doomed arrival in New Orleans, where, to reach her sister Stella's apartment, she must transition from the streetcar named 'Desire' to the one named 'Cemeteries'. Tennessee's 'jacking-off' on the page, as an act, expression or mode of desire, was therefore also a way of trying to be fully, completely alive: writing as a life force that could forestall death. In many ways it recalls Whitman's poetic project, that blending of the textual and seminal, books and bodies, a never-ending artistic project that is itself 'alive'. (In *Battle of Angels*, Val, the would-be writer, says of his eternally unfinished book: 'it's got life in it'.)

Such an interpretation of Tennessee's body of work might fall flat if it weren't for his own admission that he consistently cannibalised his real life, and the people in it, for his art. *The Glass Menagerie* centred on the shy, reticent, but quietly visionary Laura. Laura's nickname is Blue Roses, an appellation given to her by a love interest, who misheard when she explained she had been sick with 'pleurosis'. She is a character cast in the explicit mould of Tennessee's beloved sister, Rose, who, after years of mental ill-health, had been institutionalised, diagnosed a schizophrenic, and, in 1943, subjected to a prefrontal lobotomy. Characteristics of Tennessee's lost love, Kip Kiernan, can be found in the many young, handsome men scattered throughout his oeuvre, and would be made explicit in his autobiographical play *Something Cloudy, Something Clear*.

In Stanley Kowalski, many of Tennessee's friends noted, there are more than a few echoes of Pancho, his explosive, raging lover, who had, by the time rehearsals for *Streetcar* were in motion, attempted to run over the playwright in a Pontiac. And as more than one of *Streetcar*'s directors concluded, if Stanley is Pancho, then Blanche is Tennessee. 'My heroines,' Tennessee remarked, 'always express the climate of my interior world at the time in which those characters were created.' This fascinating interpellation between Tennessee's self-identity and those of his heroines – not unlike Carson McCullers' imaginative occupation of her character's subjectivities – is boldly labelled by Camille Paglia as his 'transsexual self-projection'.

The Broadway version of *Streetcar*, however, is much more than a paean to the erotic power of the male body. *Streetcar* is the story of Blanche DuBois, who, while seeking sanctuary at her pregnant sister Stella's claustrophobic apartment in New Orleans, bullies and is bullied by Stella's husband, Stanley. It's a conflict shot through with a simmering, wet-mouthed eroticism, one charged by dominance and fear, and exacerbated by their class differences. The DuBois are from a (formerly) wealthy Southern family, Stanley is a working-class Polish immigrant. There's a kind of sex tourism at play: the ostensibly refined, proper, educated ladies desire the ostensibly brute, animalistic, uneducated man, and vice versa. Blanche, however – who, later in the play, begins a burgeoning romance with Stanley's shy, ineffectual buddy, Mitch – is harbouring secrets, which Stanley discovers. At *Streetcar*'s tragic climax, he rapes her. Stella, opting to believe Stanley's version of events, rather than her traumatised sister, dispatches Blanche to an asylum at the end of the play.

Building on a few scenes temporarily titled 'The Poker Night', Tennessee penned the final draft of *Streetcar* in just six weeks and sent it off to the director-producer Elia Kazan. 'It may not be the sort of play that interests you,' Tennessee wrote with studied casualness, 'but I hope so.' He capped off the submission with a number of compliments. Elia Kazan, a first-generation Greek immigrant who wasn't drafted during the war for dependency reasons, was a Broadway giant. Tennessee had been impressed by his production and direction of Arthur Miller's *All My Sons* earlier that year – for which Kazan won the first Tony Award for Best Director – and felt he and Kazan would make the perfect match. He described himself as a 'cloudy dreamer type' who needed to be paired with an 'objective and dynamic worker'. Uniquely, he thought, Kazan had the dynamism and the know-how (the director's nickname was Gadg, short for Gadget, for his imaginative ability to fix any problem related to the staging or filming of a script). But Kazan was *also* a dreamer, a quality that helped him to create 'vastly provocative' theatre.

As discussions between playwright and director ignited, Tennessee urged the script be accepted without additional rewrites. Kazan, meanwhile, felt the toughest job for him would be how to keep the play '*truthful, faithful* [. . .] not an oversimplification into the easy categories of our theatre'. His concern was warranted. For the American stage in 1947, there was little conventional about the story of *Streetcar* or its heroine, Blanche DuBois.

Blanche has a vicarious, never satiated sexual appetite for 'young men'. Depending on consent laws in her fictional hometown of Laurel, this appetite might possibly be criminal. As the snooping Stanley comes to learn, Blanche had to flee from Laurel after becoming 'mixed up' with a seventeen-year-old high-school student. This revelation is prefigured in the play by Blanche's flirtations with a nonplussed 'young man' who tries to sell her a newspaper: in an effort to prevent him leaving, she quizzes him about his predilection for soda ('Cherry,' he says. 'Cherry!' Blanche laughs, 'you make my mouth water') before planting an unsolicited kiss on his mouth. 'It would be nice to keep you,' she says, 'but I've got to keep my hands off children.' But Blanche isn't cast as a two-dimensional nymphomaniac. Tennessee's compassion for his heroine, or at any rate his fluency in the truth of love and desire, doesn't countenance this. For Blanche, we come to learn, has a hole in her heart. She is eternally mourning her dead husband, Allan Grey – 'the boy, the boy', in Blanche's words, or 'the degenerate' in Stella's – whom, years before, when they were both teenagers, she caught in bed with another man.

'You disgust me,' Blanche had told him. This vicious rebuff contributed to a shame so intense that Allan committed suicide.

Blanche carries this tragedy, and her guilt, around with her, keeping Allan's love letters ('poems a dead boy wrote') in a tin box tied with ribbon. Blanche's desire for young men is, at least in part, a desire to reclaim 'the boy', to relive and rewrite their relationship: she seeks, in the youth of her male partners, substitutes for the departed Allan. Then again, Blanche might not be looking for substitution but emulation, attempting to bring her husband back by becoming him, by trying to see what he saw, to desire what he desired. This is a complex, layered projection which powerfully evokes the terrible truth of a love warped by grief, a grief warped by love; that need, that hunger, to literally subsume and be subsumed by the beloved, the missing, the dead, the drive to merge oneself into them, in an effort to be reunited and become one. But in the masculinist world of *Streetcar*, Blanche's forthright, autonomous desire for young men has no place. It is not allowed to exist on its own terms. She must be punished for it. Blanche understands this intuitively when Stanley, rifling through her papers, carelessly rips the ribbon off the stack of Allan's poems, so that they cascade to the floor.

'I hurt him,' she tells Stanley, 'the way you would like to hurt me.'

Blanche punished Allan for his queer desire. Stanley will punish Blanche for her female desire. Both, in this world, are unserious, marginalised, disallowed.

Stanley's brutal rape of Blanche at play's end is facilitated and enabled by the other men in the play, whose intractable relationship with Stanley, and each other, lets him off the hook. As *Streetcar*'s original title suggests, the poker game is central to the play's structure. Poker – a kind of microcosmic, dolls-house mimicry of the male world of commerce and generalship – should not be played, Mitch drearily repeats, 'in a house with women'. In *Streetcar*, it is during the initial poker game that Stanley commits his first act of off-stage battery. Five men 'at the peak of their physical manhood' sit around Stanley and Stella's kitchen table, cast in the 'raw colors of a children's spectrum', eating melon, hurling insults at each other, dealing cards. Mitch, despite being one of Stanley's war buddies, is frequently in his crosshairs, ridiculed for being an unmarried man who spends his nonworking hours looking after his ailing mother. Ridiculed, in other words, for doing the 'women's work' of caregiving. When Stella and Blanche return from a night out, things quickly turn sour. Blanche turns on the radio, and solicits the bumbling, dopey-eyed Mitch into an awkward waltz. This enrages Stanley, who hurls the radio through a window, charges at the protesting Stella and strikes her.

What happens next is powerful. The poker-playing men amass around the hot-headed Stanley, push and pinion him into the bedroom, until he suddenly goes limp. The men 'speak quietly and lovingly to him and he leans his face on their shoulders'. They then take him to the shower – to cool him off – at which point the brief, mollifying effect of their momentarily shameless intimacy wears off. Stanley again flies into a rage and punches them. The men flee, leaving Stella and Blanche alone with him. But not before they sweep up their poker winnings on the way out. Poker, Mitch repeats sadly, should not be played in a house with women.

Piss-taking and poker-playing: this is the cover which enables these men to spend time alone together. Their fleeting 'loving words' represent a brief moment of intimacy, in which the men shirk off their learned masculine roles and seek an alternative way of relating to one another. One which could include care and compassion, in an attempt to dispel the violence at hand. But Stanley's violence instantly overwhelms them, and the men relent. The way they abandon this path might be bleak; but their wilful ignoring of Stanley's final crime is tragic. The second poker game occurs in the final scene, after Stanley's rape. The men are again sitting around the kitchen table, dealing cards, volleying monosyllabic insults at one another. Stella and Blanche are also there, except now Blanche is packing her things. She believes that she is going on a vacation, but her sister has arranged to have her institutional-ised. 'I couldn't believe her story,' Stella says, 'and go on living with Stanley.'

The doctor and matron arrive to incarcerate Blanche, who resists. In the ensuing chaos, Mitch momentarily lunges at Stanley – his single, facile protest – and is struck back down. Blanche is led away. Mitch stays silent. The crazy, sex-hungry woman, along with the ghost of her dead, queer husband, is gone. But the men and their card game remain. To underscore the crime of their indifference, *Streetcar's* brutal, final line belongs not with Blanche, but with one of the poker players, Steve, whose only notable characteristics up to this point are his penchant for poor boy sandwiches, Jax beer and blonde women.

'The game,' he says, against the sound of Stella's agonised wails, 'is seven card stud.'

With *Streetcar*, Tennessee Williams stretched the conservatism that plagued much mainstream, mid-century theatre to its limits. It wasn't merely a question of taste and convention, but one of law and legality. From 1927 to 1968, Broadway operated under the Wales Padlock Law, censorious restrictions which made it illegal to depict 'the subject of sex degeneracy, or sex perversion' on the stage: a direct assault on queer visibility in theatre. Hence Allan's subplot occurring offstage, a canny get-around of these limits. And when *Streetcar* was adapted for film, it posed a problem for the puritanical Production Codes Administration. This administration enforced the so-called Hays Code, a set of industry guidelines which governed Hollywood filmmaking from 1934 to 1968, and aimed to ensure that no film would 'lower the moral standards of those who see it'. For *Streetcar* to make it onto celluloid and become an immortal, pop-cultural touchstone, several key elements of its story were forced to change.

Blanche's unquenchable sexual desire for young men was significantly diminished; explicit reference to her deceased husband's queer sexuality – what the PCA termed 'sex perversion' – was removed; and the story's climax considerably softened, with the rape being implied, and ending on the apparently optimistic 'kindness of strangers' line. Still a powerful depiction of desire, male violence and broken masculinity, the Hollywood *Streetcar* nevertheless fails to evoke the subtle intermeshing of competing desires, between and across gender and sexualities, found in the stage play. And its desensitised ending doesn't do justice to Tennessee's searing critique of the ways that a masculinist, heterosexist social order has the final word on how desire should be delimited, meted out, quashed or imposed.

Why Do They Strike Us?

Exactly one month after Brando and Tennessee invented the modern erotic male, one month after *Streetcar*'s Broadway debut blew the puritanical cobwebs off the American stage – setting raw, messy, fluid desire under the spotlights and critiquing male relations – another century-defining event occurs in America. *Sexual Behavior in the Human Male* hits bookstands, a publication which will reshape the world of masculinity, and the public's perceptions of male sexuality, forever. Eight-hundred pages thick, sold for $6.50 – or *sex-fifty*, as some streetwise booksellers quip – this dense statistical study, authored by Dr Alfred Kinsey and associates, quickly came to be known as 'the Kinsey Report'. It contains thousands of anonymous interviews with men, conducted over a fifteen-year period, in which they were asked explicit, candid questions about their sex lives, desires and histories.

Only weeks after publication, Dr Kinsey – a former zoologist who completed his doctoral thesis on the mating habits of gall wasps, of all things – becomes a household name. He's in *Time* magazine. He's compared to Darwin. The press dub him 'Dr Sex'. The Kinsey Report places the topic of male sexuality right into the mainstream, into the workplace, into the household. The Report is deemed salacious, scandalous – and people can't get enough of it. The book becomes a bestseller. The simultaneous fascination and revulsion with the publication was later satirised by Carson McCullers in her final novel, *Clock Without Hands*, where Judge Clane – a racist former congressman – bans the Report ('pornographic filth') from the local library, while secretly relishing his own copy, replacing its dust jacket with the cover of an (unread) *History of the Decline and Fall of the Roman Empire*. Like many readers, the fictive Judge would have been entranced by the Report's findings.

Sexual Behavior in the Human Male found that sexual experiences between men are commonplace, and what is thought of as 'normal' male sexuality – the exclusively heterosexual – is anything but. A third of interviewees in *Sexual Behavior* reported having at least one post-adolescent sexual experience with another man. Half of interviewees reported experiencing, at some point, sexual arousal for another man. Four per cent had exclusively same-sex histories. These findings indicated that incidence of same-sex desires and practices between men are everywhere. Kinsey concluded that 'males do not represent discrete populations, heterosexual and homosexual . . . Only the human mind invents categories and tries to force facts into separate pigeon-holes. The living world is a continuum in each and every one of its aspects.'

For Kinsey, this data – which he considered objective and empirical – provided the perfect opportunity 'for understanding the futility of classifying individuals as normal or abnormal . . . when in reality they may be nothing more than frequent or rare, or conformists or nonconformists with the socially pretended custom'. Those customs, he argues in the Report, are sustained by nothing other than 'ignorance and superstition'. The call is simple: sexuality among men is objectively varied and unfixed, and this should not be condemned but accepted. In his review of the Kinsey Report, published in April that year, the cultural critic Lionel Trilling describes the study as a characteristically

'American document', calling it a 'recoil' from the 'brutal rejection which society has made of the person it calls sexually aberrant'. It represents an attempt, he argues, to establish a 'democratic pluralism of sexuality' in the US.

The scientific community, however, were quick to point out biases in Kinsey's sampling methods. He was accused of actively seeking out interviewees he already knew to have had same-sex experiences, thereby skewing the data set. Crucially, the interview subjects were heavily weighted towards white college-educated men; on that metric alone the Report could only ever offer an impoverished characterisation of the national male sexual persona. Certainly, today, the Report appears flawed in many ways; several more recent surveys with refined sampling methods fail to demonstrate comparable frequencies of same-sex behaviours in men, suggesting Kinsey's findings radically overestimated such behaviour. Irrespective of these flaws, the social and cultural power of the Report is immense, evinced as much in its explicit rejection of 'ignorance and superstition' as in the ideologically driven criticisms of its most vociferous detractors. Chief among them was the prominent psychoanalyst-psychologist Dr Lawrence Kubie, who, back in 1943, penned the Sexual Perversion passage that was sent out to thousands of doctors at draft boards, which explicitly fused 'homosexuality' to 'effeminacy' and established it as an abnormal, unhealthy condition. In a scathing attack on the Kinsey Report, recirculated by *Time* magazine, Kubie argues that Kinsey's conclusions are predicated on the assumption that 'because homosexuality is prevalent we must accept it as "normal"' – something he deemed 'wholly unwarranted'.

Kubie's criticism anticipated a quick, concerted reversal of Kinsey's call for a democratic pluralism of sexuality. Far from seeing the Report as an affirmative document which proved there was nothing 'deviant' or 'aberrant' about same-sex desire between men, many readers and commentators concluded that the Report merely showed the extent to which 'homosexuality' was spreading through the country, and needed urgently to be stopped. In the US military, there was an increased effort to institutionalise its homophobia by indoctrinating its men into a vehement detestation and fear of the 'homosexual'. New army recruits were given lectures which trained them to identify a homosexual, resist his advances and actively report him. In some cases, these lectures drew false and spurious connections between violent murderers and homosexuality. In the navy, men discharged for homosexuality were required to sign statements waiving their rights as veterans. The situation for lesbian women was, in some ways, even more extreme: welcomed into recruitment during the war effort, women in the military were expected to return to the household in peacetime and fulfil their domestic gender roles. Merely staying in the armed forces as a woman was enough to risk accusations of 'deviancy'.

The explicit indoctrination into homophobia for new recruits in the post-war years was accompanied by similar endeavours in government agencies. In 1950, the Senate ordered an investigation into 'sexual perversion' in the government, soon issuing a report which found that 'sex perverts [. . .] must be treated as transgressors', concluding that 'one homosexual can pollute a government office'. Homosexuals are weak, corrosive, corrupting, and corruptible, the report said. Same-sex acts and desire between men was now, officially, an active threat to the government and the country: the Kinsey Report merely indicated how colossal a threat this was. This same year, under the all-seeing, autocratic rule of J. Edgar Hoover, the FBI began to collaborate with local police departments, pooling data on the 'gathering places' of queer men, arrest records related to charges of deviancy, and channelling all this information to the government. A file was also opened on Alfred Kinsey himself, whom Hoover – in a menacing note – thought should be 'put up or shut up'.

In this environment, this callous hothouse of suspicion and shifting eyes, the paranoia is potent. These nonconformists, these transgressors, these subversives are everywhere, hiding in plain sight. Your neighbour, your closest friend, could be one. It's no great leap to see how this virulent, paranoid homophobia, this belief in an insidious, invisible and ever-present sexual threat, mapped onto the fear of communism – the Red Scare – that emerged at the start of the Cold War, in 1947. So intertwined are these paranoias that historians have labelled the homosexual panic the 'Lavender Scare' in reference to a then Senator's use of 'lavender lads' as synonym for 'homosexuals'. The conflation of the Red and Lavender Scares is neatly demonstrated by Republican National Committee chairman Guy Gabrielson, who wrote in a 1950 article published in the *New York Times* that homosexuals are potentially 'as dangerous as actual communists'. Or, later, by Senator Joseph McCarthy, that aggressive, megalomaniac demagogue who fuelled and incited fears of communist subversion. He would pithily – and bleakly – characterise the climate by telling reporters that if you're against McCarthyism, you're either 'a communist or a cocksucker'.

It is against this background that *Streetcar*'s success rages on. Debuting in December 1947, it runs for two years, closing in December 1949. Two years of Brando–Kowalski strutting about the stage, hurling his red-stained package at Stella, in all his lurid virility. Hundreds of instances of Blanche DuBois mournfully lusting after 'young men' in an attempt to suppress the guilt over her own deleterious homophobia and reclaim her lost queer lover. By the time *Streetcar* closes, Tennessee is temporarily living down in Key West, Florida. He's in a new relationship, now, with Frank Merlo, a working-class,

Levis-wearing Italian American whom Tennessee affectionately calls 'the Little Horse', and with whom he'll spend the next fourteen years. But, as ever, he's hard at work. Among the stack of correspondence he has to answer is a letter – a fan letter of sorts – from Dr Sex himself, Alfred Kinsey.

Kinsey informs Tennessee that he intends to undertake an extensive study of the erotic in the arts. Attuned to the sexual innovation of *Streetcar* and Brando–Kowalski, Kinsey describes his deep interest in Tennessee's play, and claims to have studied it in great detail. He and the Kinsey Institute, he says, have even set about interviewing the cast of *Streetcar*, to ascertain their sexual histories in an effort to uncover any correlation between their sexualities and their choice of pursuing careers as actors. Tennessee, replying to Kinsey from Key West, writes that he is gratified by the attention the Kinsey Institute is paying to the play. He tells Dr Kinsey that his research, and the revelations of the Report, is of tremendous social value, because, he feels, 'understanding' is one of the most desirable things in this world, particularly a world characterised by bias and ignorance.

The two men will later meet, briefly, in New York. In the 1950s, when Tennessee, suffering from severe depression, decides to pursue psychoanalytic treatment, he asks if Kinsey might recommend a good analyst. For whatever reason, he didn't take Dr Kinsey's proffered suggestion. Instead, in an ironic twist, he sought treatment from another well-known analyst, the former president of the New York Analytic Society, a famed, sophisticated maverick who had, in previous decades, attempted to exorcise 'homosexuality' from his roster of artist-patients: Dr Lawrence Kubie. Indeed, Kubie thought Tennessee 'should be heterosexual' and tried to convince him to separate from Frank Merlo. At this suggestion, instead of breaking up with Frank, Tennessee broke up with Kubie.

At the time of Tennessee's first correspondence with Dr Kinsey, the effects of the nation's redoubled homophobia could be seen and felt everywhere around him. The atmosphere among Key West's queer community, formerly famed for its bohemian, freewheeling, sexually liberal leanings, was shot through with anxiety. Then, in March 1950, 'the thing which we all dreaded but expected', Tennessee wrote to a friend, 'has finally happened'. A young sailor from the USS *Tringa*, named John Collins, murdered an older queer man, an artist from New York named Atherton Foster. He struck him with a wooden ashtray stand, after the artist – in Collins' words – made 'unnatural advances'. Both men were found, disrobed, in bed.

With this murder, Key West changes overnight. Tennessee records his impressions on the murder and its aftermath in a lengthy letter to Carson that spring. The town police, he says, 'have been prosecuting everyone around here who is a bit different-looking'. An intensely ugly atmosphere has developed, and all the 'bohemians' have left. A young man is picked up on the sole charge of having a 'sissy walk'. Tennessee is afraid to walk the streets, lest he get picked up himself. He feels like a target, and understands that he has little in his arsenal with which to defend himself. He has only intelligence, quick wit and a Southerner's sense of social poise: when confronted by a sailor who takes Tennessee's cigarette holder as a sign of queerness, pointing out that Oscar Wilde also used a cigarette holder, Tennessee's response is one of fast, feigned ignorance: 'Who,' he replies, 'is Oscar Wilde?'

The murder of Atherton Foster causes painful memories to flicker in Tennessee's mind. Seven years ago, in New York, while staying at the St George Hotel – a known cruising spot – Tennessee was himself struck and beaten by a sailor. The 'entertainment' that Tennessee offered the sailor, in his private hotel room, had been 'accepted with apparent gratitude' until other sailors burst in, at which point the sailor punched Tennessee. He did so, Tennessee understood, from shame and guilt. Because his friends, these other men, discovered what they were doing. The following day, he recorded in his diary that he would remember the abusive sailor as 'a lover, not antagonist'. It's a remarkable gesture of humanity and generosity, a celebration of the plurality of desire, sexuality and love, rather than an accession to the cruel tactics of division, mistrust and violence that typify the masculinity of those sailors, that group of men and the nation as a whole. Why, Tennessee asked himself, 'do they strike us? What is our offense?' He knew the answer. It is because 'we offer them a truth which they cannot bear to confess except in privacy and the dark – a truth which is inherently as bright as the morning sun'.

The System of Mendacity

Tennessee's been through several weeks of hell. Exhaustion. Drink. And a head cold, no less. There's relief – some, scant relief – in pills. Pinkies, his pleasantly devitalising pet name for Seconal, a highly addictive barbiturate that, he hopes, will send him back to sleep, to the realm of dreams. Whether knocked back with a cool glass of milk, or washed down with scotch and water, by the mid-1950s pinkies have become a constant presence in Tennessee's life. His anxiety attacks and heart palpitations have mutated into a permacrisis of panic and exhaustion, one only temporarily allayed through self-medication. Sometimes, he can't walk down the street without ducking into a bar for a stiff drink, much less stomach rehearsals without popping a pill. At the height of his fame – toking on a crystal-filtered cigarette holder, attired in his iconic dark sunglasses and double-breasted chalk-stripe suit – such was the extent of Tennessee's narcotisation that a critic likened him to a man who 'swats flies in outer space'.

Currently, his lurch towards sedation is driven by a bitter run of bad luck. One that's hounded him since at least last winter, when the problems with his latest play, *Cat on a Hot Tin Roof*, calcified. Problems related to plot, pace and structure. Problems related to patience. The script was rushed into rehearsals, even though neither writer nor director was happy with it. 'A black day to begin a blue journal,' Tennessee fatalistically penned in his notebook, on the first day of rehearsals. There, he was confronted with further problems: what he saw as an inadequate cast, actors performing like stuffed turkeys, and a pretentious set design that bore no relation whatsoever to the imagined world of his play.

The life of *Cat* started well enough. On reading a draft of the stage play, Tennessee's long-time friend and editor at New Directions, James Laughlin, found it shattering, strange and true, and thought it contained the power of 'a small atom bomb'. And when he sent a first draft to Elia Kazan, the director's reply was similarly encouraging. 'I don't get but one play I really want to do every three years or so. I sure want to do this one,' Kazan wrote, also noting that he believed it demonstrated Tennessee to be on the threshold of his 'richest creative period'. But the compliments don't ring true to Tennessee. Success, for him, had always been a double-edged sword, and *Streetcar*, his greatest success of all, caused the spectres of doubt, creative impotence and paranoia to flourish. Firstly, how could he ever hope to write as fluently, as fiercely, as in *Streetcar*? The critical reception of his subsequent Broadway efforts – *Summer & Smoke* and *Camino Real* – seemed to prove this, the former receiving lukewarm reviews, the latter, perhaps worse, met with muted indifference. Secondly, what if people thought Kazan, and only Kazan, was truly responsible for the success of the work? What if they were right?

With *Cat*, these concerns are reaching boiling point. Tennessee feels that he's lost the spontaneity of youth which had formerly swept him over 'many past obstructions', and that he can now only create with a 'tremendous wrenching of the brain and nerves'. And what he has created with *Cat* is not, it seems, good enough. Now that the play is in rehearsals, Kazan

– Catch-as-Catch-Can Kazan, as Tennessee refers to him in private correspondence – is vocal with his criticisms. He thinks that the heart of the play simply doesn't work. What, he wants to know, is the play's truth? What is the truth of its protagonist, Brick Pollitt? Kazan doesn't like Brick, much less understand him, and Tennessee's attempts to illuminate his fictive character through a real-life comparison – Marlon Brando, he wrote to Kazan, 'is the nearest thing to Brick that we both know' – don't seem to help. Kazan's digging in his heels: there's no character development with Brick, no progression, and the audience will lose interest in him and the play completely.

Brick Pollitt is an embittered former football star. Throughout *Cat* he hobbles around on a crutch, having sustained a broken ankle attempting to reclaim his adolescent, athletic prowess by jumping hurdles at his old high school, tanked, in the middle of the night. Brick is also an alcoholic. His addiction – which hasn't yet tarnished his physical beauty, but paradoxically, seems to have enhanced it – represents an obstinate refusal to conform to the role expected of him as fêted heir to his father's plantation and inheritance. Consistently cooled by drink, as immutable and inert as his name suggests, Brick won't follow through with the heterosexual imperative: he won't sire the child, with his fierce, dynamic wife, Maggie the Cat, that will make their marriage 'good' and ensure the completion of dynastic succession.

But the addiction isn't the cause of his obstinance. It's the cover. There's something restless and raging at the core of his character – 'like lightning in a fair sky' – that prevents him from blithely falling into place and fulfilling his role. He is haunted by Skipper, a man with whom he shared a deep friendship, and his guilt and broken-heartedness at the part he played in his friend's death. After Skipper had a faltering affair with Maggie, he confessed his true feelings for Brick. But

Brick simply ignored him, a snub so brutal it caused Skip to 'crack up' and commit suicide. Together, Maggie and Brick's father – the plantation patriarch, suitably named Big Daddy – attempt to unearth and expose the truth at the core of Brick's character, thus aiming to resolve it. Their attempts, and Brick's resistance, create *Cat*'s driving action, what Tennessee, with typically poetic aplomb, described as the 'true quality of experience in a group of people, that cloudy, flickering, evanescent – fiercely charged! – interplay of live human beings in the thundercloud of a common crisis'.

But what, Kazan wants to know, is this action driving towards? What will Brick do at the end? Compromises are being made, and they come at great pains, and pinkies, to Tennessee. Kazan asks him to redraw and rework the characters of both Brick and Big Daddy, and to bring the tensions in their relationship into sharper focus. It's a deviation from Tennessee's original draft, in which Big Daddy fades into the background after the second act. And so, in rehearsals, each night, a different variation on the third act is staged. Audience reaction is gauged, and edits, alterations and concessions made. But disaster looms, Tennessee's sure of it. At this point, it hardly seems likely *Cat* will make it to Broadway at all.

A roster of celebrities has turned up to pre-judge the out-of-town show, some, no doubt, intrigued by rumours that the play will be a complete washout. Marilyn Monroe attends repeatedly, sometimes in a black mink coat, sometimes in blue jeans and a pink headscarf. Two giants of American fiction have come to watch: William Faulkner and John Steinbeck. And on the opening night of try-outs, sitting in the gallery is a smaller circle of friends: Gore Vidal, Christopher Isherwood and Tennessee's eternal creative ally, Carson McCullers.

When Carson arrived at the Forest Theatre, Philadelphia, for *Cat*'s try-outs, she was first mistaken by a stage assistant for a vagrant or bag lady who had wandered in off the street. By early 1955, Carson has experienced several severe strokes, resulting in temporary blindness, nerve damage and partial paralysis in both her face and left arm, which left her needing to wear, in Isherwood's acerbic words, an 'unnecessarily repulsive brace'. She is also grieving. Scarcely over a year ago, in a Paris hotel room, Reeves had committed suicide. Though her husband had openly contemplated suicide for some time, it wasn't always clear to Carson how serious his intentions were. Nor had it been clear to Tennessee, who, on visiting the couple in Paris, witnessed an erratic Reeves in the midst of a suicidal gesture.

As Tennessee later recounted, Reeves was threatening to jump out of a second-storey window, because he had 'discovered' that he was 'homosexual'. Tennessee – disbelieving the legitimacy of Reeves' suicidal ideation – erupted with laughter and told Reeves that he shouldn't jump out of a window if he believed he was homosexual; he should only jump if he were forced to be anything otherwise. Though this appeal to queer self-pride temporarily soothed Reeves, the former soldier remained deeply depressed. And in the late summer of 1953, he sought company in his quest for oblivion, attempting to force Carson into a double suicide by driving out to the woods near their Paris lodgings with two coils of rope and suggesting they hang themselves from a tree. When Reeves insisted they stop to buy a bottle of brandy before completing the act, Carson ran from the car and hailed a passing vehicle to make her escape, subsequently flying back to America, leaving Reeves for the last time.

For Carson, still coming to terms with the loss of her beloved, despised husband, who was driven to obliteration through the combined forces of alcoholism, displacement and a sense of having failed as a man, watching Tennessee's *Cat* has personal resonances. She surely understands the playwright's artistic convictions, and the character he wants to portray in Brick Pollitt: a man caged by the expectations of his masculinity, a man made to feel alienated by the potentiality of queer desire, a man whose ultimate failure to reckon with that has led to a crisis, manifesting in an addiction (gin, for Reeves, was cool spring water; for Brick, opening the liquor cabinet is 'a trip to Echo Spring'). And, finally, a man who does not necessarily change, despite recognising that he must.

Tennessee wrote to Kazan that 'even if *Cat* is not a good play, it's a goddam fiercely *true* play'. Carson stood in staunch agreement. One stage assistant remembers that she came to try-outs almost every day, and, in defence of Tennessee's original ambitions, simply whispered in her Southern drawl, 'But it's the truth.'

Cat on a Hot Tin Roof is a play about masculinity in crisis. A crisis of purpose and desire, provoked by the terms of compulsory heterosexual coupling and procreation, and the stifling homophobic social mores of mid-century America. It is also a play about the 'shocking duality' of the heart, and the lies we tell ourselves to hide this truth. *Cat* unfolds in a large bedroom–living room occupied by Maggie and Brick, in a grand plantation house in the Mississippi Delta. Tennessee wanted the stage roofed by sky, illuminated with a blurry wash of starlight and moonlight, and backed by a soft, amber glow. The situation is this: it is Big Daddy's birthday, and the family are here to celebrate. Big Mamma (Daddy's wife – who else?), Brick's elder brother Gooper and his wife, Mae, and their five screaming, troublemaking offspring – 'no-neck monsters', in Maggie's words, or '*naw-mal rid-blooded children*' in Mae's. This isn't a happy occasion, however. In this house is the stench of mendacity: lies. Big Daddy is dying from cancer, and the family are keeping it from him. His imminent death ratchets up the urgency with which Gooper and Mae battle against Maggie for accession. Who will inherit the estate?

'They're sittin' in the middle of a big piece of land,' Brick, indifferent to the inheritance, explains to his father, 'each determined to knock off a bigger piece of it than the other whenever you let it go.'

For Maggie, the drive to win accession isn't from greed, but from a need to survive. Maggie comes from nothing. She has been 'so goddamn disgustingly poor' her whole life, and if her situation implodes, as it appears it will – her husband drinking himself to death, Gooper and Mae inheriting – she's had it. You can be young without money, she repeats, but you can't be old without it. But for Maggie to be in with a chance, she must fulfil the heterosexual imperative. That is, she must have a child by Brick to prove that procreation and lineage are assured outcomes of their union, that all is well in their marriage, that all is 'normal'. An impossible task, given Brick's insistence that he won't sleep or share a bed with her, and that she should, instead, take a lover to compensate. It wasn't always this way; Brick used to be a wonderful person to go to bed with, according to Maggie. What made him such a good lover, she says, was his aloofness: 'your indifference made you wonderful at lovemaking – *strange?* – but true.' It all changed after his friend Skipper died.

Gooper and Mae assume themselves the fêted couple. Gooper is the eldest son, and has achieved an apparently normal, successful marriage with Mae, who has reared those five children. The couple have been spying, eavesdropping, listening through the wall and sending reports back to Big Mamma that Brick and Maggie simply aren't having sex. Their pathetic, snivelling subterfuge and sabotage echo the climate of the Red-Lavender scare: anyone could be spying on your private sex life, ready to rat you out should it appear abnormal. In a moment alone with Maggie, Big Mamma chides her, pointing to the bed: 'when a marriage goes on the rocks, the rocks are right *there!*' But why, Maggie asks, doesn't Big Mamma ask after her own happiness, her own sexual satisfaction? 'It goes both ways!' she shouts, a rebuttal as powerful as it is futile. The onus, in this masculinist regime, falls on Maggie. If the marriage is failing, it's because she's sexually inadequate.

Maggie is, therefore, the play's cat on a hot tin roof: set upon from all sides, trapped in a room where the walls have ears; with a man, whom she loves, as unresponsive as stone; and little time left to secure her future. At play's end, she must find a way to win. She claims to the family that she's pregnant with Brick's child, and attempts to coerce Brick into making 'this lie true' by craftily turning his addiction against him. She locks away his liquor and will not let him have more until they have sex.

Maggie's cunning – her manoeuvring – exposes the heterosexist world of the plantation house for what it is: a performance. A game to be won, with opponents to be beaten. Coupling, matrimony, procreation: in *Cat*, these are combative, potentially monstrous situations sustained by deceit. So thin is the veneer of this artifice that Big Daddy comes right out and names it. In an extended, impassioned confrontation with Brick, he claims he could write a book on mendacity. He only pretends, he says, to be fond of Gooper ('that son of a bitch') and Mae ('that bitch') and their kids ('five same monkeys'). Likewise, he only pretends to care for Big Mamma, though he hasn't 'been able to stand the sight, smell, or sound of that woman for forty years now'. It's a grim assessment, made more troubling by the fact that he actively promulgates this heterosexist rule of law himself, despite acknowledging the lies necessary to sustain it. For Big Daddy, this is what life as a man, as a patriarch, amounts to: pretences. '*I've* lived with mendacity,' he tells Brick, 'why can't *you* live with it?'

There's a key detail in Tennessee's play which throws this artifice into starker relief. It's the literal and figurative stage upon which these lies are acted out. Big Daddy, we learn, didn't inherit the plantation through the same patrilineal rule he himself enforces. Far from it. Through a smattering of details, we come to learn that Big Daddy, in his youth, was firmly working class: a vagrant, freight-hopper and transient labourer. He was taken into this plantation by its former owners – two men, Jack Straw and Peter Ochello – who bequeathed it to him after their deaths. Straw and Ochello, 'a pair of old bachelors', worked together. They also lived together, sharing the same room: the bedroom–living room in which Maggie and Brick have been given lodgings. In his set notes, Tennessee wants this captured: 'the room must evoke some ghosts, it is gently and poetically haunted by a relationship that must have involved a tenderness which was uncommon.' Big Daddy's heterosexist rule is *superimposed* atop something altogether different, a planation and estate whose success was generated through a professional and intimate relationship between men, one that doesn't fit conventional definitions of masculinity. This superimposition gives the lie to the notion that heterosexual, procreative marriage is the de facto 'true' way of living, against which anything else (a childless marriage, for instance) is different or wrong.

The Straw–Ochello backstory not only haunts the room, it also haunts Brick. In their confrontation, Big Daddy embarks upon an excavation of Brick's soul, sloughing off the layers of armour he's built around himself to eke out the truth behind his present condition. He hits upon a sore spot when he brings up Skipper, suggesting that Skipper's death was the genesis of Brick's alcoholism. At this point, Brick explodes into a kind of quivering, spluttering mess of fear, homophobic disgust and anger. He demands to know if Big Daddy thinks he and Skipper were 'a pair of dirty old men' like Straw and Ochello, a couple of 'sissies? Queers?' Is that why he and Maggie have been given this room – as an accusation? Why can't an 'exceptional friendship,' he asks, 'a *real, real, deep deep friendship!*' between two men, as he and Skipper had, be accepted, without the two men being thought of as '*fairies*'? In this utterance, the stage directions tell us, 'we gauge the wide and profound reach of the conventional mores he got from the world that crowned him with early laurel'.

We might expect from the brusque, misogynistic Big Daddy a homophobic tirade to further legitimise Brick's fear of accusation. But none comes. Big Daddy, instead, offers a curious compassion, extolling the values of tolerance and denouncing the 'infectiousness' of others' ideas.* His overtures towards

---

* Some critics have traced Big Daddy's tolerance to his rambling pre-plantation youth, seeing this backstory as emblematic of an early twentieth-century American working-class lifestyle termed 'hobohemia'. This all-male, bachelor subculture – which consisted of seamen, agricultural workers, manual labourers and the like – rejected domesticity, emphasised an ethic of male solidarity and was surprisingly lenient towards certain kinds of homosexual activity. In hobohemia, virility was demonstrated through sexually dominating women, as well as other men, so-called 'fairies' who would often ape feminine dress. On the road, meanwhile, same-sex relationships and activity were widespread, with couplings and partnerships often falling along an age rather than sex axis: older men partnered with younger men, who were sometimes referred to as 'wives'. This might explain Big Daddy's tolerance towards the prospect of same-sex coupling, while also remaining steadfastly patriarchal and misogynistic: queer sexuality as another province in which men can demonstrate power. In this sense, his confrontation with Brick is a confrontation between two kinds of American masculinity: the vanished homosocial world of hobohemia and Big Daddy's youth, and Brick's paranoid, rigid, Cold War-era manhood.

tolerance must surely have their origins in that uncommon tenderness he witnessed between Straw and Ochello: having lived, worked with and inherited from the two men, Big Daddy has cultivated a more holistic understanding of the kinds of relationships available between men, whereas Brick descends into panic and vituperation simply because he intuits that fraternity and friendship might exist on the same spectrum as sexual intimacy. Brick becomes, in this scene, an exacting example of that beleaguered Cold War masculinity: paranoid, panicked, unable or unwilling to embrace the diverse and variegated nature of male desire.

Big Daddy knows that Brick's terror at being perceived as a 'fairy' is merely the toughest, outer layer of his armour, and that his youngest son's trauma runs deeper still. 'Why did Skipper crack up?' he demands, 'Why have you?' Brick reveals that Skipper and Maggie had an affair, yet another blow to the apparent 'truth' of monogamous matrimony. In Maggie's eyes, this affair enabled her and Skipper to get closer to Brick. 'We made love to each other,' she tells Brick, 'to dream it was you, both of us. Yes, yes yes! Truth, truth!' It's an explicit version of the same slippery, scavenging desire that characterises Blanche's lust: sex with stand-ins or surrogates as a conduit, a way to reclaim or reunite with the lost or departed lover. According to Brick, however, Skipper slept with Maggie to prove his and Brick's relationship was normal, and nothing like 'that ole pair of sisters', Straw and Ochello. But Big Daddy still isn't satisfied. There's more to the story. He prods, and prods, until Brick reveals the final piece of the puzzle: after these revelations, Skipper, drunk, confessed his true feelings to Brick over a long-distance phone call. And what did Brick do? He simply hung up. And the two men never spoke again. 'You,' Big Daddy summarises, 'dug the grave of your friend and kicked him in it! – before you'd face truth with him!'

Thus, Brick drinks to kill his disgust with himself: because he couldn't handle his friend's feelings. Did he reciprocate them? Is he in denial about his own queer sexuality? Is Brick's love for Skipper – that deep, true friendship – romantic or platonic? The goddamn fierce truth of *Cat* is not – as Tennessee will later say himself – about 'the precise sexual orientation of these two men'. It is not whether Brick is really self-hating, closeted and queer, or homophobic and straight, or driven mad by the paradoxes of bisexuality. It is that Brick is a man whose inability to act upon the revelation of someone's truth, whose inability to communicate, to offer compassion, to do anything, renders him inert. He's a man who, through fealty to a rigid, conventional notion of masculinity, fails to acknowledge or recognise the truth of another's heart, and the consequences of this have thrust him towards alcoholic oblivion.

In Tennessee's original *Cat*, Brick doesn't suddenly change in the wake of this revelation needled out by Big Daddy. His relationship with Maggie is not miraculously made rosy. Rather, Brick remains stuck fast in monosyllabic near-silence, dumb with drink. When, in the play's final scene, Maggie declares her own love for him, in a moment of tenderness that punctures through the convoluted tactics and power plays of accession, Brick merely smiles, and, with charming sadness, says: 'Wouldn't it be funny if that was true?' It's an ending that emphasises the severity of Brick's spiritual disrepair. The lies that structure his world – what he calls 'the system' of mendacity – and his own complicity in them leave him in a pose of wry, sardonic cynicism: a broken man in aspic.

The Broadway ending, however, as extracted by Kazan, is more ambiguous. In the final scene, when Maggie announces her fake pregnancy, Brick joins in with her ruse, baiting the disbelieving Gooper and Mae with hints that, despite their eavesdropping, he and Maggie may have been making love all along. When Maggie tries to make this lie true, checkmating Brick by locking up his liquor, he replies, 'I admire you, Maggie.' The system of mendacity, this ending suggests, cannot be escaped, but to master its rules is, if nothing else, a laudable endeavour. Though it seems a minor change, Brick's shoulder-shrugging readjustment to the heterosexual dyad dulls the subversiveness and true power of the original, which, though a tough pill to swallow, delivers a staggering truth: people do not always change in the wake of revelation, and the trappings and constraints of conventional masculinity can be fatal to the soul.

There were many other edits Kazan convinced Tennessee to make, many of which made *Cat* a far better play; without Kazan's criticisms, the Brick and Big Daddy showdown would never have been so thoroughgoing. The director's input helped transform *Cat* into Tennessee's greatest Broadway success. It earned him a second Pulitzer and ran for nearly seven hundred performances. But the tweaked ending that Kazan coaxed from Tennessee paved the way for the play's Hollywood adaptation, which took this alteration and shot it full of steroids. Richard Brooks' *Cat on a Hot Tin Roof* (1958), which imprinted Brick and Maggie into the pop cultural canon, intentionally perverts the play's complex criticisms of masculinity and patriarchy almost beyond all recognition.

Starring a searingly handsome, blue-eyed Paul Newman as Brick, to Elizabeth Taylor's courageous, pitch-perfect Maggie, the film removes references to Jack Straw and Peter Ochello. The Brick–Skipper relationship is dialled down, becoming nothing more than a titillating gesture to 'deviancy,' a nod-nod wink-wink subtext ultimately supplanted by the marriage bed.

And the ending sees Brick determined to make true Maggie's lie; he demands Maggie lock the bedroom door. No longer needing to nimbly mastermind a way to coerce Brick into bed, Maggie obeys. The two share a kiss; the camera lingers on the bed; they will certainly fuck, is the implication, and fulfil the heterosexual imperative. Brooks' *Cat* is no longer about a beleaguered masculinity and the lies necessary to sustain patriarchy. It becomes, instead, a celebration of marriage and coupling according to the terms of a heterosexist, masculinist world.

When the script of *Cat* was published in book form, Tennessee included both his original ending and the Broadway version, with an accompanying 'Note of Explanation' that sought to explain his original artistic convictions – that Brick's unchanging moral paralysis and spiritual disrepair are essential to his tragedy. The note goes on to concede that Kazan's edits created a successful play, but wonders if the original ending wouldn't have been received just as well. Kazan and Tennessee's working relationship was one of collaboration, based on mutual trust and respect for each other's talents and expertise. The reality of the tussled-over alterations to *Cat*'s ending is certainly less straightforward than the story of directorial authoritarianism that Tennessee actively created following the play's success. Unsurprisingly, Kazan saw it as a betrayal. The two men, while publicly professing to be on amicable terms, privately felt hurt by one another. It was an altercation that neither fully recovered from, and it heralded the eventual end of their professional and artistic collaboration.

Tennessee couldn't let the *Cat* conundrum go. Made rich from the sale of the film rights and showered with critical accolades, he felt that his art had been cheapened, its truth diluted. It was two decades before he would lay this particular unease to rest, by restaging *Cat* in 1974, with his original ending reinstated, and publishing the script as the definitive version for posterity. By that time, however, Tennessee's critical star had long since faded. He also found himself under fire for reasons that, twenty years before, he could scarcely have imagined. A new generation of openly gay playwrights and artists was emerging, and, from a post-Stonewall standpoint, some felt that *Cat*, and much of Tennessee's oeuvre, was problematic. Why didn't Tennessee write a play about an openly gay relationship? An article in the *New York Times,* published by a gay playwright under a pseudonym, castigated Tennessee for not having contributed any work of understanding to the gay theatre, for substituting women characters for gay men in his work, and for not standing up for the homosexual. Another article, published in *Gay Sunshine Press,* struck a similar note, accusing Tennessee of disguising homosexual characters as women, a criticism Tennessee felt was 'dangerous to the whole art, to all the written arts. It won't hold water. It don't stick.'

This tension was not merely a product of generational misunderstanding – a pre- versus post-Stonewall attitude to the political or community duties incumbent on gay and queer people – it drove right to the heart of Tennessee's convictions about life, art and society. In an interview with the New York-based playwright and poet George Whitmore, Tennessee was asked why he didn't now choose to write openly gay characters in his plays. Whitmore was a sensitive interviewer, and, unlike those other critics, sympathetic to Tennessee's personal history as a queer man whose major works were crafted in an intensely homophobic cultural climate in which the gay liberation movement did not yet exist.[*]

But Whitmore leans on this question. Is Tennessee not

---

[*] Whitmore also conceded that Tennessee's mid-century fiction contained many representations of openly gay men.

interested in writing gay characters for the stage? Tennessee first replies that he is doing just that, in a play tentatively titled *The Wild Horses of the Camargue*. But he goes on to emphasise that he's always written about whatever interests him, echoing earlier comments that human relationships, not homosexuality, is the theme of his work. The theme of any play, he tells Whitmore, should not be impeded by 'a tangential thing like the precise sexual orientation of characters, in fact,' he concludes, 'I don't think there is such a thing as a precise sexual orientation. I think we're all ambiguous sexually'. Whitmore then draws Tennessee into a debate about the revolutionary potential of theatre for the gay community, asking if Tennessee thinks any of his own plays could be considered revolutionary in this sense.

'Revolutionary plays?' Tennessee replies, 'Every goddamn one of 'em.'

Coda

Tennessee Williams' and Carson McCullers' friendship was essential to each of them throughout their careers. Particularly in those dismal, dejected moments when they received negative criticism so fierce their artistic self-assurance might have been destroyed, were it not for their genuine, full-throated championship of one another. But their relationship went beyond creative advocation. 'Next to my sister Rose,' Tennessee told the broadcaster and historian Studs Terkel in 1961, 'Carson is, of all the women that I know, now living, the one closest to me.' In Tennessee's estimation, what kept them close, even when they went 'many months' without seeing one another, was their shared 'attitude' towards life, and towards those people whom society makes 'incomplete'. People, like themselves, who didn't fit society's brutal frameworks and restrictions and must instead 'fight for their reason'. Carson and Tennessee's pursuit to portray and critique the broken masculinity of their day, and to speculate on alternatives, reflects this mutual sensibility. That this was a joint artistic undertaking is wonderfully captured in a collaborative performance, of sorts, that they undertook in the spring of 1954.

Carson had been invited to give a lecture on the craft of her fiction, at the 92nd Street Y Poetry Center, on Manhattan's Upper East Side. Shortly before her appearance, she felt nervous and unable to read from her own work. One passage, in particular, frequently gave Carson trouble whenever she tried to read it to an audience: the 'coda' of her fairy-tale novella, *The Ballad of the Sad Café*, which describes a chain gang of black and white men. Carson's voice would often break when reading it aloud; it would even move her to tears. And so, at the last minute, she reached out to Tennessee and invited him to join her on stage. He accepted.

In front of a packed audience, with a pitcher of martinis strategically set between them in place of water, Carson begins her lecture by explaining her writing process. Though she sounds shaky at first, she soon relaxes, and her giggling, giddy Southern drawl laces and intertwines with Tennessee's languorous, relaxed voice, who occasionally interjects with a quick aside, or encouraging laughter at Carson's comic anecdotes. These include Carson's recollections of that 'sea-summer lit with the glow of a new friendship' way back in 1946, when they first met in Nantucket: every morning, she tells the audience, she'd step out of bed in her bare feet, right onto a fish head that the stray cat had brought in through the broken window.

Towards the end of the lecture, Carson cues Tennessee to read the coda out loud to the full room. 'The gang,' Tennessee orates, in his honeyed, smokey voice,

is made up of twelve men, all wearing black-and-white striped prison suits, and chained at the ankles. There is a guard, with a gun, eyes drawn to red slits by the glare [. . .] All day there is the sound of picks striking into the clay earth, hard sunlight, the smell of sweat. And every day there is music. One dark voice will start a phrase, half-sung, and like a question. And after a moment another will join in, soon the whole gang will be singing. The voices are dark in the golden glare . . .

The music that these incarcerated, imprisoned, labouring men make is so rapturous that it 'causes the heart to broaden and the listener to grow cold with ecstasy and fright'. It is so mesmeric that it appears to come from the earth and sky, rather than lungs and vocal cords. These men are chained, bound to one another in an intractable, imprisoned formation. The weight and threat of violence hangs over them in the form of a loaded gun, those red, all-seeing eyes – another man, a symbol of power, authority and hierarchy – keeping them in check. They are men who wish to convert those cold iron chains into ligatures, threads of affirmative connection and communion with one another. Who is it that creates such music, Carson's narrator asks? The answer is as bathetic as it is revelatory: 'Just twelve mortal men who are together.'

This enigmatic coda might be read as a parable for the quandary of male relations *in toto*; the nature of men's relationship to one another is regulated and governed by that demon-eyed guard with the gun, a surrogate, perhaps, for the heterosexist rule of patriarchy and its attendant gender codes. Thought of this way, the coda casts traditional masculinity as a form of incarceration. Certainly, this resonates with Carson and Tennessee's fictive men. Brick is nothing if not a man caged and dehumanised by his perception of what patriarchy demands of him. Singer is locked into a putatively ordinary existence, which he finds unbearably lonesome, simply because his relationship to another man was deemed abnormal. Penderton, shackled by the martial hierarchy and rigidity of the fort, cannot find positive expression for, let alone comprehend, his desires. These men suffer because the terms of masculinity, patriarchy and compulsory heterosexuality seek to set men against one another; to denigrate both women and the so-called 'feminine' in men; to sustain relations antithetical to the truth of the heart, the truth of love and desire; and ultimately constrain men in this deleterious gender ideal. And often, as a result, men seek to constrain women in turn: Leonora is diminished as a bargaining chip by the captain, and a static object of indulgence by Williams; the masculinist system of mendacity seeks to reduce Maggie to a 'breeder'; Blanche is despatched to the asylum.

Despite the critiques that both Carson McCullers and Tennessee Williams level against this mid-century masculinity and its corrosive impact on men and women, there are also bright moments of possibility and optimism scattered throughout their works, which gesture to a different way of living; alternative masculinities that have greater fidelity to the vagaries of love and desire, inclusive of care, friendship, love and sex. The poker-playing men's brief break from their performance of aggressive hostility and turn to compassion and loving words; Captain Penderton's powerful burst of anti-authoritarian, transgressive protest at the major's insistence on the rule of conformity; Big Daddy's surprising tenderness and tolerance when confronted with the possibility of queer love, a trait that he learned after being adopted and cared for by two men who themselves shared an uncommon bond. And these twelve mortal men in Carson's coda, who yearn to transmute their bondage into something else, something beautiful, ecstatic and awe-inspiring.

These promises of transformation spark and flare in the murky twilight of Carson and Tennessee's fiction, offering windows into a world of positive or affirmative relations between and among men. Both writers sustain their critiques of masculinity in order to show why such alternatives are desirable, why they are, in fact, needed. And their works resonated with one of their contemporaries, a man who, like them, felt that the norms associated with his gender amounted to a kind of incarceration; a man who feared being an 'outlaw' of masculinity, a fear matched only by his intense, lifelong quest to transgress and break free from its constraints.

PART THREE

What Did I Desire?

The Prison Guard and the Prisoner

Camp Gordon, Georgia, 1942

John Cheever stands guard over a group of prisoners, holding a loaded gun. He's recently completed infantryman training, and is now stationed in Camp Gordon, outside Augusta, in Georgia. The thirty-one-year-old aspiring writer, a shortish man with vivid blue eyes and an infectious grin, enlisted in the US Army last spring. But, so far, military life isn't quite what he expected. Camp Gordon is surrounded by desolate, earthy, red-yellow countryside that stretches for hundreds of miles, broken up by poisonous swamps and one-horse towns, whose chief inhabitants appear to be razorback hogs kicking up dust on deserted main streets. This is the Deep South that Carson McCullers writes about, he thinks: the vast cloudless skies, the deep-blue afterglow at dusk. It's a culture shock for Cheever, who has never before stepped foot in the South. He was born and grew up in the leafy Massachusetts South Shore town of Quincy, a stone's throw from Boston, and a universe away from Georgia. Cheever's so homesick, in fact, that his dreams in the barracks allegorise the end of the war as nothing more than a return to the East Coast, 'where there is grass and where there are elm trees'.

Today, Cheever is on guard duty. In the camp, every man has his duties, a fixed point in the hierarchy. And everything – from the rows of white clapboard barracks to the shined shoes and clean-shaven faces – is structured according to rigid rules. The prisoners he's tasked with guarding broke those rules: they're American men, many of whom have been incarcerated for desertion. But Cheever doesn't see them as unpatriotic. It's not as though they've abandoned their fellow soldiers in combat. None of the men has seen 'anything resembling war' yet, and the days in Camp Gordon are dull, marked by sex starvation and boredom, albeit laced with anxiety that, at any moment, orders might come down from on high and ship them all off to Europe or North Africa. But the way things are going, Cheever has concluded that the average American soldier is more likely to be killed by 'kindness and indigestion' than by the Germans.

Despite the culture shock of army life, Cheever gets on well with his fellow infantrymen, writing Mary, his newlywed wife, lengthy descriptions of their idiosyncrasies and quirks. There's the underworld-type guys from the East Coast – former New York loan sharks, pimps and hustlers. There's the 'southern boys', of whom he's especially fond. Cheever will remember and recount the antics of one of these Southerners for the rest of his life: a scrawny farm boy named Caleb Muse, who believed in ghosts, stashed a stolen chicken in the boiler room during inspection, and – in a moment of naive indifference, or barefaced contempt of the masculinist mores of army life – painted his toenails bright pink, and showed them to Cheever in the shower, asking, '*Ain't that pretty?*'

In some ways, the quiet purgatory of the camp suits Cheever. He isn't your typical soldier. When the regiment marches in formation, other men can pick him out immediately: there's a dreamlike quality about him. It's not that he feels disenchanted with the war effort (excepting, perhaps, the military's 'titanic inefficiency'); Cheever's head-in-the-clouds attitude is simply down to the fact that he'd rather be *writing* instead of carrying out his military duties. He spends so much time 'mooning over literary ideas' when he should instead be 'chasing a training stick with a bayonet'. Whenever life in the army makes him wonder if he ought to stop his literary contemplations altogether, his clarity and conviction soon returns: '*Fuck that,* as they say around here.' After all, it's a conviction he's had since childhood, when he declared his intent to be a writer at the age of eleven. And except for this stint as a soldier, it hasn't occurred to him that he could be anything else.

Besides, Cheever has good reason to keep up his literary daydreaming. He's a writer on the ascent, or so it seems. His short fiction is finally getting traction with the *New Yorker.* Though his work first appeared in the publication's pages as early as 1935, it's not until recently, under the new editorship of a man named William Maxwell, that Cheever's name has become a semi-regular feature in the magazine. He's built up enough solid material, in fact, that he's ready to publish a book. *The Way Some People Live,* his debut collection of stories, will appear in early 1943, while he's still in the army.

For now, however, Cheever's interred in Camp Gordon. He escorts the prisoners, those deserters, to the exercise yard. He watches them run around 'like a pack of dogs'. It's not scorn he feels towards them – on the contrary, it's *admiration.* He thinks that the prisoners are 'the finest looking group of men' he's seen during his time in the army. Their eyes are 'bright and clear' as though the 'stigma of their confinement' has produced in them a 'kind of fire and dash' absent among the ordinary enlisted men, who appear drab by comparison. When tasked with taking two of the prisoners out to the camp's wood pile, where he keeps his rifle trained on them as they carry out their sentence of 'hard labor' – cutting up kindling – he also admires their easy camaraderie, the way they rib and joke around with one another, a carefree fellowship discordant with their captivity. So enamoured is Private Cheever with these prisoners that he agrees to play, in his words, the 'gullible guard' and covertly mail their letters for them, a blatant contravention of regulations.

He sympathises with them, these men who, through some impulse, have broken rank, have shirked their duties, and been summarily penalised. The role of gullible guard – a liminal place between liberator and jailer, admiring the men who have transgressed on the one hand and enforcing their punishment on the other – mirrors an inner disorientation that Cheever will wrestle with throughout his life. John Cheever is a man caught in constant conflict. His romantic and sexual desires include both women and men. But his attraction to men disturbs and terrifies him, to the point of self-hatred. It manifests, too, in vocal homophobia along gender lines – a regurgitated repudiation of the so-called 'feminine' in men. In the words of his son, Benjamin, Cheever 'was a bisexual who detested any sign of sexual ambiguity'.

Cheever himself would use the word 'bisexual' to refer to his sexuality only rarely. When speaking in affirmative terms, he would imagine instead a 'sexual iridescence'. Most frequently, however, he would cordon off that part of himself that felt attraction to other men, labelling such desires as 'aberrant' and 'perverse'. He deems his same-sex desires incompatible not only with society's – and his own – expectations of masculinity, but with his own sincerely held wish to raise a family and make a life with them. They will seem to threaten the very foundations of that life – his 'credentials as a gentleman' – which he will work so hard to build: a marriage, children, a home in a leafy New England suburb. But at the same time Cheever will come to see this life as a kind of imprisonment, the 'confinement of traditional values and nostalgia' which prohibits him from realising his instinctive feeling that life and love 'flows or should flow like the waters in a stream'.

In a bid to understand and explore his sexuality, Cheever will fight against an urge to escape – in his daughter's analysis – 'the trappings and traps he had so carefully constructed for himself'. And against this lifelong inner conflict, Cheever will craft some of the finest twentieth-century American fiction. He will use the short story form, in particular, as a means of skewering, celebrating and probing the paradoxes of the middle classes and their social values, all the while trying to 'divine the motives of human conduct'. Alongside his fiction, he will dedicatedly maintain a journal, committing to the page millions of words of diaristic writing that offer a portrait of a man caught up in the sexual binary of his time, a man of conservative queerness who felt himself to be like 'a naked prisoner in an unlocked cell', a prisoner who, despite knowing that freedom is within arm's reach, can't fathom how he will escape.

Relics of the Past

'Our lives,' Cheever wrote, 'are not long and well-told stories.' Just as he believed that real life was not like fiction, he insisted, time and time again, that fiction is not 'crypto-autobiography'. The pressing need to distinguish between the two, however, suggests that they are not all that different, or at least that there is an easy slippage between them. Cheever maintained his journals in twenty-eight loose-leaf notebooks of lined white paper – demarcating them from the yellow foolscap he'd use for his fiction – from the late 1940s up to his death in 1982. Despite that material difference, and Cheever's outward protestations, he was intimately aware of the porousness between the two strands of his writing.

He understood that language, metaphor, anecdote and imagination are necessary tools to help us make sense of the 'incongruities' of waking life, just as they are necessary devices for writing fiction. Equally, he understood how to extract from the experiences of real-life images, ideas and emotional states that could be channelled into the universe of his fiction, enriching and complicating it, so that he could offer readers, if not reality, then 'verisimilitude'. It's an abstracted, strange symbiosis. Just because one can invent landscapes and relation-ships 'to illustrate one's most intimate feelings about life and the mysteriousness of one's own nature' does not mean, Cheever thought, that one can 'discourse with lucidity and brilliance on this process'. Perhaps we could envisage the pages of Cheever's journals to be like stepping stones across the deep pond of his fiction, and vice versa.

During the Great Depression, when Cheever was starting out as a writer, learning the hard way that short stories don't make for easy riches and overnight notoriety, he was thrown into a crisis of class, sexuality and masculinity, one that would not only haunt the pages of his journals, but create the thematic climate of his fiction for years to come.

After being expelled at seventeen from the Thayer Academy, a prestigious college in Braintree, Massachusetts, the young, devil-may-care Cheever spent the first years of the 1930s living in Boston. There, he cavorted with a crowd of socialist poets and writers, wore his hair long and generally felt 'lousy with adolescence'. During these Boston days, he lodged with his brother Fred, a handsome, athletic, Coca-Cola-swilling 'boy of summer' seven years Cheever's senior, in whom he sought and found protection and a sense of belonging. Fred became 'the center of [his] world', a much-needed anchor following their parents' financial and marital collapse, in 1932, when Cheever was just twenty.

Cheever's father, Frederick Lincoln Cheever, was a 'Massachusetts Yankee who looked forever like a boy', albeit one with a hacking cough and shabby ash-covered clothes. After losing his job in the shoe business – a not uncommon occurrence for men working in manufacturing in the Depression years – Frederick senior subsequently sunk his life savings into a fraudulent investment company, Kreuger and Toll, with predictable results. The company collapsed, and he lost all his money. The bank then foreclosed the mortgage on the family's grand, eleven-room Victorian home in Wollaston, Quincy, razing the property, and Frederick senior nosedived into alcoholism and defeatism. The family's ruin would have come much earlier but for the income of Cheever's ever-industrious mother. Mary Liley Cheever ran a gift shop in Quincy – selling trinkets and tea sets, painted lampshades and seashells – and redoubled her efforts there following the foreclosure.

To John, his mother's occupation was tacky and low-class. Moreover, he felt that her adopted role as business-*woman* emasculated his father. It exacerbated, Cheever thought, Frederick senior's defeatism by perverting the Yankee male ethic – which holds men as the breadwinners and women as housewives – that he so cherished. It also blemished the pride Frederick senior took in his patrilineality, which, so family legend had it, could be traced to an Ezekiel Cheever, a commanding Bostonian schoolmaster who crossed the Atlantic and landed in America in 1637. For the Cheever ancestry to end with an uxorious, penniless Frederick supported by his business-owning wife was, it seemed, indicative of just how far the men in his family had fallen.

Frederick senior had little reason to believe the Cheever male line would be restored to its former glory by his youngest son. Physically awkward and athletically disinclined, as a boy Cheever struggled to match his father's enthusiasm for the virile sports of boxing and horse-riding. He avoided team sports, too, especially baseball, that national pastime which evokes so powerful an image of the normal, all-American boy that to snub it seemed, at times, tantamount to treachery, both of country and of gender.* Cheever's diffidence was obvious to other boys in the neighbourhood, who would hoot and whistle when they spotted him raking leaves on the lawn of his family home, a public shaming that remained lodged in his memory well into middle age. So out of step was the young Cheever with his father's idea of masculinity that Frederick feared he had 'sired a fruit'. To cruelly underline Cheever's sense of estrangement, his father

---

* Years later, in fact, Cheever will turn to baseball as a kind of sobering, normalising salve to the torturous labyrinth of his secreted queer sexuality: 'play a little baseball and the Gordian knot crumbles into dust'.

often repeated that he should never have been born: Frederick was drunk on the night of his conception, and later tried to convince Mary to have an abortion. John Cheever learned from his father that he was unwanted, unplanned and abnormal.

Even still, in the wake of his parents' financial and marital woes, John's sympathies lay, for a time, more firmly with his father. Where paternal disparagement of a son along gender and sexuality lines was simply the natural way of things – where Frederick was in some sense 'right' in encouraging John to toe the traditional masculine line – a mother's emasculation of a father, to him, was unforgivable. She became the 'iron woman' whose outsized 'feminine interference' in John's life only consolidated his apparently stunted masculinity. Later in life, with a neophyte's grasp of Freudian psychoanalytic theory, Cheever will wonder if his own confused and contested sexuality couldn't be traced to his mother's apparent 'unmanning' of his father, whether his attraction to men was symptomatic of 'some uncured image of women, those creatures of morning, as predators, armed with sharp knives'.

Meanwhile, the manly successes of his older brother Fred – a 'quarterback [. . .] happy with his friends, nimble with his girls' – only stressed Cheever's masculine failings. By the time of their parents' separation, Fred had a steady job, a Dartmouth education and city lodgings. He seemed to embody that sturdy, gentlemanly, capable ideal of Yankee masculinity that their father had so valued. Given the wreckage of their parents' marriage, Fred was happy to take his little brother under his wing, and, living together in Boston, Cheever was offered a sense of security that enabled him to pursue his literary ambitions. More than this, Fred became a rock, a mentor and – despite harbouring a wayward interest in bloodlines, eugenics and fascism that perturbed John – a symbol of probity. For a time, he felt safe with Fred. No harm could befall him while his brother was at his side.

The intensity of their relationship – one which excluded all others – is mirrored in 'The Brothers', an early short story of Cheever's, which tells of two Yankee brothers whose 'devotion to each other is stronger than the love of any girl or even than their love of the world'. Like those fictive siblings, Cheever began to think of Fred not only as his brother, but his mother, father and sister, too: an unrealistic, impossible role that no one person could possibly fulfil. And so when Fred inevitably failed to live up to such expectations, the brothers' relationship pivoted from intimacy and support to a rivalry so intense it sparked, for Cheever, feelings of fratricide.

Fred's chief betrayal was romantic. He took an interest in a young woman whom Cheever was dating, and she promptly ceased relations with the breezy, long-haired would-be writer, opting instead for the ruddy, business-suited Fred, whom she subsequently married. This love triangle – as is typical of love triangles involving two men and one woman – was primarily about the relationship between the men. There was the inevitable sense of having been made a cuckold, that Fred's masculinity and virility had won out against his. But moreover, for Cheever, this romantic betrayal left him feeling that he had been jilted. Not by his girlfriend, but by Fred. Because there was something else in the brothers' relationship, a frisson which contextualises the simultaneously 'murderous' and 'loving' rivalry that brewed between them, and which explains the seamless switch from John's brotherly camaraderie to fratricidal ideation. Their attachment during the Boston years was so intimate it became, as Cheever later remarked, 'morbidly close'. When they were together they were inseparable; if Fred went away, Cheever would lie on the couch in anguish, crying with longing for his departed brother. Their relationship took on the quality of lovers, or, at any rate, John's attachment and desire for Fred resembled the lover's desire for the beloved. Later in life, John will trace the root of his frequently illicit romantic trysts with other men back to the 'love' he had for Fred. Not only that, he indicated to more than one man that his relationship with Fred, in those Boston years, had included sexual consummation.

Love and dependence, murderous rage and fraternal incestuousness: something had to give, or someone had to go. It was John, a departure enabled by his unlikely acceptance onto the fabled Yaddo's artist colony. Having unsuccessfully applied to Yaddo in 1933, he was admitted on a second try, announcing his intent to write about how 'relics of the past continually pierce the present'. He was referring, literally, to the city architecture of Boston, unaware that such a description will capture one of the essential themes of his entire creative oeuvre, what Joan Didion classified as Cheever's unique ability to chronicle the ways in which the 'twilight world of the old American middle class' – a lost world, a country of the mind – haunts the present, subsequently 'paralysing its exiles'.

And so Cheever spent the summer of 1934 among the pines, ponds and bronze-statued corridors of Yaddo, discovering there a green-tinged realm of leaf-light and tree shadow, a timeless haven sealed off from the real world and the pains of his family life, where he could meet and talk with established writers, spend all day at the typewriter – 'writing, writing, writing' – and drink gin with wild abandon. The bookcases were bedecked with marble vases depicting classical scenes, and statuettes of Roman gods and nude putti. Watercolour paintings portraying American pastoral landscapes hung on the walls, lit by the crepuscular glow emanating from pink Tiffany lampshades. It bespoke elegance, resplendence and Arcadia. For Cheever, as for many writers of his generation, Yaddo became a refuge and retreat that he would return to again and again, and where he would forge lasting friendships, as well as romances. After that first trip, returning to Boston and Fred, he knew things had changed for good. He gathered his possessions, shook his brother's hand and set off for New York. Leaving his brother was a departure that would literally haunt Cheever's dreams – and recur as a theme in his fiction – for the rest of his life.

Near-penniless in New York, but with the credentials of a Yaddo alumnus up his sleeve, Cheever set about making it as a writer, alone. He was determined to pull an entire life and career out of nothing but the 'rich air of his imagination' and leave the ghosts of the past behind him for good. He would do whatever it took to keep his head above water without sacrificing his literary ambitions, and his life in the mid- to late 1930s was itinerant and addled with money anxieties. He attended literary cocktail parties in Greenwich Village, getting soused on bathtub liquor and vomiting between handshakes with editors and authors. He worked a number of odd jobs, as a script reader, a copyeditor, and even as darkroom assistant for the photographer Walker Evans – with whom he had a brief fling, later recalling how Evans' eyes seemed specially designed to 'peer at the sexual acrobatics' of others. Some of Cheever's temporary lodgings evoked an atmosphere of New York City squalor so archetypal of the Depression era that Evans saw fit to immortalise them on camera film: 'Bedroom in Boarding House in Hudson Street, Residence of John Cheever' hangs in the Metropolitan Museum of Art to this day.

And then, of course, there was the writing. Among many abandoned projects – unfinished novels, a junked biography on Hart Crane – Cheever was producing short fiction at a prolific rate. He had acquired a literary agent, the formidable Max Lieber (who would later represent Carson McCullers for a short while). When visiting Lieber's office in the fall of 1939, to collect a cheque for a published short story, Cheever had a chance encounter that changed the course of his life: he met Mary Winternitz, his future wife. Mary – twenty-one years old, academically gifted, middle-class, with a fondness for

Henry James – was working as an unpaid intern for Lieber. She knew him to have a reputation for representing left-wing writers, and this aligned with her personal interest in pacifism and political activism. At Lieber's office, John and Mary found themselves in the elevator together. He was wearing a rainsodden overcoat several sizes too large, which made him look 'miserable' and in need of care. Cheever later recounted their meeting as though it unfolded with the inevitability of a meet cute: 'I asked her for a date. And presently married her.'

With representation from Lieber, and – as he saw it – a wife to support, Cheever became newly committed to his craft, and 1940 was a bumper year: he published fifteen short stories in reputable magazines, pocketing larger payments for his work (though still a long way from earning anything like a salary). He remained steadfastly dedicated to his work even after enlisting in the military, in 1941, and being sent to train in the South. For a time, during his Camp Gordon days, he relied on Mary as something of a go-between, asking her to type up story drafts and correspond directly with magazine editors. With so many publications under his belt, the time was apposite for a collection, and *The Way Some People Live* appeared in 1943, published by Random House, while Cheever was still stuck in Georgia.

Reviewing the collection in the *New Republic*, Weldon Kees – the literary critic and creative polymath – praised Cheever's 'acid accounts of pathos in the suburbs', but also cautioned him to avoid the superficial, shallow, episodic style he thought typical of *New Yorker* fiction. Another critic called the publication a 'more important event in American writing than most people realise', betting that Cheever would, after the war, pull off the 'ancient triple feat' of success as a short story writer, novelist and playwright. But with that brief flutter of critical interest, *The Way Some People Live* more or less vanished. It did not fling Cheever to fame after the war, and the author himself later dismissed its stories as juvenilia, destroying any copy of it he came across. The book scarcely had an impact. Besides the small matter of saving John Cheever's life.

When *The Way Some People Live* landed on the desk of a Major Spiegelgass, he was so enamoured by the sensitivity and 'childlike sense of wonder' of Cheever's writing that he deemed it 'unpatriotic' for him to remain in the infantry. In 1943, Spiegelgass arranged to transfer Cheever to the Signal Corps Motion Picture Center, in Astoria, Queens, a communications unit where writers, actors and cameramen create army training and orientation videos. Cheever was whisked away from his fellow infantrymen and spent the majority of his army days living in a cramped apartment in Chelsea, Manhattan, with Mary and their first child, Susan, who was born that year. On the back of his short stories, he went 'to war each morning on the Eighth Avenue Subway', swapping the daily rigours of camp life for a commuter's breakfast of bagels, lox and cream cheese, and getting blitzed on martinis at lunch. His former regiment, meanwhile – all those East Coast crooks and storied Southern boys – were sent to Europe, to storm the beaches at Normandy.

In addition to his work, Cheever was committed to building a successful marriage and family, those respectable 'credentials as a gentleman' which his father had failed to hold onto. As much as he coveted these credentials, however, they also exacerbated an almost unbearable – and paradoxical – inner crisis. The closer he came to attaining them, the more he felt he had to lose, and the more he felt confined. His sexuality at once seemed to threaten the coherence of this life, and was stifled by it. As he and Mary settled down to an unsteady existence as newlywed parents in post-war America, Cheever's bisexuality and its attendant lusts made him feel like an imposter, a fraud, 'abnormal'. Cheever was becoming a man estranged from his understanding of what a man should be.

Mortal Love

Spring 1948, New York City, New York

'There was something different about the boy, a nervousness, a softness and tenderness which wasn't like a man's, although he wasn't the least bit effeminate looking.'

The actress Jessica Tandy is on stage at the Ethel Barrymore Theatre, in the heart of Broadway. She is Blanche DuBois, in the original production of Tennessee Williams' *A Streetcar Named Desire*. It's the middle of the play and Blanche is bathed in soft light, wearing a faded white-grey dress, delicate as gauze. She's on a late evening date with her suitor, the downbeat bachelor Mitch. Overcome by a wave of loneliness, she begins a monologue, releasing a torrent of recollections about the man she loved and lost, the poetry-penning ghost from her past: her queer husband, Allan Grey.

'Then I found out. In the worst of all possible ways. By coming suddenly into a room that I thought was empty – which wasn't empty but had two people in it . . . the boy I had married and an older man who had been his friend for years.'

Music accompanies Blanche's monologue. It's a feverish polka tune, in a three-four time, mimicking and mocking the urgency of her speech. Blanche – swaying now, near collapse – then reveals the secret grief at the core of her character. After discovering her young husband with another man, and subsequently reviling him, he committed suicide.

'Allan! The Grey boy! He'd stuck the revolver in his mouth and fired.'

In the audience, a married couple sit side by side and watch: John Cheever and his wife, Mary, who is expecting their second child. It's a destabilising encounter for them both. Listening to Blanche's backstory unfold, Mary sees a correspondence between the marriage subplot and her own relationship, sensing that perhaps, like Allan, there is 'something different' about her husband. After all, Mary has always suspected that John Cheever isn't – as she sees it – 'entirely masculine'. So powerful an impression does *Streetcar* and Allan Grey's off-stage suicide leave on Mary that she can recall its leitmotif – that nauseating, merry-go-round-like polka – decades later. But whatever connection she intuits between Allan and her husband remains unnamed, a vague, unarticulated doubt in the back of her mind.

That night, Cheever dutifully updates his journal. He records his own impressions of Tennessee Williams' revolutionary play, dashing off a staccato list of images and themes – 'a torn evening dress, a crown, a homosexual, a beast, insanity, crimes, dim lights' – that evoked its particularly 'decadent' nature, and its atmosphere of anxiety and 'confinement'. But Cheever takes something else from *Streetcar*. Exposed to its unbridled decadence, that unflinching portrayal of sexual desire, Cheever concludes that his own writing is lacking by comparison. He finishes his journal entry with an injunction, telling himself to 'write passionately, to be less inhibited [. . .] to recognise the power of as well as the force of lust'. Recognising the force of lust isn't something Cheever struggles with. But recognition is different from reconciliation.

By the end of 1948, nearly a decade into his marriage, with a four-year-old daughter and infant son, Cheever's sexuality is precipitating an almost all-consuming inner crisis. Having a young family – a 'good wife' and 'lively children' – is the realisation of a dream he's long harboured. But the dream seems about to implode. He thinks that if anyone discovers his sexuality – worse, if he *acts* on his same-sex desires – it will all come crashing down. The anxiety that one might be discovered, or even suspected, is fed by the paranoid cultural climate – the Lavender Scare – which sought to make queer people as reviled in the public eye as political enemies of the state. This ambient atmosphere of 'homosexual panic' is felt everywhere. It is the year, Cheever will later recount, where 'everybody in the United States was worried about homosexuality'. While the men might seek to prove their heterosexuality through a renewed emphasis on 'masculine' activities – hunting, fishing and the like – Cheever imagines lonely wives wondering 'glancingly' about their husbands. The husbands themselves, meanwhile, wonder with whom they share 'a rude bed of pines'.

Cheever's crisis of sexuality isn't driven only by fear of 'discovery'. His same-sex desires also conflict with his rigid, sincerely held notions around correct masculine behaviour. His sexuality exacerbates feelings of guilt and disgust, and an acute sense that he has done something wrong. His mind, he writes, is 'stained with desire'. Repeatedly, he labels such desires as 'aberrant'. In clinical psychology, the term 'aberration' has long been fused with same-sex attraction; Freud's *Three Essays on the Theories of Sexuality* categorises homosexuality as one of several 'sexual aberrations'. By the mid-century, such language is echoed in politics and media, too: in 1947, the US Attorney George M. Fay ignited public panic by claiming that 'the sexually aberrant male' was so endemic in Washington, the nation's capital, that two such men are arrested on sex charges there every day. Cheever, writing in his journal that same year, desperately hopes that most of his own 'aberrations' belong to the past.

Walking through a public park in Manhattan, not long after his and Mary's evening at *Streetcar*, Cheever's gaze is drawn first to the body of an attractive young woman, illuminated beneath a streetlight, but also to the 'young men travelling in pairs, in threes, whooping, wrestling in the grass'. It's an image that recalls both nocturnal cruising and the Grecian manly games, the latter echoed in Cheever's wish to be told that 'the smell of laurel is not an aberration' (the winning athlete of these ancient games would be crowned with a laurel wreath). Cheever found that his wandering, roaming desires situated him in a kind of 'erotic purgatory'. This image suggests that Cheever didn't see bisexuality as a stable state, but as a waiting room for the apparent heaven or redemption offered by heterosexual love, or the inferno of same-sex love.

But Cheever's sense of legitimate masculinity isn't only under threat from his queerness. In tandem with his inner crisis of desire is a very tangible crisis of *cash*. The Cheevers, living beyond their means in the Upper East Side, have never been so poor. The rent is late, the bills are overdue and dinners are proletarian: canned tongue and eggs. They can't even afford to tip the doorman. The shame this causes Cheever is mixed with bitter disappointment; he had reason to believe, at the end of the war, that his penniless days would soon be over. In 1946 he had signed a contract with Random House to write a novel, securing a handsome advance. But that advance has dried up, and the novel remains unwritten. Pages and plots and ideas are drafted, redrafted and abandoned entirely. He's forced to beg his editor, with increasing desperation, for extension after extension, praying that the publisher won't suddenly demand the money back.

There was then a brief possibility that riches might await him on Broadway. He'd sold several of his *New Yorker* stories to a playwright, Max Gordon, who adapted them for the stage. But the resulting production, *Town House* – despite Gordon's conviction that they'd sell it to the pictures for 'a million dollars' – was a flop, closing after just twelve performances, and netting John a sum total of fifty-four bucks in royalties. To add insult to injury, a puff piece intended to celebrate *Town House*, published in the local newspaper of Cheever's hometown, described him as sharing with 'Peter Pan a look of guileless youth', of being 'shy' and 'Bambi-like'. No doubt a distressing read for a man who already felt his masculinity was under threat from all quarters.

Cheever's failure as a writer in these years is coequal with his failure as a breadwinner, and therefore his failure as a man. The only solution to this 'strain of debt', he thinks, is to write himself out of it. And so, throughout their Uptown tenancy, Cheever wakes every morning, dresses in his good suit and hat and rides the elevator with the building's well-salaried businessmen and office workers. But he doesn't decamp at the ground floor, like them. His commute ends in the building's basement – a windowless 'chamber-maid's cell' – where he's set up a makeshift writing desk. There, he hangs up his suit jacket and trousers, sits at the typewriter in undershorts and shirt-sleeves, and begins hammering at the keys with two fingers, hunt-and-pecking style, hoping to crank out short fiction that he can sell at speed.

His daily routine is productive but torturous. The writing process is tantamount to a painful, physical purge: he speaks of stories being ripped from his brain, stories sweated from his pores. He is struck with the combined terror that he has failed as a man sexually, financially and artistically. And yet, down in this dim, sweltering basement, pounding the

typewriter keys with the speed and ferocity of a spring hail-
storm, John Cheever produces some of his finest work, short
stories which will come to be regarded as masterpieces of
American fiction.

The best work that Cheever produces during his basement-
dwelling days is gathered in his second collection, *The Enormous
Radio and Other Stories* (1953), a book that represents a significant artistic development from the almost exclusively realist
fiction of *The Way Some People Live* (gruff 'army prose', as he
recalled it, spoiled with 'poorly informed snobbism'). In these
stories, Cheever begins to carve out the vivid, recurrent themes
and situations that become characteristic of his later work. The
territory is almost exclusively East Coast, veering between
Manhattan and the South Shore. The characters are the aspirant and precarious petite bourgeoise, 'shoestring aristocrats'
like him, only a whisker away from one kind of ruin or another
– married couples, new families, upwardly mobile professionals – and the superintendents and elevator men who serve
them.

Frequently, the stories are written in the third person, but
the narrator – 'like a cultivated and slightly superior museum
guide', according to one critic – becomes a character, recount-
ing the events with a 'wry yet knowing shrug'. Thematically
they are linked, as literary critic James Kelly saw it, by 'the abrasive loneliness of drifting people who uneasily tell themselves
that things are bound to work out' despite all evidence to the
contrary. Cheever's cast of characters are involved, wrote Kelly,
in an 'uneasy adjustment to [the] alien pressures' of a modern,
post-war America, desperate to maintain a veneer of social
respectability and financial security. The stories that Cheever
has begrudgingly sweat from his pores aren't just pay cheques

for the impoverished writer: they are innovative, masterful, and unlike anything in modern American short fiction.

The collection's titular story – 'The Enormous Radio', which first appeared in the *New Yorker* in 1948 – is prototypical of Cheever's new style. Set in a Manhattan apartment, a married couple, Jim and Irene – who have achieved 'that satis-factory average of income, endeavor and respectability that is reached by the statistical reports in college alumni bulletins' – find their complacent existence brought to crisis by Jim's purchasing of a new, expensive radio. The couple soon discover this modern appliance has an inexplicable fault: it transmits their neighbours' private conversations, and they are shocked to find 'demonstrations of indigestion, carnal love, abysmal vanity, faith and despair' coming from their co-tenants. Irene develops a voyeur's obsession with these private goings-on, and, having attained an intimate knowledge of the infidelities and financial woes of her neighbours, comes to see her own 'normal' existence as fragile, under threat from the superfluity of morbidities that surround her.

After begging her husband to confirm that their shared life is better than the sordid lives of their neighbours, Jim consoles her (of *course* they're happy; they have two beautiful children) and pays a mechanic to fix the radio. It's an expense the couple can scarcely afford, and it pushes Jim over the edge. He begins to verbally assault Irene with a list of grievances, and so, as the radio is repaired, their relationship breaks. 'The Enormous Radio' certainly extracts the theme of surveillance from the paranoid cultural climate instigated by the nascent Cold War. More simply, it is a story about two people forced into a new, painful encounter with a harsh reality, which they had hoped, in being satisfactorily average, they were insulated from.

Included in *The Enormous Radio and Other Stories* is another piece which builds upon this quintessential Cheever theme, in

which a protagonist is brought to crisis through a new, destabilising encounter with something alien to him. First published
in the *New Yorker* in 1951, 'Clancy in the Tower of Babel' (an
early draft of which was titled 'Clancy in Sodom') also takes
place on Manhattan's East Side. The titular James Clancy, a
middle-aged Irish immigrant who lives in a slum tenement
with his wife, loses his factory line job after sustaining an injury.
But he soon finds new employment running an elevator in a
fancy apartment building, and the couple are saved from ruin.

There, he feels alienated from the environment and its
inhabitants – all their cocktail parties, flashy jewellery and
poodles – but the assiduous Clancy soon memorises the tenants'
floor numbers, learns the ways in which each is inextricably
'secured to the world' by friends, debts and jobs, and finally
gets everything 'straight' in his mind. He begins to see himself
as the building's guardian, tasked with protecting its community. But an intruder arrives into this scene: Mr Rowantree, a
'bachelor' recently returned from a 'summer in Europe',
bywords which would signal to a cosmopolitan *New Yorker*
reader (but not to the naive, fictive Clancy) that Rowantree
may be a homosexual man.

Clancy can't get Rowantree 'straight'. The man doesn't
seem to keep any social appointments. He's good-looking,
Clancy thinks, which makes his bachelorhood all the more
confounding. After needling the mysterious Rowantree about
his private affairs, the man invites Clancy to visit his place of
work, an antiques store which he owns. There, Clancy is
perturbed by the eclectic objects kept in the dimly lit interior,
finding it troubling to think 'of the energy in a man's day being
spent in this place'. Soon after this encounter, Rowantree
brings a young man, Bobby, back to his apartment, politely
introducing him in the elevator to Clancy, who is deeply
distressed to find that on a closer look 'the young man was not

a young man' but middle-aged, and that 'the qualities and airs of youth, which a good man puts aside gladly when the time comes, had been preserved obscenely in him'.

Clancy is shocked to see Rowantree take Bobby's arm as though he were 'a pretty girl', and, with a fierce rebuff, refuses to let them ride the elevator ('I'm not taking *that* up in my car'). His dismissal of the couple sets Rowantree on the warpath. He complains to Clancy's boss, who himself threatens to fire the elevator man if he doesn't recant. Thus, James Clancy's livelihood – the wellbeing of his family – depends upon his having to adjust to working and living, as he sees it, 'in Sodom'. In Cheeveresque fashion, the narrative then pivots towards the absurd. Rowantree attempts suicide, not once, but three times in rapid succession, first by putting his head in the oven and then by trying to scarf a bottle of pills. Each time he is rescued by Clancy, who is dumbfounded by this turn of events – 'Dear Jesus!' – while the enfeebled Rowantree confides in him the source of his anguish: Bobby has left him. Though Clancy thinks that Rowantree should be placed in an insane asylum, he does everything in his power to save the man's life, only to learn, soon after these high dramatics, that Bobby has reconciled with Rowantree. What's more, the couple immediately restart their campaign to get Clancy fired.

It's a turn of events so mind-boggling to the elevator man that it plunges him into a state of literal paralysis: he becomes dangerously ill and is forced to convalesce. Some weeks later, the building's doorman visits and hands him an envelope full of cash donated by the tenants, the result of a collection organised by none other than Rowantree. This further twist provokes a vision in Clancy, in which he sees his own funeral. Among his mourners stand the queer couple, expressing their grief more vociferously than his own wife. Such a morbid reverie has an ameliorating effect, and Clancy returns to work, all the while wondering what he should say to that erratic 'pervert', Mr Rowantree. But Clancy says nothing. Rather, he resolves to pass Rowantree in silence, concluding that 'half-blindness was all that he himself knew of mortal love'.

Clancy's final, begrudging admission that both his world-view and understanding of the human heart is limited may feel like nothing more than a mandatory concession he is forced to make, in order to keep his job. When we consider exactly what Clancy relinquishes, however, in order to make such an uneasy adjustment, it appears instead to be a radical shift in character. The root of Clancy's homophobia doesn't need spelling out – he is, after all, a God-fearing middle-aged married man living in 1940s New York – but Cheever grants it depth through an aside about Clancy's academically gifted son, an inestimable source of pride for his father. One evening, Clancy is struck by the realisation that his son's face is *his* face, and that when he dies, 'some habit or taste of his would live on in the young man'. As such, there is 'no pain in death'. Clancy's faith, his belief in the afterlife (or, less generously, his need for posterity) depends on progeny, and the succession of the male line. In this light, the incursion of Rowantree and Bobby into the neat, 'straight' building represents a threat to the very foundations of Clancy's faith, the tenets that help him contend with the reality of death and the mysteries of our existence. In order to admit that he has insufficient knowledge of 'mortal love' – and there-fore to accept the possibility of love between men – Clancy has to also cede that his faith must be open to revision.

But what is it, really, about Rowantree's actions that force Clancy to make this shift? The depiction of the bachelor plays with familiar 'homosexual' literary conceits: that, like Singer and Antonapoulos in *Hunter* (a novel Cheever once said resem-bled his idea of 'excellent' modern writing) or Allan Grey in *Streetcar*, queer men either commit suicide or end up in the insane asylum. With Rowantree, however, Cheever nods to these conceits but plays them to comic rather than tragic effect. Rowantree's suicide attempts are slapstick, Clancy's grouchy talk of having 'heads examined' in the aftermath is facetious because of its unsentimental pragmatism. We are not asked to feel sympathy for Rowantree in his distress and heartbreak – it unfurls with such speed it appears to the reader, as it does to Clancy, exaggerated – and his subsequent attempts to fire the man who saved his life seem outright malicious. In other words, Rowantree is not an especially sympathetic figure, and Clancy's final change of heart isn't inspired by empathy.

It's Rowantree's inconsistent behaviour – heartbreak and reconciliation, malicious intent and guilt-ridden generosity – which complicates Clancy's 'simple worldview' and thus corrodes his adamantine belief in the corrupting nature of Sodom. At the end of the story, Clancy gazes at his wife and son in admiration, but concedes – for the first time – that others may find them unattractive and idiotic. Rowantree's queerness is what first forces Clancy into crisis and alienation; but it is Clancy's recognition of Rowantree's complexity as an individual that brings him to a new awareness of the vagaries of the human heart, and to at least begin the process of locating mortal love where he once saw nothing but Sodom. He becomes, in the end, an uneasy custodian of pluralism: an elevator man in the Tower of Babel.

It is tempting to imagine Cheever writing 'Clancy in the Tower of Babel' as a way to workshop or test his convictions around queer sexuality, to chart, through storytelling, the fault lines of his own ongoing crisis of sexual identity and argue himself towards a reconciliation between his homophobic instincts and his more progressive ones. Certainly, that porousness between fiction and autobiography is obvious in the story: Clancy's rebuke of the antiques store recalls the excessive 'feminine' interference Cheever felt his gift store-owning mother inflicted on his boyhood. Both function as symbols of emasculation. Where Clancy believes the antiques store is a 'waste of man's energy' – analogising common denunciations of gay sex or sodomy, in which energy or 'ejaculate' is *wasted* because gay sex acts are non-procreative – Cheever felt his mother's occupation castrated his father.

But it is the glanced-at character of Bobby where Cheever's lived insecurities around queer sexuality seem most clearly transposed into fiction. Bobby is a kind of prop character. His apparently garish and sad attempts to cling to the image of youth function in the narrative as little more than a screen upon which Cheever's own obsessive anxieties around 'homo-sexuality' are projected. Namely, that queerness is tantamount to repellent vanity and the so-called 'feminine' in men (Bobby is like 'a pretty girl'), and that queerness is associated with an obscene and unmanly attachment to bygone youth. Despite the somewhat open-minded, even optimistic resolution of 'Clancy', it will take Cheever the following two decades to work through these deeper anxieties in both his journals and fiction.

Although *The Enormous Radio and Other Stories* contains work that later critics found exemplary, at the time Cheever struggled to find a publisher. Random House certainly didn't want it. He ultimately settled for the independent press Funk & Wagnalls, which specialised in reference books. Cheever also had a difficult time gathering pre-publication accolades, desperately sending galleys to 'old, tender-hearted, soft-brained friends' – including Spiegelgass, whose admiration for the writer's work had, a decade prior, saved his life – in the hope of a kind word. On publication, reviews were scant and mixed. Cheever was concerned by a review in the *New York Times* which commented on the 'neurosis' evident in the work, and which concluded that fourteen Cheever stories in a row could be 'a lethal dose' for the 'too-sensitive reader'. Perhaps more damning was the response from Cheever's mother, who, on receiving a copy of the book, merely commented on her son's author photograph. If she knew that there would be an ashtray in the photo, she wrote, she would have sent a 'lovelier-looking' ashtray.

The muted reception to the book confirmed to Cheever that his career and finances had permanently plateaued, a sensation only exacerbated by his departure from New York. By the time *The Enormous Radio* was published, the Cheevers had migrated to the suburbs, where life was less expensive, cramped and hectic for a small family. They moved twenty-five miles north of their former East Side dwellings, to a small rental house in Scarborough. For Cheever – seventeen years a New Yorker – the move seemed to represent yet more failure, a kind of creative, artistic and intellectual calcification. The suburbs: this is where men go to rot. Unbeknownst to him at the time, however, the move would provide him with access to a milieu and culture that would help him build on his ideas of sexuality and masculinity in his fiction, and to create a fictive landscape that would come to be known as 'Cheever country'; one which would have a lasting impact on American literature and cultural imagination.

Freud Versus the Earth

John Cheever lifts a razor to his neck and drags the blade against his stubble. He studies himself in the bathroom mirror, trying to form a clear picture of the bleary-eyed man in the reflection. His eyes are wide and aquatic. The scent of gin carries on his breath. Steam mists the glass. An infinite hangover fogs his thoughts. Who is he, this man, this forty-four-year-old writer, father and husband? He's a lonesome figure – 'a bone, a stone, a stick, a receptacle for Gilbey's gin' – and he's been drinking far too much. Each afternoon, Cheever ritually mixes a martini. This unleashes a steady stream of cocktails which flow freely into the evening, so that by supper he's cloaked in juniper fumes. Looking at his haggard reflection, Cheever wishes that he had oriented his life around healthier, more active lines. He has an urge to hurl himself into a pool – one of his favourite pastimes – or to stride out into the countryside, where the air smells perpetually of grass and leaves. He imagines climbing a mountain, or cutting down a tree, a friend at his side.

He dips the razor into the basin and sloshes it around.

Cheever's reverie brings something else to mind, something he saw recently. A young man, white shirtsleeves rolled above the elbows, sitting idle in the shade of an apple tree. Looking at this carefree youth, Cheever had longed, desperately, to be that young again. But he knows that this yearning is for something unreal, something as 'insubstantial as smoke'. He lifts the razor to his face once more. The sound of blade against stubble is like ripping paper, like tearing a page slowly from a book. His train of thought moves from the young man under the apple tree to 'old WW' – Walt Whitman – and the long-dead poet's pursuit of 'his muscular companions'. Perhaps there is some connection, he thinks, between Whitman's rich poetical imagination and his sexual ambiguity. But the thought of the poet's possible queerness troubles him, because it 'excludes Venus'.

Cheever's hungover musings reflect the erotic purgatory he's long felt trapped in, and the 'deep hue of sexual anxiety' which now colours his experiences of even the most mundane settings: train stations, grocery stores, dinner parties. Because, wherever he goes, he's hyper-sensitive to any mention of 'homosexuality' and extremely self-conscious that he might – through some tell, some inadvertent mannerism – out himself as a 'queer'. He wants to see himself as distinct from such men, particularly his contemporaries in the literary world. That year, casting a critical eye over James Baldwin's *Giovanni's Room*, Cheever finds the novel 'repulsive' and is made 'jumpy and prudish' by its portrayal of two queer men. Likewise, he dismisses Tennessee Williams' *Cat on a Hot Tin Roof* as a play about 'queers and the usual woolgathering about this bitter mystery'. But even here, Cheever is conflicted. As a corollary to such phobic dismissals, Cheever inexplicably feels his own work is more insightful about the subject of queerness than Baldwin's. And he later describes his marriage in the exact same words he uses to decry the relationship between Brick and Skipper in *Cat*: both are 'bitter mysteries'.

Cheever is caught between extremes: condemning same-sex desire on the one hand, while believing the contradictions in his sexuality are just part of man's 'divided' and 'paradoxical' nature on the other. In this contorted, conflicted state – in which he characterises himself as 'insane, neurotic, queer, impotent and worthless' – he feels a persistent need to decode or better understand his sexuality. Indeed, his current circumstances seem to mandate it. At a time when Cheever still sees his queer desires as having the potential to destroy his marriage, family and career, there's never been more to lose. In 1956, the Cheevers – with two children and a third on the way – have settled into the suburban lifestyle. Though not wealthy, they are no longer perilously suspended above financial ruin. Their rented house is humble, but it's situated in glamorous surroundings, perched on the edge of a leafy, verdant and prosperous estate. Growing up in these foothills of the upper middle class, the Cheever children can't figure out if they're rich or poor. But for their father, being able to afford this fair-to-middling lifestyle is more than enough. It means he's close to attaining his long sought-after badge of breadwinner.

Cheever's recently struck gold, selling the rights to a short story to MGM for $25,000. Artistically things are looking up, too. Despite the critical and commercial failings of *The Enormous Radio*, his fiction – still appearing regularly in the *New Yorker* – is finally garnering the kind of acclaim he's dreamed about, earning him recognition from the National Institute of Arts and Letters as well as a Guggenheim Fellowship. What's more, he's finally finished his overdue novel. *The Wapshot Chronicle*, a picaresque family saga set in a South Shore town, centres on a near-senile patriarch, Leander – who idly wonders whether he might be a 'pederast' – and his two sons, brothers who each struggle to enter the adult world of marriage and employment. In 1958, the novel will win the National Book Award for Fiction. And yet, against this backdrop of relative success and security, Cheever's sexuality has pushed him into a dysphoric state of existential terror.

'I would like some business to transact,' he writes, 'other than asking myself: Am I real?'

This unstable sense of self-identity is intensified by marital difficulties. Though his marriage appears perfectly normal from the outside, communication between the couple has all but broken down, verbally and – more pressingly for Cheever – in the bedroom. To be sure, being permanently saturated in gin doesn't facilitate 'carnal acrobatics', he understands. But what if the booze *itself* is a symptom of his sexual aberrance? More than once, Cheever speculates in his journals that there is some connection between alcohol abuse and moral 'degeneracy'. It is not just that his sexuality poses a threat. It has now become actively corrosive, eating away at the foundations of the life he's built, eroding his marriage, transforming him into 'a small and dirty fraud, a deserved outcast, a spiritual and sexual imposter, a loathsome thing'.

But if he can better understand his sexuality, perhaps its corrosive effects can be neutralised. Where, though, is the answer? Standing in front of the mirror, razor in hand, with the echo of dripping water against white porcelain, Cheever thinks there are two places he can look. Perhaps an answer lies – mysteriously – in 'the fragrance of the natural earth'. For Cheever, the natural world is almost invariably associated with sexual potency. Ever since he was a child, engaging in the 'vices' of his adolescence – 'masturbating in the mouldy-smelling woods' – Cheever has found nature to be a virilising force, a source of succour. On almost every page of his journals there can be found transcendentalist imagery – he relishes the 'heavy succulence in the woods after the smashing rains' and the 'grass root and flower root and leathery smelling streams' – and Cheever repeatedly records fantasies about returning to a state of nude innocence in the natural world, of running naked through the woods, swimming in the nude and lying on warm rocks in the sun. And the sexual potency he finds in the natural world is specifically queer. Time and again, he conflates this pastoral, transcendentalist imagery with his same-sex lusts. He daydreams about having sex with men in ponds, beneath leaf canopies and on riverbanks, as if, just like in Whitman's poetry, the luxuriance of the natural world both fuels and gives cover for such imagined and idealised queer encounters, providing a space where the rigid limitations of modern masculinity can be suspended.

The second place Cheever thinks he can find an answer to his contorted, paradoxical sexual nature is less poetic. If not the fragrance of the natural earth, perhaps, Cheever wonders, he 'can pin the tail onto Freud'.

As a keen reader of Freud, Cheever was familiar with psychoanalytic concepts of sexuality. Indeed, he could hardly have ignored them. The entire generation, he later wrote, had to suffer years of 'prolonged psychoanalytical conversations' at dinner parties and the like. The popularity of psychoanalysis peaked in North America in the 1950s, before it met its 'paradoxical fate of mass diffusion and precipitous decline' in the 1960s. So well known was Freud's name in the cultural mindset that President Eisenhower saw fit to pay tribute to the centenary of his birth in 1956. Some of Cheever's closest friends and collaborators, including William Maxwell, his editor at the *New Yorker*, were undergoing Freudian analysis. Cheever would go to see his own Freudian 'shrink' in the early sixties, though he'll only stick it out for eight sessions and barely skirt the subject of his sexuality.

Unlike Carson McCullers, Cheever rarely spoke of himself as an 'invert'. Rather, he conceptualised his same-sex desires as a force to be reckoned with, and the men he was attracted to as temptations to be resisted. During this time of his life he only infrequently characterises himself as a 'bisexual', speaking instead about his homosexual 'instincts' and 'anxieties'. His 'erotic nature' is both 'terrifying and changeable'. In tandem, his homophobia towards other men – and himself – often manifested as a hatred of *vanity* in men. Cheever hates being caught looking in the mirror. He refers to a colleague who had been accused of homosexuality as a 'mirror-person'. Certainly, this is a variant of homophobia as a repudiation of the so-called feminine in men. But for Cheever, vanity represented something more. It suggested a narcissistic attachment to bygone youth and adolescence, a failure to mature into manhood: recall the middle-aged Bobby's 'garish' attempts to cling to his youth in 'Clancy in the Tower of Babel'. Both of these sentiments – same-sex desire as instinctive and changeable, and a connection between narcissism and homosexuality – carry echoes of Freudian language and thinking.

Freud's work precipitated a revolutionary change in conceptualisations of sexuality. But the revolution didn't come all at once, and inversion theory remained prevalent in the first decades of the twentieth century. As contemporaries, Freud and Havelock Ellis developed their theories concurrently, each acquainted with the other's work. Freud even recommended Ellis's writing to at least one of his correspondents who asked for advice on how to better understand 'homosexuality'. Despite such nods of recognition, however, their ideas were radically different. Where Ellis and inversion theorists understood sexuality and sexual desire to be the unfolding of some innate process riveted to a binary view of gender, explained as a discrepancy between biological sex and internal psychology – a man who desires other men is *internally* a woman – Freud 'doubt[ed] the very existence of such a thing as innate inversion'. He believed, instead, that each person makes a sexual 'object choice' towards which their desire is directed.

According to Freud, homosexual or same-sex object choice is just one possible outcome of each individual's unique 'psychosexual development'. And what shapes that development is complex, a 'plural history of urges, memories and emotional constellations'. This notion – that sexuality or sexual object choice can be described as something which *develops* according to a range of factors, rather than something congenital or inherited – was a radical innovation. Not only did it destabilise the characterisation of the 'homosexual' or invert as a static and totalised subject, represented in an anomalous subset of the general population, it also wrenched apart the conflation of sexuality and gender. Freud moved away from the characterisation of sexual desire as a mere conflict or confluence between one's fixed biological sex and gender, as proscribed by inversion theory, towards something altogether more nebulous and strange.

To explain psychosexual development in men, Freud hypothesised the existence of the Oedipus complex. During this ostensibly universal stage in boys' infancy, the child's sexual desire is unconsciously directed to his mother. This is accompanied by feelings of rivalry towards the father, as he is the competitor for the mother's love. Through this rivalry, the infant boy fears literal and figurative castration by the father. The so-called positive outcome or resolution of the Oedipus complex occurs when, because of this castration fear, the infant boy resolves to identify with rather than compete with the father, and sublimates his sexual instincts towards the mother into affection. The result is 'normal' psychosexual development or maturation that tends, in adult life, towards stable relationships and heterosexual object choice.

However, through case studies with several male patients, Freud came to describe 'negative' outcomes of Oedipus. Here, the boy seeks out his father's love – rather than seeing him as a rival – and identifies instead with the mother. This might occur for a multitude of complex (theoretical) reasons, but it is typically reified in the image of a passive or 'emasculated' father and domineering mother. Such negative outcomes of Oedipus lead to abnormal psychosexual development, Freud thought, and partially explain why in adulthood men might express conflict around same- and opposite-sex object choice. In this context, the notion of bisexuality as we currently understand it began to emerge. In Havelock Ellis's thinking, bisexuality problematised the simplistic view of sexual inversion, in which one's mental and physical masculine or feminine elements were mismatched. True to inversion theory's commitment to the gender and sexuality binary, inversion theory could only explain bisexuality through 'psychosexual hermaphrodism'; a bisexual is psychologically intersex, so to speak. The bisexual is not an invert, but psychologically possesses both sexes. Freud liberated bisexuality from this formulation: bisexuality comes to refer to those who have a conflicted or ambivalent sexual object choice.

Another crucial tenet of Freud's thinking around sexuality was the concept of narcissism. As with many of his ideas, its significance and meaning waxed and waned across his writings. Freud eventually came to configure narcissism as another transient stage in psychosexual development, where an infant temporarily takes themselves as the love object, before directing their desire to 'other' object choice. In Freud's earlier works, however, he uses narcissism almost analogously with 'homosexuality', hypothesising that men who exhibit same-sex object choice underwent short-lived and intense identification with their mother in childhood, after which they 'take *themselves* as their sexual object', proceeding from this 'narcissistic basis' to seek out 'a young man who resembles themselves and whom *they* may love as their mother loved *them*'. Appended to this observation, Freud emphasised the radical divergence between his ideas and aims, and those of typical inversion theory. 'Psychoanalytic research,' he noted, 'is most decidedly opposed to any attempt at separating off homosexuals from the rest of mankind [. . .] it has found that *all* human beings are *capable of making* a homosexual object-choice.'

Though not as vocal as Havelock Ellis in calling for social and judicial tolerance towards the 'invert' or 'homosexual', Freud rarely cast an explicit moral judgement on homosexual versus heterosexual object choice. Nevertheless, there is implicit in his thinking, both around Oedipus and narcissism, a suggestion that homosexual object choice represents a thwarted or arrested psychosexual development which is in some sense abnormal, regressive and immature. Additionally, the very idea of psychosexual development – sexuality as something which emerges as opposed to being innate and fixed – opened the doors to the notion that homosexuality could be 'cured', that, through therapy, a patient's desire could be reoriented to the 'correct' or normal heterosexual object choice.*

For these reasons, Freudian terminology was rarely utilised by well-educated queer men and women in the interwar years who wished to advocate for tolerance, or better understand their sexuality, and many – like Carson McCullers – continued to cast their sexual selfhood in the language of inversion. Additionally, where many of Freud's writings were based on his psychoanalytic interpretation of case studies, Ellis's work – inspired by the methodology of John Addington Symonds – utilised direct interviews with so-called inverts, allowing these men and women to express themselves in their own language, and on their own terms. Queer readers were more likely to recognise their personal experiences

---

* Many mid-century Freudians – besides Kubie – also believed homosexuality could be 'cured'. Charles W. Socarides, for instance, cast 'homosexual' men as addicts: they 'hope to achieve a "shot" of masculinity in the homosexual act [. . .] they must have their fix'. This curious interpretation characterises same-sex behaviour between men as a compulsive, remedial redoubling of manhood, a line of thought also concurrent with the (homophobic) notion of the homosexual-as-narcissist.

in such testimonies. But the profession of psychoanalysis – Freud's theories and associated therapeutic techniques – grew steadily as a movement in the USA and Britain, and by the 1950s had all but supplanted inversion theory. By comparison, Ellis's work came to appear both redundant and severely lacking. He had merely *identified* the so-called sexual invert. He hadn't *interpreted* anything. As one of Ellis's biographers remarked, Ellis may have been a pioneer who 'ploughed the fields in the valley', but Freud 'surveyed the shattered detritus of the nineteenth century from a summit only he could ascend'.

The rise of psychoanalysis in the US was partially expedited by the military's unprecedented introduction of psychiatric exemptions into the draft, which resulted in widespread diffusion of Freudian ideas among medical professionals (epitomised in the Sexual Perversion amendment, penned way back in the early forties by Tennessee Williams' one-time analyst Dr Lawrence Kubie, who was a staunch Freudian). But the psychoanalysis of the post-war years embodied a distinctly American appropriation of Freud's theories, shaped by (and in turn shaping) a cultural ideology that evolved in the 1950s. This is the decade of the baby boom. The decade of extraordinary economic prosperity. In America, divorce rates plummeted. Fertility rates skyrocketed. The suburbs grew and grew, with new families – like the Cheevers – migrating in droves from the cities. Traditional class differences were beginning to erode through sudden, mainstream access to consumer goods. In the Depression years, class and community had been key, structuring social forces. But in this newly prosperous post-war world, the nuclear family took precedence: a heterosexual married couple who live together alone (as opposed to living in multigenerational family households) with their children.

Consequently, in psychoanalysis, the cohesion of the domestic family realm took on heightened significance. In America, the profession took a decidedly conservative turn, becoming ideologically invested in sanctifying heterosexual love and marriage. Senior analysts began to stress a new ethic of maturity and adulthood, qualities deemed necessary for maintaining a successful nuclear family. For men, this implied a 'rejection of the homosocial, adolescent world of "mates" or "buddies"' – male relations inscribed during the war – in order to meet the 'responsibilities of marriage'. The implication is that positive, affirming homosocial bonds between men are juvenile, incommensurate with the 'adult' task of being a father and family man, and that maturity in men is analogous with successful heterosexual relationships. Such an ethic is an analogue or extension of the Freudian suggestion that homosexual object choice indicates immaturity or arrested development: both represent a turning back, stunted growth, a kind of infantilism. Both run in opposition to the supremacy of the nuclear family, which demands mandatory heterosexuality.

Cheever – a married family man, breadwinner and certified tenant of suburbia – was attempting to make sense of his queer sexuality while saturated in this cultural ideology. Unsurprisingly, he was aware of the Oedipus paradigm, wondering if his same sex desires represented an urge to flee from that 'uncured image' of women carrying sharp knives, instilled in him by his apparently domineering mother and 'emasculated' father. But it is the notion of immaturity and infantilism in men that haunts him most. He loathes vanity and narcissistic behaviours in other men, and in himself, because it represents regression, arrested development, a return to the adolescent, all of which might be symptomatic or symbolic of the Freudian homosexual: an inappropriate attachment to youth is a conduit for sexual aberrance, or it carries the potential for sexual aberrance.

Cheever writes about this particular anxiety repeatedly in his journals. In one entry, he imagines having sex with a man in a lake or pool, before telling himself that such fantasies represent 'an *infantile* country of irresponsible sexual indulgence' that have nothing to do with the real 'facts of life'. More succinctly, he writes of homosexuality as a false 'promise of recaptured youth'. Cheever's feelings for his older brother Fred are related to this conflation of adolescence and homosexuality: his departure from Fred, when he was still a young man, left him with 'a lack, a longing [. . .] a sexual tristesse' that was never repaired, as though his and his brother's severance, at Cheever's own hand, was his declaration that 'morbid closeness' between men belongs to a particular time in a man's life, to youth and adolescence.

Certainly, Cheever feels that his sexual desire for men is incompatible with his desire to raise a family: the former is irresponsible, the latter is adult. Utilising classical symbols, he occasionally figures these divergent desires as a conflict between 'Venus' – the Roman goddess of love – and Ganymede. In Greek myth, the divine hero Ganymede, an adolescent boy, was the most beautiful of all mortals. His relationship to the god Zeus exemplified the ancient Greek custom of pederasty, a romantic-mentor relationship between an older man and an adolescent male. Where Cheever classifies his love for Venus as 'inalterable, pure' on the basis that he can 'inseminate' her, the adolescent Ganymede, he thinks, would only provide him with opportunity to 'demean' himself.

Cheever didn't only express and explore these ideas in his journals. As ever, there is a porousness between his fiction and journal-keeping, and in the short fiction he produces through-out the 1950s and into the early 1960s he creates and refines a recurrent fictive character: a married, adult man haunted and tantalised by the idea of the past, a man who has a narcissistic attachment to bygone youth and adolescence.

The Last Swimmer of Summer

The short stories Cheever produces in the mid-fifties and through to the early sixties are published in a trio of collections which, bit by bit, cement his critical reputation as a master of the form: *The Housebreaker of Shady Hill & Other Stories* (1958), *Some People, Places and Things That Will Not Appear in My Next Novel* (1961) and *The Brigadier and the Golf Widow* (1964). In these collections, Cheever perfects that blend of realism and lyricism, social commentary and myth, that enabled critics to compare him to (the otherwise antithetical) Anton Chekhov and Ovid. In these stories there's a shift in landscape from New York and into the leafy commuter towns of New England, fictive neighbourhoods, populated by nuclear families. It's a world where the streets are drenched in gold-green tree-shadow and sprinklers throw mist over immaculate lawns, perfuming the air with grass scent. Wives tend to their asters and rose bushes in unison and organise charity galas. After long days in the office, husbands anaesthetise themselves in bars on Madison Avenue, before catching the express train from Grand Central Station home in time for family dinner. The shared social universe takes place in parents' evenings at preparatory schools, rounds of golf at country clubs, and – most prominently – an endless roster of cocktail parties, one fading into the next. Waking life is therefore glassy-eyed, stained with booze or else submerged in the murky half-light of a lingering hangover.

Occasionally, though, the light breaks through, bringing new clarity to the lives of these sedated suburbanites. What is revealed to them, in such moments, tends towards one of two extremes: their world either appears beautiful or deplorable. A cornucopia promising a magnificent and meaningful existence, or a wasteland of moral and emotional paralysis, its material abundance a thin veil for infidelities, insanities and paranoias. These opposites reflect Cheever's bifurcated opinions about his own life in the suburbs, an existence that he finds alternately 'unbearable or transcendent'. Within this *mise en scène*, Cheever situates his haunted men: men who, propelled by the ideology of their time, find themselves coveting the ambrosia of suburbia while loathing it; cultivating a mature, adult life, while feeling confined and trapped; forever turning back to the past and their youth as a means of escape.

There is Gee-Gee, the married, alcoholic father of 'The Scarlet Moving Van', whose very name is a relic from the past: in his college days, his athleticism and beauty earned him the sobriquet 'Greek God', hence Gee-Gee. So intolerable, however, does he find the social mores, aspirational ethic and consumer comforts of the adult suburbia where he and his wife live that he can't help but make a pariah of himself. Gee-Gee gets soused at dinner parties, stripping to his underpants, smashing plates, insulting all his neighbours ('What a goddamned bunch of stuffed shirts!') and storming into the night, leaving his wife, Peaches, to ineffectually cry, *Come Back! Come Back!* It is as though, Cheever's museum-guide narrator tells us, Peaches is trying to call back the lost 'sweetness of a summer's day', to reclaim the youthful Greek God from 'ruin'.

Then there is Cash Bentley of 'O Youth and Beauty!', another married, alcoholic father. Cheever developed this story not long after a trip to the Metropolitan Museum of Art, where, viewing the Greek and Roman statues of lithe young men, he was struck by the realisation that it is men, not women, who lose their beauty as they age. Cash, a former track star self-conscious about his 'thinning hair', ends every Saturday night cocktail party in Shady Hill in the same way. Tanked on whisky, he rearranges the furniture, demands the host fire a pistol out of the window, and, not unlike the booze-fuelled antics of Brick Pollitt, demonstrates his athletic prowess through a solo 'hurdle race', vaulting himself over chairs and tables in a cocksure display of vigour and muscularity. Cash maintains this quality of 'stubborn youthfulness' as an ineffectual bulwark against the 'unbeautiful facts of life' that characterise his day-to-day: taxes, the demands of raising children, the 'elastic in waistbands', marital quarrels.

During one such hurdle race, Cash falls and a doctor is summoned to set his broken leg. Hobbling around on a crutch and prevented from his weekly ritual, Cash's world appears newly banal.* His neighbours are ingratiating. They look older than before. Even the roses, cut by his wife, smell putrid rather than fragrant. One night, sitting miserably alone at home, the sounds of a garden party – a young people's party – pour through the window, instilling him with a painful yearning. He was once a young man, he thinks. He had been 'a hero'. Why must he now feel like 'a ghost of the summer evening'? Once his leg is healed, Cash makes a final bid for lost youth via

---

* Cash and Brick – athletes-turned-alcoholics, obsessed with lost youth, who both break a leg drunkenly vaulting hurdles – bear such a superficial similarity one wonders about influence. Cash first appeared in the *New Yorker* (1953). An early version of Brick – where he is compared to a summer's day and described as a man who has 'not yet lost the slim grace of his youth' – predates this, in Tennessee Williams' short story 'Three Players of a Summer's Game' (*New Yorker*, 1952). However, Brick didn't appear with his broken ankle and crutch until *Cat* (1956). Perhaps Cash derives from Brick; but perhaps Brick's crutch derives from Cash.

his prized hurdle race. He rearranges his furniture and hands a pistol to his wife, who – unfamiliar with fire-arms – accidentally shoots Cash dead, mid-vault.

This theme, a man's attachment to bygone youth and beauty which, incommensurate with the adult world, is either vector for annihilation, in Cash's case, or indicative of ruin, as in Gee-Gee's, forms the basis for what has come to be Cheever's most famous and widely anthologised short story. 'The Swimmer', first published in the *New Yorker* in 1964, is part-Homeric odyssey in miniature, part-fever-dream. Its protagonist, Ned Merrill, is yet another married suburban father who possesses the 'especial slenderness of youth' despite no longer being young. Like Cash and Gee-Gee, Ned 'might have been compared to a summer's day, particularly the last hours of one'. Idling by a green swimming pool on a hot Sunday with his wife and their hungover compatriots, Ned has a vision: his neighbours' pools form a chain, a 'quasi-suburban stream' or river, meandering through the county back to his own house in Bullet Park. For Ned, who believes himself to be 'a legendary figure', the vision of the river is irresistible, and its significance obvious. He will – he must – swim home. There, his four beautiful daughters will be waiting, playing tennis . . .

And so Ned, our ersatz hero, departs on his odyssey. Hurling himself into the first pool, he finds that being held by its green water is a natural state, one that could only be improved by swimming in the nude. Like Private Williams of McCullers' *Reflections*, whose solo, naked sojourns to the woods represent a rejection of the army camp's artificial and fiercely prescribed hierarchy, Ned Merrill's botanical immersion in the elements is an attempt to reject the social laws of suburbia, its incapacitating, mandatory paralysis, and return to an imagined primitivism. Ned wants to feel water and light on his bare flesh. He wants to become fresh and aquatic. Through this journey, he hopes to transform the chain of pools into a *real* river, and so transform the suburban into the sylvan, a terrain of natural exuberance in which this symbol of male beauty – a nude, lithe, graceful, strong swimmer – predominates.

But as Ned progresses, pool by pool, the true nature of his journey is brought into focus. His neighbours do not cheer him on in his epic quest. Some look upon him strangely, others are outright rude. Their increasing hostility is echoed by the environment: what was a glorious summer's day has been blighted by a storm, stripping leaves from the branches. Autumnal fragrances fill the air. One of the swimming pools has been unseasonably drained. Ned must cross a busy highway, where drivers leer and hurl trash at him. Approaching the end of his journey, Ned dives into a cerulean pool belonging to a former mistress. He had ended that affair, we learn, with casual callousness. 'Good Christ,' his past lover remarks, when Ned explains the nature of his quest, 'Will you ever grow up?' This remark deals the final blow, and at the end of his swim, Ned's strength leaves him. Confused, crestfallen and exhausted, he begins to cry. Limping to his house in Bullet Park – his final destination – he finds it empty, locked up and dilapidated. His daughters are not there, nor his wife. The seasons have changed in an afternoon. He is alone.

What are Cheever's haunted men trying to flee from? The responsibilities of fatherhood and husbandhood, those twin duties that the culture's family-centred ideology demands of its adult men? The haunted men certainly embody a recoil from that conservative, psychoanalytic ethic which predominated in the 1950s: men whose regressive 'turning back' and adulation of bygone adolescence not only runs counter to the tenet of 'maturity' deemed necessary to sustain the heterosexual dyad and meet the responsibilities of the nuclear family, but represents a conscious desire to escape it. And just as that ethic was itself analogous to psychoanalytic ideas of abnormal sexual development, in which homosexual object choice is also some-how 'regressive', Cheever instils his haunted men, very consciously, with characteristics that embody his personal anxi-eties around queer male sexuality. Gee-Gee, Cash, and Ned are all *vain* men, their attachment to their youth and former beauty is narcissistic: they are so-called 'mirror people'. All signifiers, in Cheever's thinking as well as in psychoanalytic nomenclature, for arrested or abnormal psychosexual development, itself an indicator for 'homosexuality'. Indeed, Cheever wondered in his journal whether or not his own 'persistent clinging to summer when summer is over' – his need to always be the literal 'last swimmer of summer', recklessly hurling himself into pools and ponds in cold weather – was narcissistic.

Yet, Cheever's haunted men are dissimilar to the caricatured Bobby, that 'out' homosexual. Bobby's superficial appeals to youth are depicted as garish. More importantly, they are *girlish*; he is treated like 'a girl'. This is the key difference between Bobby's vanity and the vanity of Cash, Gee-Gee and Ned. Bobby is effeminate – a phobic projection of Cheever's feeling that to be an effeminate man is to be queer, and vice versa. The haunted men, meanwhile, are given a sense of grandeur and stature. The ways in which they mourn or attempt to reclaim lost youth are, despite some absurdist turns, tragic, even heroic. And their bygone youth and beauty is, or was, decidedly masculine: they are compared to athletes and Greek gods, the literal archetypes of muscular male beauty. Their veneration of this image of the male body, and their attempts to (re)claim it for themselves, symbolises a rejection of the 'feminine' in men. This is also mirrored by their rejection of domestic settings, so frequently typified as a 'feminine' domain. Cash wants to trans-form the domestic into an amphitheatre, a place of manly games, while Gee-Gee sees the domestic as something to malign and denigrate, and a place where he can embarrass and then flee from his wife.

But for Ned, his desire to reclaim lost youth runs deeper. It is not ambient existential angst and taxes that he needs to flee from. Ned's life is already a ruin. His efforts to 'return' to his past through swimming home – something that begins as a legendary quest, in which he is emblematic of 'youth, sport and clement weather', and ends with his physical enfeeblement – represent an effort to numb himself on nostalgia. It's a nostalgia which reaches far back beyond his former suburban existence to something else: a dream of pastoral primitivism, that transcendentalist zone of luxuriant elements, where the youthful male body and male beauty is somehow sustained, held in suspension by green water. Like Private Williams, that nude nature boy sunning himself beneath pines, Ned Merrill's sought-after unity with the natural world constitutes an attempt to claim an imaginary realm in which the youthful male body is both sovereign and liberated from any and all social strictures.

For Cheever, the natural world and its luxuriance – that fragrance of the earth – so often became, in his journals, a queer ecology, a source of virility and an environment which could fuel and permit same-sex romance. It recalls, so clearly, the dreamed-up homosocial utopia of Whitman's 'Calamus', which emerges from the fragrant pond waters and dripping pines of an imagined pastoral. 'In the woods, too, a man casts off his years,' wrote Ralph Waldo Emerson, the transcendentalist visionary and forebear to Whitman, whose writing Cheever was well acquainted with. 'In the woods is perpetual youth . . .' And Cheever, as his contemporary John Updike remarked, was nothing if not a latter-day 'transcendentalist'.

The genius of 'The Swimmer' is that it can be read as an allegory in multiple ways. Part-dream, part-nightmare, the story works as a metaphor for the end of the 1950s, that decade of American fecundity: what looked, through the misty veil of sprinkler spray, to be a material paradise on earth is nothing but a mirage. And once the gin fog burns off, this suburban world and its values are as empty and dilapidated as Ned Merrill's house. New cultural forces lie in ambush, ready to raze the ideological foundations of the post-war decade: the threat of nuclear apocalypse, civil unrest, free love and the never-ending war in Vietnam, which smears every household's new colour TV screen with the blood of young conscripted men. The conventions of polite, realist *New Yorker* fiction are ill-equipped to contend with such rapid and bewildering cultural changes. Hence Cheever's hallucinogenic narrative device, where the seasons change in a single afternoon,* which perturbed critics on publication ('weird' and 'sinister' were words used to describe Cheever's surrealist turn).

Then there is the evergreen correlation between Cheever's journals and his fiction: Ned Merrill's delirious, delusional journey and subsequent lucidity resembles an alcoholic's inflated sense of grandeur, before the booze runs dry and reality bites. More simply, 'The Swimmer' represents everything Cheever knew he was at risk of destroying as he sank further into his addiction.

---

* The idea of a chain of pools was not a device, however. An equivalent 'suburban stream' existed in Cheever's neighbourhood, as he was keen to point out to interviewers in his later years ('get your trunks on and I'll show you').

The Valley

September 1971, Sing Sing, New York

The writer stands in front of a group of prisoners, framed by a yellowed American flag. John Cheever – sixty years old, his mind and body saturated with alcohol – is teaching creative writing to a group of forty felons, in the Sing Sing Correctional Facility. This maximum-security prison, colloquially known as The Big House, is a stone's throw from the writer's home. At the start of the sixties, despite his editor's admonition that 'freelance writers should not own property', Cheever and Mary managed to cobble together enough cash for a down payment on a house in Ossining, Westchester County, a suburban settlement on the banks of the Hudson unusual for its socioeconomic diversity. The grand, semi-dilapidated stone colonial property they purchased – named *Afterwhiles* – is set in a five-acre estate. Through the estate's towering elm trees and pines poured shafts of light, bathing the lush gardens and lily-studded pond in a glow 'the colour of artificial lime drink'.

This idyll, however, has turned sour. The pond is silted up and swampy, wisteria chokes the trees and the garden's stone walls are crumbling. *Afterwhiles* was too much property to take on. For Cheever, the estate is a visual metaphor of sorts, both for his conflicted sense of class – a shoestring aristocrat at home among decaying grandeur – and a symbol for the overbearing weight that the domestic, family realm represents for him. In his estate, he finally embodied the patrician, capable, gentlemanly ideal of Yankee masculinity his father had hammered into him as a child. The extent of what he had to lose is now ineffable. On the other hand, the trap he has set himself, as joint homeowner of this gargantuan property, feels inescapable. He prefers to call the estate *Meanwhiles*.

And then there is Sing Sing, an unavoidable fact of life in Ossining. Not a metaphor for entrapment or confinement, but its literal embodiment. The prison illustrates, in Cheever's view, 'our world's inability to produce a workable concept of justice and penance'. Walking along the railway tracks that hug the banks of the Hudson, Sing Sing's domineering watchtowers can be seen, in silhouette, against the skyline. Cheever's children, playing by the river, could even make out the shadows of guards stalking the prison walls. In 1970, having learned that there was a shortage of teachers in the facility – something like half a dozen for several thousand inmates – Cheever volunteered his services. He wanted to conduct a course in writing, 'in making sense of one's life by putting down one's experiences on a piece of paper'. But it didn't take long for him to realise that his aspirations to be a 'fucking do-gooder' – to parachute into this world of convicts and expose them to the apparently illuminating force of literature – were misplaced. Passing through five sets of clanging iron gates, escorted by hostile guards into a room of murderers and thieves, he felt side-eyed and surveilled, conscious that he stank of gin, petrified that the prisoners might think his accent pompous.

During Cheever's tenure at Sing Sing, the Attica Uprising rages further west in New York State. Over a thousand male inmates take control of Attica Prison for four days in September 1971, holding guards hostage in a protest against inhumane conditions and systemic racial discrimination. The uprising ends in violent suppression: the slaughter of inmates, followed by illegal torture, carried out by law enforcement. To say that tensions are high during Cheever's teaching hours at Sing Sing is an understatement, and one of his students is quick to point out that Cheever – whose face had, by this point, graced the cover of *Time* magazine – would make a great hostage. Nevertheless, night after night, Cheever walks through those gates, explaining to his students that 'narrative is a synonym for life', workshopping their creative writing, and teaching a curious selection of literature (including Machiavelli, a 'cool motherfucker', in the eyes of one student inmate). Showing up in spite of Attica, Cheever earns his students' admiration. And, much like those Southern boys back in his army days, he comes to admire these inmates. Some have 'faces of exceptional goodness'. Others are 'comely'. All are 'great company'. Should an uprising occur at Sing Sing, he thinks, he'll side with the inmates over the guards in a heartbeat. This teaching gig, after all, has opened his eyes to the reality of prison life, and he now feels that the very notion of incarceration is an unspeakable horror, 'the blasphemy of men creating and building, stone by stone, hells for other men'.

Cheever becomes particularly close to one of his students, Donald Lang, a wiry, black-haired convict in his early thirties, in jail for armed robbery. Lang first dismissed Cheever as a phony, but soon came to admire his 'balls', and when he successfully got parole – aided by a letter of recommendation from Cheever – the two became tight companions. Cheever even put him up at *Afterwhiles*. There, Lang talked at length about his prison life, willingly providing Cheever with environmental details and knowledge of prison's sexual codes – where the 'dynamism between youth and age' is as powerful as the 'dynamism between men and women' – that would provide the scaffolding for Cheever's next, most successful novel,

Falconer (1977), in which he openly portrays same-sex love between men in his fiction in a light that he would previously have deemed unimaginable.

Much like Tennessee Williams, Cheever often felt that his life was determined by three interrelated forces: sex, work and alcohol. From the mid-1960s until the late 1970s – by which point he had been committed to the Smithers Alcoholism Unit in New York, a drying-out facility that finally made him sober – these forces were spinning out of control. Work is torturous, never-ending and laced with professional jealousies. He drinks himself into memory loss, and frequently loses his balance. And his sex life is far from monogamous. His infidelities with women – most prominently, a long-lasting love affair with the Hollywood actress Hope Lange – become known among the family, and were even utilised by Cheever as emotional ammunition during the never-ending wargames of his and Mary's marriage. After so many years worrying and wool-gathering about his queer lusts in the pages of his journals, his infidelities also now include men. These, however, he keeps hidden from his family.

In late September 1966, having recently quit therapy, Cheever returns to Yaddo. It is an unusually warm autumn. There, among the peach-coloured maples of the estate, he meets Ned Rorem, a handsome composer a decade his junior. Rorem is openly queer (he even wondered in his journals what a Kinsey-style report on homoerotic behaviours among male composers might reveal). A week after his arrival, Cheever knocks at Rorem's door, cradling a bottle of scotch. The nervous writer then proceeds to tell all about his unsuccessful psychoanalysis, how he equates 'writing' with 'fucking,' and why this – apparently – makes him better than his contemporaries. Drunk, Cheever insists Rorem meet him the following day at the swimming pool, which Cheever – now a board member at Yaddo – had convinced them to build several years earlier.

Cheever's first impressions of Rorem reflect the anxieties around same-sex desire he's long harboured, although there's a shift in tone away from self-repudiation to outright fear. His feelings are vertiginous, amounting to a 'terrifying erotic chaos'. Just a year prior to their encounter, another composer and fellow Yaddo alumnus, Marc Blitzstein, had been murdered in Martinique by three sailors, after apparently propositioning one of them. In his early visits to the artist's colony, Cheever had enjoyed Blitzstein's company (and the company of Yaddo's other notable queer composers, such as Aaron Copeland and David Diamond, the third player in one of Carson and Reeves McCullers' love triangles). Blitzstein's grim fate – violent death at the hands of other men – seemed to prove to Cheever that acting on queer desire amounts to annihilation, that sexual relations between men are a flirtation with death. This was first made clear to him when trying to write that biography on Hart Crane, all those years ago, whose demise – at least precipitated by homophobic violence at the hands of sailors – eerily mirrored Blitzstein's.

Such is the extent of Cheever's conflation of queer sexuality with death in these years that any man he is attracted to seems to threaten his life. A young man in sneakers, glimpsed in the corridor of a museum, appears to Cheever as his 'executioner' – yet how disorientating and cruel that the 'executioner mask may conceal a comely face'. These men signify 'strangeness, a sort of erotic darkness' that destroys the 'sensible strictures of society'. Once these sensible strictures are removed, the 'infections of anxiety and in particular the fear of death' seep in. Even still, Cheever searches for a means of rupturing this fatalistic thinking. Speculatively describing a long view of western sexual history, he postulates that 'in agricultural and maritime societies homosexuality [was] self-destructive' because such societies depended on an increasing population. And yet, there were historical periods where society 'enjoyed a forthright robustness that allowed us to see the depth and beauty of the love men feel for one another'. Here, he is possibly envisaging ancient Greece and its custom of pederasty. But all this philosophising misses the most simple solution to stymie the fear of death brought about by queer desire. Cheever wonders if that fear might be conquered by running naked through the woods.

Yaddo, a place completely removed from the 'facts of life', seems to offer an environment devoid of the fear that stalks Cheever in his day-to-day. The verdant estate and neoclassical decor – all those marble putti and statuettes of nude men playing lyres – are evocative of that pastoral imaginary he repeatedly conflates with queer desire. And this isn't only an instinctive impression. Under its director Elizabeth Ames, Yaddo has become known for its political and social progressivism, welcoming queer men and women, as well as writers with communist sympathies, under its roof.* And so Cheever and Ned begin a raucous, scarcely concealed love affair during that golden autumn, possibly the first consummated same-sex encounter Cheever has had since Walker Evans. They make love under the ping-pong table. Cheever jokes at the double entendre legible in the bronze plaque in the music room, dedicated to the philanthropist who had helped found the artist's

---

* In 1949, when a campaign was waged by a rabid Robert Lowell to have Ames removed as director on grounds of being a 'Red', Cheever, allergic to McCarthyism and its acolytes, helped lead a successful campaign in support of Ames.

colony, which reads: 'George Foster Peabody: Lover of Men'. And he confides in Ned. He tells him about the few sexual experiences he's previously had with other men. He tells him that his experience of sexual orgasm is always accompanied by visions of sunlight, and flowers.

But their affair seems to end the moment Cheever leaves Yaddo, as though that verdant estate really was imaginary. Upon leaving, a return to 'normality' has to follow, and Cheever feels he must resume his performance as an old-fashioned, patrician gentleman, a father and long-suffering husband. Arriving back to *Afterwhiles*, Cheever has a dream in which he makes love to a woman who resembles Venus, on the banks of a river. During their coupling, she proceeds to shape-shift into Adonis. Waking, Cheever returns to his long-held quasi-Freudian prejudice, noting that same-sex pursuits are an 'unsuitable pastime for a grown man'. The die, however, has been cast, and though he continues to keep his queerness a secret from his family, he needs to find expression for it beyond the pages of his journals. His latter years are full of relationships with other men, relationships that often resemble – his daughter later recalled – 'a series of younger male protégés'.

When Cheever briefly teaches at the Iowa Writers' Workshop in 1973, he becomes infatuated with one of his young male students, Allan Gurganus (who didn't reciprocate his romantic interest, finding that Cheever came on to virtually any student he found attractive, man or woman). His attraction to Allan is typically ambivalent, mixed with inquisitiveness and disgust: the openly gay lifestyle that Allan led is off-putting, indicative of an 'erotic cult that counts so on beauty'. Yet he is also mesmerised by it, receiving long correspondence from Allan about the mores of the San Francisco gay scene, while writing reams of love letters to him in return.

And then, in the years following Cheever's sobriety, he begins a long-term relationship with the young writer Max Zimmer, also a former student. Their affair is complicated by an intense mentor-mentee power dynamic, one which often perplexes Max, who also seeks creative advice and guidance from Cheever. Despite Cheever's confused declarations of love – sometimes he describes his feelings for Max as a profound romance, other times as a 'back-slapping friendship' – the young writer often feels that Cheever's interest is purely sexual. Like Donald Lang, Max also becomes a lodger at *Afterwhiles*, though none of the Cheever family know – or none want to know – the true nature of the men's relationship.

Such furtiveness engendered feelings of paranoia in Max. Strangely, however, for a man who had spent his life in a cringing position of guilt imagining the destruction that his queer desire might wreak upon his married life, Cheever appears increasingly laissez-faire about hosting his lover in the family home. Living vicariously through his young lover, Cheever foists scotch on him; they dine and talk about writing; then chase intimacy in the woods. Does such risk-taking speak to a subconscious need to come out, or is it the behaviour of a man who, after so many years successfully 'passing', believes he simply couldn't be *found* out? One can only speculate. Despite the intensity and longevity of his affair with Max, Cheever nevertheless continues to feel relief that his protégé-cum-lover doesn't show any characteristics of the sexual 'irregular'. That is, Max is not legible as an effeminate queer to others.

It is as though the 'manliness' of their relationship is, for Cheever, a necessary cover to conceal from the world what is really going on, while also being the only way he can legitimately cultivate and accept same-sex romance. It's a paradox, a way to square the circle: men can care for other men, men can be close, physically and emotionally with other men, men can have sex with other men, but only when it is 'forthright and robust', only when it is 'manly'. In order to accept his sexual iridescence, his homosexual instincts, his bisexuality – however Cheever characterises it – and not become estranged from his sense of what a man should be, he needs to find a way to deliquesce his understanding of masculinity and queerness, to bleed one into the other. 'How can this man,' Cheever wonders in a cryptic journal entry, possibly referring to himself, 'genuinely male and solid, kiss another man with such tenderness and pleasure, and plan to love the young woman with the long hair? It seems quite possible without any loss.' It seems possible to Cheever only in virtue of that 'genuine' male stolidity. His compromise is to ratify queer sexuality only if it champions a totalised concept of masculinity, one completely cleansed of the so-called 'feminine' in men, a concept of masculinity hard and clean as marble.

This logic, these agonising mental gymnastics, certainly runs through Cheever's fictional depictions of same-sex love and desire in his later works. Among the freely associative medley of vignettes that constitute his late short story 'The Leaves, the Lion-Fish and the Bear' (1974), there is a depiction of two putatively heterosexual men – a hitchhiker, Stark, and white-collar worker, Estabrook, both married, and strangers to one another – who meet and have a fulfilling night of anonymous sex in a motel room. Their coupling is couched in the language of backslapping and comradeship. The men revert to the 'makeshift sexual horseplay of adolescence', they 'joke amiably about one another's performance'. The following morning they bid each other goodbye at the gas pumps and return to their wives, never to meet again. But something deeper pulses through this depiction of comradely queerness, something of greater consequence than sexual fulfilment or exploration.

After their lovemaking, near dawn, Stark – in deep sleep – embraces Estabrook as though 'he were a lifesaver that would keep him from drowning'. In response, Estabrook – though he 'felt he looked onto some revelation of how lonely and unnatural man is' – returns the embrace, 'put his arms around the stranger' and felt 'joy'. This nocturnal, post-coital communion is a rare moment in Cheever's fiction in which intimacy been men is celebrated: 'these men were what they were – bewildered, naked, natural, and perhaps content.'

Deeper consideration is given to same-sex desire in Cheever's *Falconer*. The protagonist is a philandering, married man named Ezekiel Farragut, in whom Cheever distills a number of autobiographical life experiences. Farragut's very existence is anomalous: his father had tried to have him aborted. When reminded of this fact by his older brother, whom he detests, Farragut strikes his sibling dead with a fire iron, and is convicted on a charge of fratricide.* In prison, Farragut becomes infatuated with a handsome, lithe man in his early thirties named Jody. Their relationship starts as a friendship – 'I'm so glad you ain't a homosexual,' says Jody – but soon becomes romantic. The confined, quarantined strain of masculinity which emerges in the unique microcosm of the prison, Cheever learned from Donald Lang, will occasionally tolerate same-sex encounters on the grounds of necessity – how else are virile, manly men supposed to get off? – or else grossly permits them if used to enact hierarchal violence in the form of rape. The all-male prison environment, sustained by machismo and articulations of aggressive masculinity, might therefore seem a convenient foil for Cheever to use in order to explore same-sex desire in his fiction.

---

* Cheever apparently remarked to his older brother – 'Fred, I killed you off in *Falconer*' – on the occasion of their final meeting, shortly before Fred's death.

Cheever's characterisation of Farragut dives into profound emotional territory. Though Farragut first finds his relationship to Jody a 'grotesque bonding', it soon provokes in him 'so profound a love'. Trying to parse this new love, Farragut runs through a veritable list of long-held anxieties about sexuality that mirror Cheever's own. Chiefly, 'since Jody was a man', Farragut thinks, there was the danger that this love was nothing but narcissism, the 'danger that Farragut might love himself'. Not only this, but under Jody's affections, 'a flower seemed to bloom' deep within that 'wilderness that was himself', and he wonders if in loving Jody he not only loved himself, but had 'become infatuated with his lost youth'. Next in the list is the fear of death. Farragut broods on death's 'dark simples', and thinks that to passionately 'kiss a man on the throat' was as 'unnatural as the rites and procedures in a funeral parlor'. In kissing Jody's torso, was he not 'kissing the turf that would cover him'?

And yet, these prejudices and anxieties do not, ultimately, matter to Farragut: what matters is that he longs for Jody. He aches for him. He listens for the sound of Jody's tennis sneakers squeaking on concrete in approach to his cell, and his body is filled with radiance. When the heartbreak inevitably comes – Jody departs, via a daring prison escape – Farragut is left to stew in this newly uncovered, subterranean reservoir of love. He is numb and incapacitated. A fellow inmate, nicknamed the Cuckold (so named because he 'iced' his wife after being cuckolded) consoles Farragut, though it's really a way for the fidgety murderer to confess his own queer experiences. The Cuckold begins a meandering monologue about an affair he had with a hustler named Michael, something that completely transformed his long-held 'prejudice against faeries', whom he had always found 'silly and feeble-minded'. Michael was so gentle and affectionate, he seemed to move through reality 'like a swimmer through pure water', and though the Cuckold had long believed there was something 'strange and unnatural' in the image of two men being affectionate with each other – embracing, kissing, having sex – after sleeping with Michael he concludes that this is not the case. The only strange and unnatural thing is for a man to be alone.

And so the Cuckold introduces the heartbroken Farragut to 'the Valley': a long iron urinal trough behind the mess hall, where inmates go 'after chow' to masturbate in unison. The urinal can accommodate twenty men at any one time. It's usually stacked, with more men waiting in line. There's a code in the Valley: as inmates pleasure themselves, they can only glance at the man to their left or right. They can touch only the waist or shoulders of their neighbours. Nothing more. This image – a chain of semi-nude men reaching repeated, simultaneous orgasm, permitted to touch each other only furtively, peripherally – is somehow haunting, comical and beautiful at once. A knowing acknowledgement of the absurd compromises men might make in order to be physically close to one another, a compromise that doesn't jeopardise their 'masculine' credentials, but belies the very real, collective desire for a kind of companionship or adhesion, inclusive of sexual and spiritual proximity both.

The Valley is a convenient metaphor for Cheever's own contorted, paradoxical and awkward effort to merge traditional masculinity and queerness. He was a man, later in life, able to declare that 'as I live, homosexuality is not an evil, the evil is anxiety', yet he remained repulsed by men who lived an openly gay lifestyle. He was a man willing to weave infidelities into the fabric of his marriage, proudly declaring his heterosexual romances while secreting away his queer ones. And, as he pursued those romances, he would still ask himself, 'What did I desire? Is this some force of self-love?' In the mid-seventies, in an AA meeting, a young man opened up about his 'bisexual anxieties' and was called a 'phony' by the rest of the group. 'Perhaps,' Cheever wrote, 'I should have said if it is phony to have anxieties about bisexuality I must declare myself a phony'. And yet he didn't say anything: Cheever was also a man who remained silent.

But there is, despite this constant turmoil, a shift in his character, an attempt to craft a vision of men's capability to be close with other men, physically and spiritually intimate. A year after *Falconer* was published, Cheever felt able to note in his journals: 'I am queer, and happy to say so.' Given that he kept such prideful statements private, separate from his public persona and family both, this might seem to be only a minor development – an 'uneasy adjustment' – in Cheever's often unpalatable outlook on masculinity and sexuality. But when we consider what he had to relinquish in order even to venture such a vision – his entire concept of self-identity, forged through decades of silent self-hatred and loathing, that image of the naked prisoner in the unlocked cell – it appears instead to be a radical, transformative change.

PART FOUR

What About Love?

The American Madness

November 1948, New York City, New York

James Baldwin, twenty-four years old, is sitting on an aero-plane destined for Paris, desolate and demoralised. He has forty dollars in his pocket, a packet of cigarettes and just two words of French in his vocabulary. He carries a duffle bag with him, stuffed full of manuscript pages from half-abandoned, half-finished novels in progress. Four in total. Something's been stopping him from completing a book, from becoming a *real* writer. All the questions that *Ignorant Armies*, his latest, failed novel, sought to tackle – what it means to be a man, to love and to be loved – have proved unanswerable. The characters stopped talking, the plot lost shape and the story broke down. What those questions boil down to is self-identity; his identity, as a man. Baldwin knows that he can't resolve his fiction until he resolves himself. Who is he?

He's leaving New York, leaving America, to find out. Or to try. If Baldwin's to examine himself, to examine his life truly, he can't possibly stay in Greenwich Village, his chosen haunt of the past five years. The Village is New York City's epicentre of creativity and bohemianism. It's a scene sustained by cheap restaurants and cheap rents, an apparent haven for far-flung misfits, ne'er-do-wells and nonconformists. But life there has been 'strange, great and bewildering'. Baldwin's day-to-day is characterised by disorder, a dizzying carousel of shift work, boozy hobnobbing and artistic struggle, and it's driven him to the point of collapse. Evenings, he'll wait tables at the Calypso, a desegregated West Indian restaurant on MacDougal Street, where he's affectionately known to the jazz musicians as 'the kid'. After work he'll roam the Village bars, finding each one mired in an atmosphere of 'bottomless, eerie, aimless hostility'. These watering holes are full of radical intellectuals, artists, actors on the make, and plenty of writers, many of whom make the writer's life look plain hellish. There's a formerly famous poet-turned-barfly, shamelessly begging for drinks. There are struggling novelists, teetering on the edge of alcoholic oblivion. And once-respected kingpins of the literary world, now subsisting off a diet of champagne and opium. So many reminders of just how unlikely is sustained artistic success, and how many pitfalls there are for a young, burgeoning writer. Navigating the scene, he'll later remember, is like walking through an 'alabaster maze', one suspended 'above a boiling sea'.

And then there's the writing itself. Around midnight, Baldwin crawls back to whatever cold-water flat he's temporarily renting. There, he spends the small hours alone, chain-smoking cigarettes, 'wrestling' with his demons and his typewriter, which more often than not amounts to the same thing. He might be drunk, but he's never high: he's avoided the fate of the needle, unlike many of his friends, and steers clear of marijuana, as it fills him with a counterfeit confidence, temporarily making terrible writing appear revelatory. Finally, as the sun rises over the Village streets, he'll collapse into an exhausted sleep, waking in the afternoon to begin the whole performance again.

But it's not this lifestyle alone that's forced him to take the drastic step of expatriation. It's the perplexing social, sexual and racial codes of the Village scene. Nothing, he's found, is ever quite what it seems. There's a bewildering mishmash of liberal attitudes and bigoted behaviours – self-proclaimed radicals whose actions, or lack of action, conflict with their stated beliefs – frequently galvanised by acts of racial and homophobic violence. Greenwich Village offers an opportunity for some of its denizens to reject bourgeois values, to cast off their middle-class, conservative backgrounds. But not for Baldwin. Moving through this world – this almost exclusively white world – is like walking through a dizzying 'hall of mirrors' which constantly throw back fleeting and 'distorted fragments' of himself. Baldwin, a young man born into poverty in Harlem, a man so distressed by his ambiguous sexuality that he thinks of himself as an 'outlaw', has to grapple with racial, sexual and class difference in this ostensibly liberal demi-monde.

He finds some reconciliation, however, in literature. In the months preceding his departure to Paris, Baldwin reads widely and takes fortitude from one book in particular: *Leaves of Grass*, by Walt Whitman. Whitman's 'beautiful ambiguity' – the poet's vision of an expansive self that both courts and accepts paradox – offers validation. Whitman's poetic conceptualisation of self-identity is one that cannot be broken into fragments, because it is never static or rigid enough to be shattered. Whitman presents a fluid, expansive self, able to inhabit and speak through and across – and therefore transcend – labels of class, race and sexuality, labels that others have sought to pin on Baldwin his whole life.

Baldwin carries this idea of fluidity with him, now, as the plane rolls onto the runway. Nevertheless, the young writer is filled with fear and anxiety. What if I go mad out there, he wonders, what if I end up on the streets, homeless? What if I *die*? The only solution to his fear, he knows, is to keep moving. Otherwise he'll perish in it. And besides, he thinks, as the jet soars above the city and leaves the land behind, nothing worse can possibly happen to him out there, penniless on the streets of Paris, than what has already happened to him here in America.

'It was my season in hell,' Baldwin would later say about his years in Greenwich Village. But at one point the Village represented for him a kind of salvation. He'd resolved to make the move from the Harlem of his childhood and adolescence not long after the death of his stepfather, David Baldwin, in 1943. David, whose parents were born into slavery, was a Baptist preacher, powerful in the pulpit, cruel in his personal life and desperately proud, a pride matched only by a deep, unrelenting bitterness towards the world. Throughout Baldwin's childhood, David earned a meagre wage working at a bottling plant, providing the family's sole source of income. It was never enough to keep them out of poverty, and the family was forced to move from one apartment to another, constantly hounded by a series of 'welfare workers and bill collectors', the only white people ever to set foot in their lodgings.

David Baldwin could emanate both a terrifying charm and fill a room with unconquerable tension. Often, he would puncture that tension with violence. As a child, James Baldwin and his siblings were regularly beaten by their stepfather. David once lashed Baldwin with an iron cord, because he'd slipped on an icy street, accidentally dropping a dime that was destined for a can of desperately needed kerosene. And the violence inflicted upon him by his stepfather was verbal as well as physical. David always found his stepson 'strange', and was quick to tell him so. But his criticisms were usually more venomous. He'd call his stepson the 'ugliest boy' he'd ever seen. He'd make constant reference to his bulging 'frog eyes'. This seeded a painful body dysmorphia in Baldwin – he struggled for years to imagine that his body could be desirous to another – but even as a child he intuited that his stepfather's relentless verbal onslaughts had hidden motives.

Baldwin shared his prominent eyes with his beloved mother, Emma Berdis Jones, unquestionably 'the most beautiful woman in the world' to him. Baldwin saw that David's constant attacks on his appearance were actually a way for his stepfather to attack his *mother's* appearance: a way for David to call his wife ugly, without saying it directly. Channeling his misogynistic ire through the boy, he thereby abused them both. And Baldwin saw evidence of similarly convoluted tactics elsewhere in his adolescent world. He was frequently on the receiving end of verbal abuse from other boys in his neighbourhood (in part because of the Boy Scout shorts David insisted he wear, well beyond commensurate age). They would hurl insults at him, calling him a 'sissy'. Baldwin knew that these attacks, too, had a misogynist dimension: they sought to denigrate him by implicitly comparing him to a woman. These experiences shaped Baldwin's understanding of masculinity. He saw, early on, that men's relationship to one another is so often inflected or coloured by men's relationship to – most often denigration of – women.

The 'strangeness' that David located in Baldwin wasn't only about his looks. It appertained to his stepson's preternatural thirst for literature. From a young age, Baldwin had devoured books 'like some weird kind of food', always reading, even as he cared for his younger siblings. By the time of his early adolescence, he was penning poems, plays and stories, finding encouragement in his literary pursuits from a schoolteacher, a kind-faced Midwestern woman named Bill Miller, who was quick to pick up on her student's evident artistic talent. She wanted to help that talent flourish, taking Baldwin, at age thirteen, to see his first play: an all-black production of *Macbeth*, staged in Harlem's Lafayette Theatre, directed by a twenty-year-old Orson Welles. But Ms Miller's mentorship distressed David. He remained suspicious of her – what did this white woman *really* want with his stepson? – waiting, just waiting, for the mask to drop, and her true motives to be revealed. Besides, this literary bent interfered with the path he had envisaged for his stepson. The young James should turn his bookishness to the study of religion. He should preach.

'When I was fourteen I became a preacher,' Baldwin later recalled with sharp laconicism, 'and when I was seventeen I stopped.' By all accounts, just like his stepfather, Baldwin was outstanding in the pulpit. He fervently studied scripture, absorbed the plain-spoken language and authoritative cadence of the King James Bible, and then improvised luminous, stem-winding sermons based off a few scribbled notes. He was a performer, and the pulpit was his stage. But the church didn't help clarify the chaotic thoughts that, as a teenager, were at the forefront of his mind: thoughts related to desire, sex and the body. If anything, the church seemed to confuse them. After one of his sermons, a member of Baldwin's loyal congregation – a young woman – solicited the sixteen-year-old for sex. The teenage preacher may have gone through with it, too, were it not for the untimely interruption of her boyfriend.

Other complications lay beyond the church walls. Outside of his sermonising, Baldwin was spending a lot of time in Harlem with an older man, a 'moustachioed, razor toting' Spanish Irish racketeer, who said he was 'in love' with him. Baldwin loved him, too, 'in a boy's way'. He would later credit the relationship with this older, whisky-swilling white man with having 'shattered' the categories – black and white, straight or homosexual – which had previously appeared monolithic and unyielding to him. But the conflict between his sanctimonious preaching and this decidedly sacrilegious union precipitated an identity crisis. He came to feel that his performance, up there on the pulpit, was inauthentic and fraudulent, that he was wearing a mask.

Baldwin's attraction to the Village began while he was still a preacher. Part of what pulled him to the scene in the first place was the presence of one man in particular: a modernist expressionist painter two decades his senior, named Beauford Delaney. Emboldened by a streetwise friend, who'd made Delaney's acquaintance while playing hooky, one day Baldwin walked up to the painter's door, a modest SoHo apartment, and knocked. The door opened. Baldwin walked in. And what he walked into changed his life. He stepped into a world of light, 'into Beauford's colours' – the magic, multicoloured oils of his easel, the bright white sheets flung over canvasses, and the 'black-blue midnight' that Delaney carried around inside of him, the dark times in Tennessee, full of sorrow, from which he emerged.

Delaney taught Baldwin to see. The painter's artistic vision of the world forced Baldwin's inner and outer eye into a 'new confrontation with reality'. The light, Delaney showed him, falls 'on everything, on everybody', and that light is always in flux, 'always changing'. Delaney also taught Baldwin to hear: not only to listen to music, but to experience it. The needle on his small, old record player coursed through the grooves of records by Ethel Waters, Ma Rainey, Louis Armstrong and Fats Waller. He wanted Baldwin to understand these musicians were not mere celebrities to be admired, but part of his inheritance. Delaney became a kind of ersatz father figure, a spiritual guide, an artistic mentor and a shining example of 'absolute integrity' and remained so for the rest of Baldwin's life. Moreover, Delaney was a man, he was black and he was queer. He may not have been *rich*, but he was surviving, making art, and didn't kneel for anyone. Delaney was Baldwin's first 'living proof' that 'a black man could be an artist'. Delaney would often sing an old, traditional Christian song: 'Lord, open the unusual door'. For Baldwin, that door opened right in time.

'You'd rather write than preach, wouldn't you?' Baldwin remembered his stepfather saying, not long before he renounced the ministry. Yes, he would. A fire had been lit, and it wouldn't go out. But as David became increasingly ill, Baldwin knew that the task of financially supporting his family would fall to him, as the eldest of seven siblings (eight, by the time of David's death). This was the reason he wasn't drafted into military service. His exemption, most likely a III-D – 'Deferred by reason of extreme hardship and privation to wife, child, or parent' – kept him from combat, but exacerbated the pressure he felt to renege on his artistic aspirations and instead go to work.

After finishing high school in 1942, Baldwin first took a labouring job in New Jersey, working in an outfit of ten men laying track for the army. There, he earned more money than his stepfather, which was perceived by David as a threat to his position as paterfamilias, a challenge to his authority. But the teenage Baldwin – though well liked by his peers – was soon fired. He simply didn't conform to his employers' 'conceptions of a good American labourer'. As an itinerant labourer back in the city, this became a pattern: he'd lose work as soon as securing it. The prospect of doing this forever, trying to scrape together enough cash through manual labour to support his mother and siblings, filled Baldwin with a 'choking desire to scream'. Harlem, by now, seemed like 'a prison' to him. His future there, he felt, was written on the wall: by the time his youngest sibling would be old enough to take care of herself, he calculated, he'd be thirty-six years old, living in a basement, working manual jobs. Like so many other brilliant people he'd seen get trapped in their poverty, he feared he would become 'monstrous'.

And so, when he took the leap from Harlem to Greenwich Village after David's death – when he made the decision to write more and more, and eat less and less – the stakes were incredibly high. He was striking out alone, pursuing a life that the circumstances of his upbringing seemed designed to keep him from pursuing. In taking the leap, however, he didn't only wrestle with feelings of betrayal – that he should stay and support his family – he had to wrestle with the ghost of his stepfather and all that he represented. Baldwin imagined David sitting at a window, watching him, and hating him for 'reaching towards the world that had despised him'. Leaving Harlem for the Village in order to write was not just a matter of relocating to another part of the city. It was challenging that looming, dominant masculinist figurehead, it was choosing to be 'strange'.

Fortunately, Baldwin's artistic mentor, Delaney, provided assistance in this passage: it was he who helped Baldwin secure the job at the Calypso. And Delaney was there, too, to boost Baldwin's morale, as he came to learn that Village life wasn't the artistic haven it might have at first seemed. Although the Calypso, with its racially diverse, sexually liberal clientele, offered something of a retreat, Baldwin and Delaney were nevertheless two of very few black men in the Village scene proper – there were virtually no black women there at that time – and Baldwin was 'decidedly the most improbable' of them all. He was 'monstrously young'. He still looked sixteen – hence the nickname 'the kid' – and was eager yet shy, tongue-tied but ambitious, and patently lonely. These qualities marked him out and made him an obvious target for the racial viciousness that, he soon learned, was rife in Greenwich Village. Partly, this viciousness came from white 'tourists' to the Village. Partly, it came from the Village 'natives' themselves, those middle-class kids play-acting radicals, the first tremors of the nascent Beat Generation, people he 'thought were friends'. But always it came from the cops. They would either commit racially motivated acts of violence themselves, eagerly egg it on, or, at best, turn a blind eye.

One night, Baldwin was drinking in the San Remo, an Italian-run joint a few doors down from the Calypso. He'd often go there after work, sitting on a barstool in the window. On this night, however, a mob formed outside, demanding that Baldwin come out into the street. The owners of the San Remo shut out the lights and ensconced themselves with Baldwin in the backroom, where they sat in darkness until the mob had dispersed and the coast was clear. Though a terrifying experience, the aid offered by the Italians signalled to Baldwin that it is possible to get 'beyond the obscenity of colour'. After that evening, Baldwin thought, 'I was no longer black for them and they had ceased to be white for me.' Thereafter, the San Remo owners were unfalteringly amicable with the kid. They accepted him totally, and not only in terms of race. They didn't care in the slightest what his 'sexual proclivities' happened to be: the fact that Baldwin was, at the time, openly seeing and sleeping with both men and women. It was as though, having accepted him in terms of race, they'd found new interpersonal territory where they could accept him entirely.

That race and sexuality are inextricably connected had become clear to Baldwin in his brief romances with white women during his Village years. With one girlfriend, the couple couldn't walk the streets in public without being spat on by passersby. The wrath that the mere prospect of interracial coupledom incites has its roots, Baldwin would later articulate, in a persistent fear that haunts white America, a fear born of a history of racist, masculinist misogyny and violence. Black masculinity and sexuality are always deemed threatening to white women. The 'black man' is characterised by racist white America as a latent rapist who wants to inflict himself upon and 'desecrate' white women, a symbolic (and literal, given marriage law) desecration of a white man's property.

Baldwin postulated that this racist trope, as with racism *in toto*, reveals little about the experience of blackness but tells us everything about whiteness: 'by means of what the white man imagines the black man to be, the black man is enabled to know who the white man is.' What this tells us, Baldwin would argue, is that white America wishes to avoid being 'called to account' for the crimes committed by their forefathers during slavery, that 'bloody catalogue of oppression'. Among these horrific crimes are the countless, unrecorded, tragic acts of rape that white slave-owning men inflicted upon black women. This is precisely why black masculinity-sexuality is cast as a threat to white women: the racist trope is a direct analogue of those historic crimes, it emerges from that same nightmare. White America wishes to remain innocent, and so projects its most horrific sins onto black men, keeping them forever at a 'certain human remove'.

But Baldwin learned he also had to guard against other threats in his couplings with white women. He knew that racial fetishism could be a driving factor behind his partner's desire, that he might be reduced to an 'appendage' in the bedroom, desired because of white myths around black men's virility, or be used as a pawn: sleeping with a black man was one way a white, middle-class Village 'intellectual' might seek to rebel against their bourgeois upbringing. But this was only one side of a 'double fear' in such couplings, and the other was more urgent. There was a very real power dynamic that could be actively dangerous. More than one white woman had already let Baldwin know that the power of her skin could be instantly used against him. During an argument in Washington Square Park, a partner slapped Baldwin in plain view of passersby. He understood she was metaphorically crying 'rape!'. His partner's willingness to mobilise the immense power of that racist trope, and thereby incite violence, in response to a lovers' quarrel was shocking. In that moment, Baldwin did the only thing he could do: he fled.

Baldwin's same-sex encounters in the Village were no less fraught, and likewise revealed the inextricability of race and sexuality. Though the Village was home to an effervescing queer scene, homophobia was still rife, and sometimes the two clashed in perplexing ways. A man who called Baldwin a 'faggot', safely cloistered in a crowd of other aggressive men, was just as likely to solicit him for sex later, in private. This paradox spoke to the scripted nature of masculinity, revealing a divide between a man's public and private desires. Baldwin had already experienced such jarring Janus-faced attitudes, back in his days as an itinerant labourer. After work, he'd occasionally hit up the Apollo Theater on 42nd Street, which showed foreign films. A combination of 'innocence and terror' prevented Baldwin from understanding that the theatre was a cruising spot, though his innocence was broken when a young man, in the darkness, grabbed his crotch. But the men's toilets held the real revelation. The men there frightened him. They looked like the kind of men who'd 'beat faggots up' – they looked like 'cops, football players, soldiers, sailors [. . .] they had wives, mistresses and children'. And yet they were sometimes 'on their knees,' sometimes 'stroking themselves' at the urinal, 'staring at another man'. Baldwin would occasionally go to bed with men like these – men whose 'daytime' gender roles conflicted with their nocturnal cruising – and they could confide in Baldwin the true scope of their sexual desires, only because they felt that a black man could never 'betray' them: no one would believe his testimony.

These encounters showed Baldwin that 'male desire for a male roams everywhere, avid, desperate, unimaginably lonely'.

And he, too, felt alone. Away from the often clandestine world of casual sex, he struggled to be honest with other men for whom he fostered deep, romantic feelings. This was complicated by the fact that the men he tended to desire were those whose outward personas were traditionally masculine, and whose sexuality, while fluid, primarily moved towards opposite-sex romances. One of Baldwin's crushes was a Midwestern man, an aspiring actor who used to hang out at the Calypso, prior to landing his breakout Broadway role: a young Marlon Brando, who, in 1947, would awe America in Tennessee Williams' *Streetcar*. Though Baldwin thought of Brando as a 'beautiful cat' – he was flirtatious, so obviously attractive to 'both women and men', and 'race truly meant nothing to him' – the crush was successfully converted into a long-lasting friendship.

Conversely, Baldwin found that being honest in his relationships with women – both to himself and his partners – was an almost insurmountable challenge. For an entire year, in the Village, he lived with a woman whom he loved, but with whom he knew he didn't want to make a life. He even bought a wedding ring, and was intent on proposing to her, before hurling it into the Hudson. Though he wasn't able to articulate it in this way at the time, he was grappling with, as he later put it, 'all the implications in this society of being a bisexual': an inability to disentangle feelings of opposite-sex love and desire from the societal pressure to fulfil the heterosexual imperative – marriage, children – while simultaneously feeling that one's same-sex desires must be relegated to the shadows.

There was one central, unrequited love of Baldwin's Village years: Eugene Worth, a man of Baldwin's age – an 'incandescent boy' – whom he met in 1943. The men's friendship was charged by a shared political fervour. They petitioned together, 'fought landlords' together, 'starved' together. They had both been victims of racially motivated violence. Worth had a roster

of girlfriends, and it didn't seem that he harboured any romantic desires for other men, until the day he idly told Baldwin, 'I
wondered if I might be in love with you'. Their friendship also
had its passionate, bitter disagreements, which often emerged
from a divergence in worldview. Baldwin had an allergy to
political 'groups' and parties, which he often felt evinced a
subtle and alienating self-righteousness. As the young Baldwin
became quasi-nihilistic, Worth – a member of the Young
People's Socialist League – held to a faith in humanity. One
evening, arguing at a diner in the Village, Baldwin told Worth
that people in the world don't want to get better. This tragic
truth, he contested, means that socialism's bitter end would
necessarily be fascism: if you want people to adopt socialism,
you're inevitably going to have to *force* them to do so.

'What about love?' Worth asked Baldwin.

'That train has *gone*,' Baldwin replied.

'You're a poet,' Worth said, with devastating finality, tears in
his eyes, 'and you don't believe in love.'

In 1946, shortly after this exchange, Eugene Worth committed suicide. He jumped from the George Washington Bridge
into the Hudson. Worth's near-final words to Baldwin – what
about love? – echoed in his mind for the rest of his life. His
friend's suicide marked the moment that Baldwin resolved to
leave the Village, to leave America. He was absolutely certain
that Worth would not have died in such a way if it weren't for
the racism he encountered daily, those millions of assaults on
his humanity, and Baldwin felt sure that he would meet the
same fate if he stayed in New York. If he didn't die, he thought,
his 'hatred' – his desire for 'revenge' – would permanently
destroy him and whatever humanity he still had left.

But it wasn't only Worth's suicide that signalled some terrible, terminal cancer had infected the Village – indeed, the
entire country – and that meant escape was necessary. Part of

Baldwin's ire at the Village scene in the mid-1940s related to its woeful ignorance of the reality of his life and experiences under white hegemony: white friends of his, for instance, would suggest Baldwin seek psychoanalysis to cure whatever was so evidently eating at him. For Baldwin, anyone who suggested he needed to be 'adjusted' to this racist society via Freudian analysis was clearly themselves ill. He came to see the entire psychoanalytic phenomenon as a get-out clause, a faux formula for safety, betraying a 'desperate moral abdication'. People went to the shrink to find justification for the empty lives they led, he thought.

By 1946, Baldwin saw how the traumatic effects of the war rippled throughout and warped the white liberal world, too. It was a time of 'terrifying personal anarchy', where drink, drugs and annihilation reigned supreme. There were men, Baldwin learned, who had had same-sex encounters while in the army, but now, back in normality, they 'dared not discover if they desired to repeat' such encounters, and 'lapsed into a paralysis'. And then there were those who had witnessed the horrors of Nazi racism and genocide in the death camps and were changed forever. As Baldwin would later articulate in one of his most famous essays, 'Down at the Cross', 'white people were, and are, astounded by the holocaust in Germany. They did not know that they could act that way.'

But Baldwin could not help but feel, in these 'sorrowful' years, that the 'human indifference' to life demonstrated by the Holocaust would be his very portion 'on the day that the United States decide[s] to murder its Negroes systematically instead of little by little'. For Baldwin, the horrors that the war had unearthed represented something different to him than his white compatriots. And as the nation headed towards this new, traumatised future, one which, its citizens were led to believe, would be befitting a country victorious in war, Baldwin 'split the scene completely'. From across the ocean, Paris looked like 'a refuge from the American madness'. And leaving his home country symbolised a putting down of all 'formulas' in exchange for the 'chilling unpredictability of experience'. He left in order to encounter himself without reservation, on clear ground, as an individual, as a writer and as a man.

Into the Land of the Living

March 1955, Yaddo, Saratoga Springs, New York

'I have many responsibilities,' James Baldwin writes, at thirty-one years old, 'but none greater than this: to last, as Hemingway says, and to get my work done. I want to be an honest man and a good writer.' This dictum is sustaining him, now, as he shoulders his way through several of the most arduous months in his burgeoning literary career. Baldwin's temporarily back in America, suffering from nightmares, surviving on three hours of sleep a night, living on his nerves and nothing else. But he senses that he stands on the threshold of something – creative and artistic success, notoriety, even fame – if he can only survive and get his work done. The task seems insurmountable. There's a novel to draft, a collection of autobiographical essays to complete, a long short story to finish, a lecture to prepare, book reviews to file, and a play to revise, *The Amen Corner*, which he hopes will pique the interest of the famous film and theatre director Elia Kazan. Maybe, he thinks, he can get his old friend Brando involved . . . All of this before sailing back to Paris in the summer, lest too much time back in America send him to Bellevue.

Baldwin considers huffing a ton of Benzedrine to get through such a colossal workload. But he's found a temporary oasis of peace and quiet where he can begin to tackle it:

America's most prestigious writers' colony, Yaddo. Baldwin was recommended for a fellowship by the critic Lionel Trilling. On the basis of Baldwin's first novel, published two years prior, Trilling had promised Yaddo's director, Elizabeth Ames, that Baldwin was 'one of the best and most promising men of his generation'. And Baldwin's stated plans while at Yaddo no doubt impressed the admissions committee with their super-human ambition. He sought to complete two works during his time there: a discussion of 'the status of the Negro in America at present', which will be published later the same year as *Notes of a Native Son*, and a long short story, which will metamor-phose into his sophomore novel, *Giovanni's Room*.

Baldwin's Yaddo plans demonstrate that he sees a parity between his fiction and essay writing, and writes in both forms concurrently. By design, this multi-disciplinary approach results in a crosstalk between the two. Ideas in his fiction rein-force thought and arguments in his essays, and vice versa: Baldwin is a 'Socratic gadfly', darting between different genres. Both forms enable him to realise his goal as an artist, and that goal, he believes, is to 'bear truthful witness'. And all of his writing is deeply personal. In his essays, he writes from personal experience, weaving anecdote into broader philosophical, political and cultural analysis. Likewise, autobiographical expe-riences are imagined into characters and situations in his fiction. Baldwin believed in the adage that one can only write out of one's experience. And he believed that everything and anything can happen to you. This is what Walt Whitman meant, Baldwin once said, when the poet wrote, in *Song of Myself*: 'I am the man, I suffered, I was there' (an epigraph that opens *Giovanni's Room*). It is the notion of an expansive self whose experiences can't be delimited, transcending the labels and static categories of identity ('those airless, labelled cells') that keep us isolated from others, and ourselves.

This is Baldwin's second return to the USA after expatriating himself to Paris. His first, a visit for several months in 1952, provided him with an opportunity to reconnect with his family, while simultaneously reminding him of why he originally left. Baldwin had returned to a country experiencing the 'national convulsion' of McCarthyism, and he discovered that the intellectual and artistic community in New York was cannibilasing itself. Friends were betraying friends, naming names, justifying their capitulation to the psychic terrorism waged by Senator McCarthy – 'a coward and a bully' – through 'learned discourses'. Baldwin already knew that the white liberal community sought to insulate itself from the true implications of black suffering through similar displays of 'ignorance and arrogance'. But he hadn't anticipated how easily they would relinquish the artistic and intellectual values they had, seemingly, held so dear. For Baldwin, 'truth *is* a two-edged sword': a real artist and intellectual must accept this, even if it means risking 'dying' by that sword.

Baldwin's other motivation for that first return was more practical. He needed to meet with his publisher, to discuss edits on the manuscript of his debut novel. For Baldwin's Paris years had also provided him with the creative breakthrough he so needed. Though his arrival in the French capital was, initially, a devastating shock – his attempts to settle in a 'wild process' typified by 'failure, elimination, and rejection' – Baldwin eventually got used to the lack of home comforts (Coca-Cola, dry martinis, an 'American toilet'). And he soon discovered that Paris was no less littered with American writers and artists than the Village – Richard Wright and Carson McCullers were among the many expatriate luminaries Baldwin met during his first months there. But this was not the same destructive, ruinous and grief-flooded world. The codes were different. He was able to examine himself honestly and, in turn, complete a book. Published in 1953, *Go Tell It on the Mountain* tells the story of John Grimes, a teenage preacher in Harlem, his relationship with his fanatically religious stepfather and John's struggles to reconcile his uncertain adolescent sexual awakening with life in the church. The book received largely positive – though not earth-shattering – reviews. But it was enough. It incentivised him. In Paris when *Mountain* was published, a friend recalled how 'regal' Baldwin looked afterwards, how he brimmed with new ideas and talk about future projects. He had become a real writer.

Something happened to Baldwin while in Paris which forced him to confront those questions of sexual disorientation, emotional authenticity and masculine identity that had pushed him to breaking point in New York and stymied his artistic growth: he met the love of his life. In 1949, Baldwin was drinking beer in a dive bar when he met Lucien Happersberger, a blond, skinny, seventeen-year-old Swiss boy who had fled from his home in Lausanne with a thirst for adventure and a yen for painting. Their meeting was magnetic. Others in Baldwin's entourage sensed something seismic had occurred that night and they were right: the painter and the writer formed an immediate, intense bond. Lucien, down and out in the city, looked to the by now streetwise Baldwin as an older brother, and Baldwin was happy to play the role of mentor. They encouraged one another's artistic pursuits. They shared everything, pooling their scant resources each night to buy dinner. Quickly, the relationship deepened from a mentor-mentee alliance into a union sustained – on Baldwin's part – by fierce emotional openness and authenticity. Baldwin later credited Lucien with shattering the pose of distrust that he'd armoured himself with in response to the physical and psychic terrorism of his New York years. He further credited Lucien with bringing him into the land of the living.

But the electric, intense bond soon showed its cracks. Where Baldwin was beginning to become more comfortable as a queer man whose sexual and romantic interests primarily, though not exclusively, tended towards other men, Lucien's tended in the other direction, and he wanted – desired – women lovers, too. And where Baldwin wanted their relationship to be totally, mutually sustaining, marked by attachment, the Swiss youth saw it as something more relaxed. So began the Lucien problem: he was – and remained – central in Baldwin's life, but the nature of their relationship would undergo endless and often dramatic metamorphoses.

A year into their complex, frenetic pairing, Baldwin met someone else in Paris who would become almost as important to him as Lucien: Mary Painter, a laconic, well-educated Midwesterner who worked at the US embassy. Baldwin and Painter bonded over a shared disillusionment with the expat community in Paris, and, with Lucien in convoy, an unlikely threesome was formed. The trio would cook together at Painter's apartment, get drunk, listen to classical music records and lie together on the floor, smoking. Baldwin's feelings for Mary were a kind of love, he felt. She was the only person – excepting Beauford Delaney – with whom he felt he could be entirely honest, safe in the knowledge that his honesty would be returned. But he also knew that he couldn't form a traditional romantic and sexual relationship with her, even though a part of him desired this. When he realised he couldn't marry Mary, he later remarked, he 'realised he could marry no-one'.

Part of Baldwin yearned for a so-called 'normative' relationship, for a domestic life, and the sense of safety and stability it promised. But he worried such a relationship was impossible to have with another man, because it would require one of them to willingly relinquish his manhood, in turn eliminating or quashing something essential about what they desired from one another in the first place. Implicit in this thinking is the notion that there exist power dynamics inherent to heteronormative domestic coupling that always necessitate one person yield to another, and that these lines of power – dominance and submission – inevitably fall along the axis of gender. Men and women are conditioned, the thinking goes, to fit this unequal mould (or, more accurately, men are conditioned to force women to fit this mould) but men and men aren't. Though the former relies upon man's proprietorship over a woman, its false promise of security was nevertheless seductive, and Baldwin would covet such a relationship, on and off, for many years. His relationship with Lucien, meanwhile, fuelled his pessimistic belief that domestic harmony was impossible for him to attain with another man.

In the winter of 1951, Lucien and Mary both encouraged Baldwin to hunker down in the tiny Swiss village of Loèche-les-Bains (population 600), where Lucien's father owned a chalet, in order to finish a draft of *Mountain*. He set off with Lucien that November. While the winter months proved creatively productive (and sociologically fascinating: a man of colour had never set foot in the village before*), the domestic union he'd hoped to enjoy that winter was thwarted by visits from Suzy, a girlfriend of Lucien's. The following February, shortly after Baldwin posted a tattered, ink-stained draft of *Mountain* to Knopf, his publisher, Lucien delivered a brutal blow: Suzy was pregnant, and she and Lucien would marry. Signalling the first of many transformations in their relationship, Baldwin – though cut up and heartsick – outwardly encouraged the marriage, and later became godfather to Lucien's child.

* An experience he would write about in his famous essay 'A Stranger in The Village', collated in *Notes of a Native Son*.

Now, sitting in front of his typewriter, strung out, surrounded by draft manuscript pages, illuminated by the pollen-thick light of Yaddo in spring, Baldwin is trying to tease out the problems of his second novel, *Giovanni's Room*. Lucien – who is currently planning to move to New York and make a life in America – is at the forefront of his mind. So, too, are all the attendant concerns and issues Baldwin was confronted with and purged through this relationship, the conflicts inherent in same-sex relationships, the knottiness of bisexuality and the notion of emotional and sexual honesty and dishonesty. He will, in fact, dedicate the book 'To Lucien'. But as he teases out these threads, another Lucien resurfaces, a Lucien who has remained, splinter-like, in Baldwin's memory for many years: Lucien Carr.

A decade earlier, Carr – a precocious, attractive twenty-year-old student at Columbia University – murdered David Kammerer, a man in his early thirties. Kammerer had been obsessed with Carr for years, an obsession that, to some, occasionally appeared to be reciprocated. In court, central to Carr's defence was that he was not a 'homosexual', and that Kammerer posed a nonviolent sexual threat. This was an early version of what would come to be known as the 'homosexual panic defense', in which the defendant claims they were subject to unwanted same-sex advances so frightening they were provoked into a state of temporary violent insanity, and that this should therefore mitigate the severity of their crime and punishment.*

The defence has its roots in a mental health disorder known as 'homosexual panic', hypothesised by Dr Edward Kempf, an early proponent of psychoanalysis and sceptical follower of Freud. Curiously, however, 'homosexual panic' as a mental

---

* A version of which still exists in the USA today.

disorder – which was listed in the DSM-1 – maintained that panic arose because an individual's latent 'homosexual cravings' had been aroused, and not, as the legal defence has it, because the presumption that a man might be receptive to same-sex advances is enough to trigger a manic episode. In other words, Kempf suggested that many men may have dormant same-sex attractions or desires, and if these are brought to the surface – if these are suddenly made conscious – a state of panic can follow.

It was from the ashes of the Carr–Kammerer case that the Beat scene emerged. Jack Kerouac and Allen Ginsberg were close to Carr at Columbia, and both men harboured feelings for Carr that veered between comradeship, idolatry and romantic attraction. Kerouac, whose intense, close relationships to his male friends were encoded with 'homophobic homoerotic[ism]', even helped Carr hide the murder weapon – they threw the knife down a storm drain – before convincing him to turn himself in. Kerouac recounted the murder in an auto-fictive novel, co-authored with William Burroughs, *And the Hippos Were Boiled in Their Tanks*. Ginsberg, meanwhile, dedicated 'Howl' – that defining poem of the Beat Generation – to Lucien Carr, as though literally beatifying him (Carr, unmoved by such acknowledgement, asked for his name to be taken out of future editions). But the Carr–Kammerer case also fascinated James Baldwin, and he followed it closely. The murder said something about fear, and about the possible ramifications of denying the complexity of one's sexuality. It said something about the pendulum-like nature of desire, how it swings back and forth between violence and attraction, an action so common in relations between men.

Baldwin would distill these ideas, just as he would distill those experiences with Lucien Happersberger, the love of his life, into *Giovanni's Room*. In the spring of 1955, at the end of his Yaddo residency, Baldwin believes he's finally completed the novel manuscript. He senses that the book will have an enormous impact on his career, but worries, privately, that his motivations for writing it have become confused. In correspondence with his friend Mary, Baldwin confesses that his artistic aims are intimately bound up with his ego, and wonders if his desire to write stems from petty pride, a need to triumph against adversity and become famous against all odds, simply to prove to the world that had so mistreated him that he could. Later in his life, however, Baldwin will be able to look back with clarity on his true reasons for writing *Giovanni's Room*. The novel, he said, 'comes out of something that tormented and frightened me – the question of my own sexuality'.

The Light of a Smashed Flower

Baldwin was back in Paris when his second novel hit book-stands in the summer of 1956. It was published only a few months after *Notes of a Native Son*, his series of autobiographical essays largely about racial issues in Harlem and America. *Notes* was embraced by a white, liberal audience. In part, this was by intention: Baldwin sought to lead 'the white consciousness through the horrors of the black dilemma' by adopting a seemingly objective perspective, which white readers would recognise, by default, to be their own. There were unintended consequences, however. Such a reader may have felt their homework, so to speak, on the 'Negro problem' was complete upon reading *Notes*. To them, Baldwin was an intelligent black man who spoke their language, and whose rightful position was to be their educator and ameliorate their guilt. These racist tactics made Baldwin 'safe' to the white audience and, in doing so, made him feel trapped. But he confounded their expectations with *Giovanni's Room*, which, in setting, is about as far away from Harlem as Baldwin could get.

The novel is neither explicitly about the 'Negro problem' nor is it set in America. *Giovanni's Room* tells the story of two men in Paris – a white American and an Italian – who form a sexual and romantic relationship, even as one of these men, David, is engaged to a woman. For Baldwin's editors at Knopf, the queer male characters alone made the novel a risky proposition. At the time, there were precious few American novels which depicted overt queer relationships between men in a sympathetic or affirmative light: *The City and the Pillar*, Gore Vidal's 1948 novel, is often cited as the earliest such work, and the negative reception it received almost destroyed Vidal's career. The fact that *Giovanni's Room* not only centred on two queer men, but was also written by a black man, was altogether too much for Knopf. They dropped Baldwin, warning that the book would alienate his audience and leave him 'dead' as a writer. Even Baldwin's agent told him to burn the manuscript. But Baldwin persisted, and he eventually found a willing publisher with the Dial Press.

Baldwin had predicted the controversy his novel would court. It would be condemned, he thought, as one of the most unpleasant books ever published in America. But this didn't matter to him. Baldwin considered his novel to be 'truthful' and this superseded any anxiety around critical reaction. The notion of truth, in fact, is key to *Giovanni's Room*. It is a novel about the cost of denying one's true self. David, the protagonist, is forced into a position in which his masculinity is revealed to him as a scripted identity. The drama hinges on whether or not he confronts and accepts this truth.

The story unfolds against the crowded dive bars, along the cobblestoned *quais* and beneath the pearly, stultifying skies of late 1940s Paris: the scene of Baldwin's first years in the French capital. It's told from David's perspective. He's a white, blond, athletic American on permanent vacation, one financed by his father back in America, who wonders – with increasing urgency – why his son is wasting his best years on the Continent. David has recently proposed to his girlfriend, Hella, an eagle-eyed American who spends the first half of the novel sojourning in Spain, hoping to convert her ambivalent feelings for David into ardour. One evening, however, while drinking at a dive bar with Jacques, an older, sexually hedonistic man from whom David cadges drinks, David meets a leonine barman. This is the titular Giovanni, an Italian émigré who fled his hometown after his girlfriend suffered a stillbirth. He is under the employ of Guillaume, the bar owner, who hired the Italian youth after meeting him in a cinema (ironically backlit by '*un film du far west*' and the face of Gary Cooper, that icon of stolid American masculinity, the so-called 'strong and silent' type). Guillaume hired Giovanni primarily because his beauty makes him a powerful sexual lure for the queer men who frequent his bar.

With Hella out of the city, David and Giovanni begin an impassioned but short-lived love affair. This results in Giovanni losing his job: the affair becomes an open secret, denuding Giovanni of the sexual obtainability that had made him erotic bait at the bar. Meanwhile, it plunges David into a crisis: he becomes lost in a cloud of shame and confusion, though feelings of joy and exuberance, like so much forked lightning, occasionally pulse through his emotional weather. The affair reawakens in David memories of the only other same-sex encounter he's ever had. As a teenager, he slept with a friend, Joey, for whom he felt a 'tenderness so painful' it seemed his 'heart would burst'. After they had sex, however, David was overcome by terror. Joey's body – a man's body – seemed full of 'mystery' to him. It represented annihilation, a 'cavern' in which David would be 'tortured'. And so David resolved never to sleep with a boy again. He rejected Joey, first by falsely claiming he'd found a girlfriend, and then by bullying him: mandatory heterosexuality and the overt or coded denigration of queerness, those twin pillars of the public masculine identity. It is this pattern that David is tragically doomed to repeat as an adult in Paris, in his relationship with Giovanni.

David and Giovanni's affair takes place almost exclusively within the confines of Giovanni's room, a small ground-floor dwelling far from the city centre. It's a damp bedsit, its stale air sweetened by the scent of spilt wine. The floor is blanketed in plaster dust, littered with bottles, broken bricks and scrolls of wallpaper. Curtainless windows, obscured by whorls of white cleaning polish, provide a blurred privacy for their lovemaking. At first, David finds an ever-renewed sense of amazement in their coupling. But this quickly changes: as the days roll into weeks, Giovanni's face becomes more like a stranger's. Lying in bed, the ceiling seems to descend upon David, the weak ceiling lamp like a 'diseased and undefinable sex' casting a 'smashed flower of light' over the two men: a grotesquely baroque image emphasising the gorgeous, sickly rot David feels is intrinsic to their lovemaking.

Nevertheless, early on in their relationship, David attempts to domesticate Giovanni's room. He senses that, beneath the frisson of their desire, Giovanni really wishes for David to liberate him from the chaos of his life, a chaos which has been 'regurgitated' and realised as the clutter and mess enveloping his living space. David's attempt at 'playing the housewife', however, precipitates his initial crisis over the relationship. Men, David feels, 'can never be housewives'. What shape, then, should their relationship take? His thoughts begin to spiral. One moment, he tells himself, 'I am happy. He loves me. I am safe.' The next, he wishes to never be touched by Giovanni again. The room begins to become a prison, and David realises he cannot liberate Giovanni through their union. Instead, he must liberate himself.

David's inability to 'fit' his and Giovanni's affair into a recognisable domestic mould isn't the only reason he is thrown into crisis. One day, eating cherries with his lover, as they spit the stones at each other – 'two grown men jostling each other on the wide sidewalk' – David feels that 'he really loves' Giovanni. It's as though this playful, fraternal camaraderie, away from that regurgitated chaos and those limp attempts at homemaking, has liberated him to conceive their relationship in a different shape. Just then, however, a young man walks past. David's eye is drawn to the stranger. Giovanni clocks this and good-naturedly laughs at David, causing him to blush and tailspin into terrified panic: is this his future, David wonders, ogling boys, pitifully chasing them down 'dark' corridors? Is this what Giovanni has awakened in him? At this moment, David feels a 'hatred for Giovanni which was as powerful as my love'.

Giovanni – a man watching a man watch another man – unwittingly causes David's shame-spiral, by making him suddenly aware that his queer desires are visible, are legible, in a public setting. Out there, on the sidewalk, his desire is naked: his scripted masculine identity is revealed as an inauthentic pose. Elsewhere, David refers to this – more affirmatively – as an awakening, as becoming newly conscious of his 'insistent possibilities'. This beautifully abstract term signifies not merely the wider spectrum of desire that his newly unstable or fluid sexuality appears to offer, or, in darker moments, threaten. It refers, too, to that moment of love he felt for Giovanni: it refers to the insistent possibility and potentiality of finding love with another man. To accept this possibility is, by proxy, to accept the possibility of finding love anywhere, with anyone – it is to believe that love transcends categories of sexuality and gender – but he can only accept this if he moves through his shame, and relinquishes his current masculine identity. This is why David hates Giovanni: the affair has forced him into a position where he must accept and admit these insistent possibilities – what Giovanni terms the 'stink' of love – or retreat from them.

David's crisis is not one of whom to choose – Giovanni or Hella – and it is certainly not about whether he is 'straight' or 'gay'. Such a division into simple labels, Baldwin felt, is anathema to the novelist, whose task it is to reveal 'how profoundly all things involving human beings interlock': labels merely 'isolate' us from each other. Rather, it is a collision between his image of himself – the tall, American blond man taught to marry – and what he actually is, a complex human who is capable of finding love anywhere, capable of being touched and changed by anyone.

Of course, the tragedy is that David does retreat from the 'stink' of love. He retreats from this 'truth', just as he did with Joey, and reverts to his default masculinity: one structured by homophobia and misogyny. Two scenes signal this retreat. David first shames Jacques for the apparent shallowness of his liaisons with younger men, accusing him of kneeling before 'an army of boys for just five dirty minutes in the dark'. Jacques first reprimands David for denying his sexual fluidity, before explaining that his framing of these encounters as 'dirty' betrays his cowardice. He entreats David not to think of the affair with Giovanni as dirty, telling him that the men can have a lasting, affirmative impact on one another's lives, 'if you will *not* be ashamed, if you will only *not* play it safe'.

Later, after learning of Hella's imminent return to Paris, David refuses to break the news to Giovanni. Rather, he deserts him, and subsequently goes out to sleep with a woman, a blue jeans-wearing expat from Philadelphia named Sue, whom he quickly ditches post-coitus. David is aware that his actions are cruel. He apprehends a 'grave distrust' in Sue, created by 'many men' like him. He even recognises that he uses Sue as a way to 'escape' Giovanni's room: locked between her thighs, David attempts to reroute his contested masculine identity through the 'network of Sue's cries', back towards familiar ground. He feels the needs to reaffirm his status as a man, an American man who fucks American women. Sue, he hopes, will cleanse him of the stink of love before Hella's return. And this is Sue's only function: having exhausted it – discovering, in the process, that it was ineffectual – David casts her aside, full of self-loathing. It's an efficient articulation of the way in which misogyny in men often stems from the fear of contested masculinity; men reduce women to sexual objects and discard them, hoping that this exercise in dominance and power will restore their machismo.

This is to say nothing of David's treatment of Hella, beyond the obvious cruelty of his infidelities. When Hella does eventually return to the city, David rejects Giovanni, hiding the nature of their union from his wife-to-be, while making plans for married life. In the aftermath of this rejection, Giovanni – broke, lonely and desperate – tries to reclaim his job from the predatory Guillaume, reluctantly using his body as a bargaining chip: he is made into a prostitute. After Guillaume 'has his will' with Giovanni, however, he refuses to rehire the Italian. The rage which Giovanni had to suppress in order to offer his body to Guillaume violently erupts. He murders Guillaume, and is subsequently sent to the guillotine for his crime.

David is benumbed and wracked with guilt, but cannot tell Hella why. Recognising that David isn't being honest about the reasons why he is so incapacitated by Giovanni's demise, Hella pleads with him: 'Please don't shut me out. Let me help you.' But David keeps Hella locked out: his affair with Giovanni is simultaneously too 'dirty' to admit, and yet privileged as too sacrosanct for Hella, as a woman, to understand. In this cringing, contorted position, David pursues a final infidelity, falling into bed with a sailor, an effort to recapture something of Giovanni's intimacy. Hella discovers this, and leaves him. Giovanni, meanwhile, is executed. This is where the Carr–Kammerer influence is subtly imbricated: not only in Giovanni's violent murder of Guillame, but more acutely in David's 'panic' at what his lover has reawakened in him. His attempts to deny this lead to Giovanni's death. He is Giovanni's symbolic executioner.

David's crisis of masculinity is also one of nationality. He is *American*, we are relentlessly reminded, and his return 'home' must occur under the aegis of a marriage. This is how David eventually explains his long absence to his father: he has met a nice American girl. Giovanni, by turns playfully and cuttingly, needles David about his nationality. Americans always flee, he says. Americans do not believe in the 'serious things', like love and pain and death. David resists these stereotypes, until one 'harshly bright' morning in the midst of the affair, while collecting mail at the American Express office, he has a realisation. The office is full of Americans. The women appear to David 'to have had no traffic with the flesh'. More disturbing, however, are the American men. They seem 'incapable of age'. They are cloaked in soap-scent. It's like a preservative, he thinks, used to deny the 'dangers' of any 'intimate odour'. Behind the eyes of these beyond middle-aged men, David can see the 'unsoiled, untouched, unchanged' eyes of the boys they had once been. Their wives, meanwhile, might as well be their mothers, 'stuffing oatmeal' down their throats. For David, these characteristics highlight their sorrow: 'the sorrow of the disconnected', a sorrow born of isolation.

David's disturbing, uncanny vision expresses a crucial argument in Baldwin's overarching ideas around the intersection of masculinity, sexuality and national identity, which he first articulated several years before the publication of *Giovanni's Room*, in a 1949 essay titled 'The Preservation of Innocence'. A boy's maturation into manhood occurs, Baldwin argued, through a recognition of complexity and paradox in others, including – perhaps chiefly – the recognition of complexity in interpersonal relationships between men and women. However, it is one of the 'major American ambitions to shun this metamorphosis', because rejecting complexity enables American men to preserve their innocence. It enables them to remain 'clean'. David sees the boys *within* those men in the American Express office, mummified in soap, protecting themselves from 'obscene' odours.

But, of course, American men do not merely wish to preserve their innocence. American men are colonisers. They are the architects of hegemony. They wish, Baldwin wrote, to 'arrive at man's estate': to dominate, to rule. Through this irreconcilability – the irreconcilability of an untouched, innocent boy who wishes to rule the world – a particularly monstrous iteration of masculinity has emerged: the mindless 'tough' guy whose attitude towards women marries 'the most abysmal romanticism' with the most 'implacable distrust'. This is the juvenile, Tommy-gun toting effigy of masculinity found everywhere in popular culture: the good guys, the Native American-slaying cowboys, with their John Wayne stance, cartoonish machismo and attempts to woo the girl with baby talk. Their real-life counterparts, meanwhile, are left aping this ideal, resisting any more complex notion of masculinity with an adamantine will. This dominant American ideal of masculinity, Baldwin contested, is one 'so paralytically infantile that it is virtually forbidden – as an unpatriotic act – that the American boy evolve into the complexity of manhood'.

There is a division here in Baldwin's language between 'masculinity' and 'manhood'. Where masculinity refers to that scripted identity, that national ideal, manhood comes to represent a state to which men could aspire: a concept of self that accepts and embraces complexity and difference. Men's inability – or refusal – to *mature* is what prevents them from discovering manhood. And an essential part of that maturity is to accept love on an individual and social level, regardless of labels and categories. David, though he struggles to accept it, *is* one of those mummified men-children, or at any rate he has committed to becoming one: a man who wishes to remain untouched, unsoiled, a man who wishes to reject the stink of love, which is also to remain disconnected, isolated, infantile.

Critics and readers responded to *Giovanni's Room* with a mix of cautious praise and bafflement. One friend of Baldwin's, betraying a reflexive need to classify and catalogue in the wake of the novel's resistance to easy categories, was interested by his depiction of persons 'half queer, half man'. Some critics took aim at its expatriate perspective. Why wasn't the author of *Go Tell It on the Mountain*, who was so capable of making Harlem culture and the race problem legible to a white readership, offering more in that vein? Writing in the *New Yorker*, Anthony West contended that Baldwin's chosen theme – which he judged to be the conflict between a man's 'instinctive desires' and 'moral sense' – was 'legitimate'. But the Parisian setting, he argued, rendered Baldwin's treatment of this theme ineffectual. Writing among the 'unfamiliar and exotic', West contended, Baldwin's story lacked the 'validity of actual experience'. He then chided 'Mr. Baldwin', suggesting he focus more on American subjects – i.e. race and Harlem – as he had done in *Mountain* and *Notes*. Apart from West's coded racism – his effort to delimit Baldwin's scope as a writer – West doesn't consider that Baldwin's expatriate perspective is precisely what enables him to unfurl a critical depiction of a uniquely American masculinity. As Baldwin was better able to diagnose his homeland's social-cultural ailments from a distance, so the character of David only apprehends those mummified man-children cloaked in soap *because* they are so conspicuous, huddled together in the post office, alienated and estranged in a foreign setting.

Even still, Baldwin was perhaps piqued by such criticisms, as he later claimed that his immaturity as a writer, at age thirty-one, prevented him from tackling the intersections of race, sexuality and national identity in a single book. This is precisely the task he set himself for his next novel. In 1956, just as *Giovanni's Room* was going into a second printing, Baldwin travelled to L'Île-Rousse, in Corsica. There, he lived for several months and worked on a new, epic novel, appropriately titled *Another Country* (despite the protests of the house cat, which would swipe its paws at the typewriter keys whenever Baldwin started working, earning the nickname 'Nemesis'.) Baldwin travelled to L'Île-Rousse with a new lover – his first serious relationship since Lucien – a young musician named Arnold, whose sexuality was similarly fluid or equivocal. And, as with Lucien, domestic harmony with another man proved elusive yet again. One month into their trip, Arnold announced his intention to leave. A pattern seemed to be emerging. There is always a man, there is always heartbreak, there is always an empty room.

Arnold's departure effectuated a serious, conscious gesture towards suicide: drunk on brandy, shoes in hand, Baldwin waded out into the sea at night, finding in those nocturnal waters some essential force willing to embrace him in a way that the loves of his life had not. But Baldwin didn't yield to that embrace, and he returned, alone, to the typewriter. This close encounter with death – that tension between annihilation and liberation, between being caressed and engulfed – revealed to him something new about loneliness, about the terror and power of love, which he would channel into the essence of *Another Country*.

The Boys

It's the fifth week of rehearsals for *Sweet Bird of Youth*, Tennessee Williams' third Broadway effort since the runaway success of *Cat on a Hot Tin Roof*, back in 1955. He's collaborating again with Elia Kazan, though the men's relationship, tarnished by the *Cat* rewrite debacle, is more strained than ever. The situation with *Sweet Bird* isn't helping matters. The rehearsals are an utter shambles. There's an atmosphere of total chaos and 'intolerable nervous strain'. The props are tacky. The theatre is small and draughty, letting the biting, late winter air rush in and chill the cast and crew. The meagre provisions offer cold comfort: the coffee tastes 'like cardboard'. Kazan is forced to remonstrate with the cast, miming actions, trying to summon some magic. Tennessee, frogmarched again into rewrites, looks like he might storm off at any moment and declare the play a failure.

Watching the drama unfold, James Baldwin sits in the stands, clutching a clipboard, assiduously taking notes. Kazan has invited him to act as production observer for *Sweet Bird*. After all, he still holds his own Broadway ambitions, and this is an unmissable opportunity for him to better learn the ins and outs of professional theatre. Last year, after working tirelessly on a script, Baldwin was able to have a version of *Giovanni's Room* workshopped at the Actors Studio in New York. The Studio, a

255

training organisation founded by Kazan and Cheryl Crawford, specialised in promoting method acting, or the Method, made famous in America by performers such as Marlon Brando, Paul Newman and Marilyn Monroe, who trained at the Studio in the mid-fifties. When news circulated that the Studio were casting for Baldwin's play, it seemed that every young actor in the Village wanted a part. There was special interest in the role of Giovanni, a character whose fiery temperament was perhaps more attractive to aspiring actors than the comparatively subdued part of David. Baldwin had would-be Giovannis 'coming out the faucet'. He was even propositioned by one of those chasing the role, who hoped such solicitations might land him the part. It must have been curious, to see such a proliferation of men eager to bring his imagined queer character to life, in the city that had caused him so much psychic turmoil around his sexuality a decade earlier. The actor eventually cast, a Yale-educated Turkish man named Engin Cezzar, impressed Baldwin with his performance, even as the former preacher had to grit his teeth during a scene in which Giovanni-Cezzar spits on a crucifix. Following the performance, Baldwin and Cezzar became fiercely close friends, and remained so throughout their lives.

Through his time at the Studio, Baldwin forged a strong relationship with Kazan, which won him this invitation to act as would-be theatre apprentice. It was an uneasy friendship, at first: Kazan's infamous capitulation to the House Committee on Un-American Activities in 1952 – where he named eight fellow artists he knew to have had communist sympathies – had made him a controversial figure in Hollywood and Broadway.*

---

* Once the convulsion of McCarthyism ended, he was almost a pariah: 'Elia Kazan is a traitor,' Orson Welles famously remarked, long after the dust had settled, 'he is a man who sold all of his companions to McCarthy, at a time when he could continue to work in New York.'

Baldwin had his own reservations about Kazan's betrayal, but felt more at ease with him after the two men toured the Harlem nightspots together. Perhaps Baldwin found in Kazan none of the literary and artistic pretensions that were rife elsewhere.

Despite the chaos, the weeks in rehearsals for *Sweet Bird* haven't dampened Baldwin's enthusiasm for the stage. He sits hypnotised by the 'inexplicable transformations' that the actors undergo when bringing Tennessee's characters to life. He is inspired by watching Kazan in his element. And Baldwin admires Tennessee, too, in a 'visceral' sort of way. Partly, as Kazan later remembered, because 'Tennessee didn't sit in judgement of anybody'. Baldwin no doubt also found resonances between the themes of masculinity and maturation in his own work and that of Tennessee's: *Sweet Bird* centres on a beautiful male sex worker and aspirant movie star, Chance Wayne, whose inability to accept the passing of his youth leads him to ruin.

The theme is neatly evoked by the play's epigraph, taken from a poem by Hart Crane: 'Relentless caper for all those who step / The legend of their youth into the noon.' Baldwin, as an avid reader of the poet, would have passed Tennessee's 'Crane test', where the playwright found immediate affinity with fellow admirers, as he had done minutes after meeting Carson McCullers a decade beforehand. And like Tennessee and John Cheever, Baldwin found that Hart Crane's mythology and tragic demise – suicide by drowning, in the aftermath of a homophobic assault – evoked something of his own struggles with sexuality. At thirty-two, the age at which Crane committed suicide, Baldwin had written to his friend Mary that he understood why Crane had done it (this was in the wake of his lover Arnold's departure from Corsica, and Baldwin's own late-night walk into the water). In the middle of rehearsals, however, Baldwin receives some monumental news that takes his attention away from *Sweet Bird*. He has won a grant from the Ford Foundation, totalling $12,000, to be paid across two years: a hefty sum, equivalent to around ten times as much today. The grant is to help him finish *Another Country*, the draft manuscript of which he's now been carting around for years. To celebrate, Baldwin goes out for a raucous celebration, with Tennessee Williams and Elia Kazan in tow.

Even with the Ford grant in his back pocket – which Baldwin suspects the Foundation have awarded to prove to themselves how liberal they are – it's no small miracle that Baldwin manages to finish his third novel by the close of 1961. Just as he had worked on *Giovanni's Room* alongside *Notes*, so, too, does he write *Another Country* alongside a second collection of autobiographical essays, titled *Nobody Knows My Name*. And, somehow, he writes both books while maintaining a calendar and itinerary that would send most people to an early grave. Indeed, it almost does: he frequently exhibits symptoms of chronic stress, occasionally collapsing and staying bedridden for days at a time. Baldwin's diary, from the late fifties through to the publication of *Another Country*, in 1963, defies belief. He becomes an international commuter, living in several time zones at once, surviving on Johnnie Walker scotch, cigarettes and scarcely any sleep. Buffeted by growing fame and notoriety – a notoriety he finds increasingly difficult to bear – Baldwin travels back and forth from New York to Paris, spending time in Harlem with his family, and hanging out in the French capital with Lucien, Mary Painter and Beauford Delaney, his first artist-mentor, who had moved to the city in the early fifties. He even crosses paths with Tennessee Williams once or twice on the Continent, and eagerly takes him to see Delaney's studio and paintings in a Paris suburb. He also accepts an invitation from Engin Cezzar to stay with his family in Istanbul, a city that will, in the coming years, become for Baldwin yet another adopted home.

However, much of his travelling in these years is within America. The burgeoning civil rights movement demands his attention. Across the South, there's an organised effort to abolish the racist Jim Crow laws through direct action and nonviolent protest, lead in part by CORE, the Congress of Racial Equality. The Jim Crow laws, which legalised segregation and racial discrimination, galvanised and gave credence to a persistent, violent, omnipresent racism. Its most hideous manifestations were realised in the murder of Emmett Till, the fourteen-year-old African American boy who was abducted, horrifically tortured and murdered in Mississippi, in 1955, by white men, for allegedly whistling at a white woman. Baldwin tours the South many times in these years, meeting with figureheads at CORE and other spokespersons and leaders in the movement, including Martin Luther King Jr and Medgar Evers. He becomes increasingly involved in the movement himself, both partaking in action and chronicling it in his writing, presciently warning that 'what is happening in the South today will be happening in the North tomorrow'.

It was Baldwin's first trip to the South, in 1957, which proved the most shocking for him, and provided yet another powerful and painful lesson in the intersection of masculinity, sexuality, power and race. On assignment for *Harper's Magazine* and the *Partisan Review*, Baldwin toured Alabama, Carolina and Georgia to cover several sit-ins and boycotts. Travelling the Southern states for the first time in his life was a terrifying, awesome experience. The entire landscape, it seemed to him, was sustained by the twin currents of desire and violence. The liquid heat, the heady, deep dark nights, followed by unrelentingly bright, fierce days: the land itself seemed to 'demand' that violence be unleashed. Had the South's rust-red earth acquired its colour, Baldwin wondered, from the blood that dripped from the trees? The trees where white men had hanged and castrated black men?

But Baldwin knew that not all such violence was so explicit. One particular incident occurred on that first tour which reminded him of this. He was groped, by 'one of the most powerful men' in one of the Southern states he visited. This white man – left anonymous in Baldwin's retelling of the incident in *Nobody Knows My Name* – got himself drunk and reached with sweaty hands for Baldwin's crotch. This was a man, Baldwin knew, 'who could provoke or prevent a lynching' with a word. He could place Baldwin in jail – or liberate him – with a phone call. Naturally, Baldwin was shocked. Not by the act itself, but by the egregious power imbalance, and the implicit assumption that Baldwin was amenable to the advance. The offender assumed that Baldwin wouldn't tell of – or in any way protest – the incident. Doing so risked death: 'as my identity was defined by his power, so was my humanity to be placed in service of his fantasies'.

Just like those 'tough guys' in the Village, the white masculinities Baldwin encountered in the South displayed a dissociation between their private and public selves – the latter rigid, inflexibly 'heterosexual', the former willing to express same-sex desire – but both the private and public remained connected by their instant willingness to utilise the hegemonic power and supremacy of their skin colour. Male desire for the male roams everywhere, to be sure. This also converges with the fact that 'men have an enormous need to debase other men – and only because they are *men*', a truth, Baldwin writes in that same essay, 'which history forbids us to labor'. Masculinity is about power and hierarchy: men affirm their status as 'men' by debasing women, and each other. When these competing or complementary forces intersect with race, as in the groping incident, this Southern white man utilises the power of his skin colour in an effort to both consummate his sexual desire and debase Baldwin, a stratagem that also ensures all evidence of his desire will remain hidden.

Leaving the identity of the aggressor unnamed in print grants the event the weight of a parable. It gives further structure to Baldwin's overarching arguments that modern masculinity is in a stalled, perplexed, and infantile state (groping – snatching at what one desires – is abhorrent, in part, because of its brainless puerility), and that the consequences of this are violent and destructive. Baldwin has an opportunity to publicly expound upon these ideas in October 1960, when he takes part in a three-day symposium in California, organised by *Esquire* magazine, on the subject of 'Writers and Writing in America Today'.

His co-panellists are a very young Philip Roth and a mid-career John Cheever, who, in typical self-satirising fashion, gloomily predicts his role will be to 'speak on the Death of The Short Story and model sports coats'. Cheever believes that the slightly incongruous line-up has been selected in order to generate 'some kind of literary blow-out'. The opposite occurs: across the three days, the authors engage in largely amicable discussion, finding many points of agreement. Baldwin and Cheever are especially friendly with each other. Despite Cheever's earlier reflections about *Giovanni's Room* – where he was made 'jumpy' by its depiction of 'queers' – he realises, after this meeting, that he has 'much more in common' with Baldwin than he had 'ever imagined'. And Baldwin would come to admire Cheever's fiction. Unlike his white contemporaries – such as John Updike, whose fiction was not 'relevant' to his experience – Baldwin would find Cheever's 'lost suburbanites' incredibly moving. During the symposium itself, Cheever's diagnosis that America has exhibited an 'abrasive and faulty surface' for the past twenty-five years certainly corresponds to Baldwin's general analysis of the state of the nation, its hypocrisies, convoluted lies, self-deception and 'system of moral evasions'. But perhaps Baldwin is just as charmed by the way Cheever shirks all literary pretensions: he insists on hurling himself into the hotel swimming pool before the first panel.

During their third and final discussion, at San Francisco State College, Baldwin pulls his ideas around masculinity and infantilism into a wider critique of America and its failures. His voice crackles through the microphone. In an exploratory, probing manner, he postulates that America suffers from a 'great cult of nostalgia and adolescence', which is evident in the country's literature, from Mark Twain to Hemingway. This cult has something to do with the American vision of the 'good life', Baldwin speculates, which is really a 'metaphor' for the Garden of Eden. Americans want to live a guilt-free, Edenic existence, one devoid of complexity, one in which everything will turn out 'all right'. This is, of course, a great lie. And this lie has prevented any real 'idea of a man' from coming into being in American society. Rather, there is an adoration of 'the boys'. This admiration is made evident, he quips, in the presidential candidates on offer that year: John F. Kennedy and Richard Nixon.

He is perhaps gesticulating as he talks, a cigarette pincered between his index and middle finger, his enormous eyes wide open, a largesse of gaze that mirrors the insight of his speech. Baldwin was a physical speaker. He'd often grip or touch the hand of an interlocutor when in close discussion, as though mere vocalisation were insufficient to communicate the urgency of his arguments; they required connection, movement, the somatic artistry of an actor. Stopping and starting, repeating to his audience and his co-panellists that he is not attempting to make an easy joke, but is being deadly serious, Baldwin submits that the 'failure in American life' – perhaps, he contends, this is not just American, but a western failure – is really a 'failure of the masculine sensibility'. Somehow, somewhere, 'something broke down', and the detritus, the contemporary 'concept of what it is to be a man' is nothing but this cult of adolescence: a masculinity which resists complexity, embraces infantilism and claims innocence. Baldwin concludes that this breakdown in masculinity relates to – or has caused – a corresponding breakdown in relations between men and women, too. As he wrote earlier in his career, 'when men can no longer love women they also cease to love or respect or trust each other, which makes their isolation complete. Nothing is more dangerous than this isolation, for men will commit any crimes whatever rather than endure it.'

Unlike Cheever's 'haunted men', who, zoned out on nostalgia and desperate to reclaim their youth, look ever-backwards to an imagined Arcadia, and Cheever's consistent personal conflation of the pastoral with queer virility and desire in his journals, Baldwin's ideas move in the opposite direction. For Cheever, the Edenic, untarnished 'innocence' of this transcendentalist landscape, all those woods and streams, all that leaf-light, represents an imaginary escape from the mandatory, social strictures of mid-century suburbia in which desire between men cannot be visibly mapped. But for Baldwin, there is no such such pastoral. There is no Eden. Innocence is not a state where masculinity can be remade or reimagined: innocence is impossible. If the nation's broken masculinity is to be repaired – and if mapping and making visible desire between men forms a part of that – the movement must be forward. There must be maturation.

Do You Love Me

The complex ideas around masculinity that Baldwin discussed during the *Esquire* panel filter into the writing of his third novel, *Another Country*. Attempting to balance such themes and structure them within a single work proved just as torturous as one might imagine: many times, Baldwin considered tearing the draft of his novel to pieces. The 'strange and frightening' messages he sought to blend into the story remained obscured to him, for so long. But he knew there was a good novel buried beneath the mess. And it needed excavating. If he failed to dig it up, Baldwin said, he'd end up in the graveyard. This idea of writing-as-excavation – a task so paramount that if the artist fails to achieve it he will himself be buried – isn't mere hyperbole. It is central to Baldwin's aim with the novel. In *Another Country*, he wanted to 'bring to the surface the buried, despised, long denied assumptions on which my liberated, graceful, agonizing colleagues have never ceased to act'. Assumptions that pertain to the two most 'profound realities' every American citizen must face: the realities of 'colour and sex'.

Another Country – at over four hundred pages – is astronomical in scope, length and ambition. It resembles, in the words of one critic, a 'long-playing record of frantic embraces and frantic questions'. The comparison is warranted: Baldwin wanted people to encounter the book as though it were a jazz record, likened his role as author to that of 'a blues singer' and the novel as a kind of 'universal blues'. The setting is mid-1950s Manhattan. The jazz joints, subway cars, tenement rooftops and dive bars of Harlem and Greenwich Village, contrasting worlds mired in that bewildering mix of circum-spect liberalism and racist hostility, brought vividly to life through Baldwin's direct experience of both. The story follows Rufus Scott, a young jazz drummer, and his relation-ship with Leona, a white woman from the South. Their rela-tionship ends, and in the aftermath – scarcely a quarter of the way through the book – the would-be protagonist abruptly disappears. Rufus commits suicide.

The bulk of *Another Country* then centres on a large cast of characters, each haunted by Rufus's sudden death. There is Rufus's sister Ida, a singer who forms a relationship with the Italian American Vivaldo, an aspiring novelist and Rufus's best friend. Ida is lusted after by the predatory talent agent Ellis; Vivaldo lives in the creative shadow of his erstwhile mentor, Richard, a middle-class writer-turned-hack. Into this social circle returns Eric, a white actor who has been living in Paris, a trip he embarked upon in order to become 'a man'. On re-entering this scene after Rufus's death, Eric has an affair with Richard's wife, Cass, and subsequently sleeps with Vivaldo, despite being in a relationship himself with a Parisian named Yves. Eric, we learn, had also had a difficult affair with Rufus prior to the events in the novel.

In plot summary, *Another Country* might sound like little more than an elaborate game of carnal musical chairs, or, as Norman Mailer put it, a 'chain of fornication'. But this entangled, reluctantly polyamorous and sexually fluid network of lovers constitutes the framework upon which Baldwin mounts a difficult, often shocking assessment of sexuality and masculinity. In their liaisons, each character navigates perilous power dynamics related to race, gender and class. They struggle to discover new interpersonal terrain, where relationships are not structured along these lines of power, or wrenched apart by difference. Baldwin's exploration of multiple, layered social and cultural forms of inequity and privilege within his characters' relationships reflect his 'intersectional[ity]', which he was exploring, notes the academic Thomas Chatterton Williams, before intersectionality 'was a thing'. It also demonstrates how, in Baldwin's writing, relationships in the present are always tethered to and impacted by relationships in the past.

And what governs, or at the very least fortifies, the power dynamics that these couples struggle against is that cancerous, broken American ideal of masculinity. *Another Country* is a novel about men's inability to trust or love one another, how this hostility engenders a space between men, a gap, an in-betweenness, an isolation, where they are locked within their scripted identities, and the deleterious consequences for men and women both. But the novel is not only a critique. It also considers the ways in which masculinity can be reformed, and the transformative possibilities offered by new kinds of radical male intimacy.

Baldwin said that Rufus's suicide was the 'hardest thing' he ever wrote. It is a conscious fictionalisation of the real suicide of his friend and unrequited love, Eugene Worth, who – like Rufus – jumped off the George Washington Bridge. And, like Worth, Rufus is driven to suicide by the psychic and physical racist terrorism wrought by Jim Crow-era America. As Rufus's sister Ida says in the novel, 'my brother would still be alive if he hadn't been born black'.

Rufus first meets his lover Leona in a jazz joint, where he is part of the band, and where the crowd – 'white and black, high and low' – ecstatically enjoys the music. Towards the

end of the set, Rufus becomes transfixed by the band's saxophonist. It appears to him that the musician is speaking
through the saxophone, a glossolalia that Rufus translates as
a repeated question or demand: '*Do you love me? Do you love
me? Do you love me?*' Rufus breathes in the 'odour of the men
around him', watching the saxophonist unleash that question across the crowd, itself a temporarily pluralistic utopia
cast in a haze of pot smoke, where boundaries of class, race
and sex have momentarily vanished. A vision that ceases as
soon as the music ends.

When Rufus and Leona meet after the set, those boundaries
reappear. Alone on the balcony at an afterparty, framed by the
bridge from which Rufus will eventually jump, they have sex.
It's a perilous, knotty scene. Rufus 'had expected her to resist
and she did'. Leona then 'ceased struggling' and the noncon-
sensual assault becomes an enthusiastically reciprocated sex act,
her tongue 'hot' on Rufus's neck. In difficult, startling passages,
Baldwin pulls us further into Rufus' perspective. Though he
feels an unexpected 'tenderness' for Leona, the momentary
assault enlarges, in his mind, into a fantasy of rape. Rufus thinks
of her as a 'milk-white bitch', his cock as a 'weapon', his semen
as 'venom'. Nothing will stop his act of penetration, not the
'white God himself', he thinks, nor a 'lynch mob'. Has the
Southern Leona, for Rufus, become a metonym for that lynch
mob, the lynch mob for the entire catalogue of oppression
wrought by white supremacist America? Is Rufus figuratively
playing the role of the 'Black rapist' – that racist stereotype
concocted by the white American imagination to deflect from
its own history of supremacist violence – as punishment for
those who invent and peddle such a myth? Rufus's real and
fantasised violent misogyny, Baldwin shows us in this moment,
is inextricable from the history of masculinist racial violence. It
is not excusable on those grounds, nor does it result solely from

that history, but it cannot be considered independently of it. *Another Country*'s first sex scene highlights the recursive nature of such violence, and suggests one of the many ways that women – including white women – can become its collateral victims.

Though Rufus and Leona form a relationship following their difficult, al fresco liaison, it soon breaks under the strain of society's racism. They encounter problems with their landlord and neighbours. Leona loses her job because she is seen in public with Rufus. Subsequently, Rufus's violence returns, and he begins to beat Leona. In his violent state, he recalls another rage – the 'same roaring in his head' – that inflected a previous relationship, his uneasy coupling with the Southern Eric. Rufus remembers how, in a confusion of 'affection, power and curiosity' laced with 'unforeseen violence' he responded to Eric's romantic solicitations ('I'll try anything once, old buddy'). But their connection was quickly blighted by Rufus's homophobia: he 'despised Eric's manhood by treating him as a woman'. In physically and verbally abusing Leona, Rufus realises that he used against her 'the very epithets he had used against Eric'. His misogynistic violence is sutured to homophobia, his homophobia to misogyny.

As a result of Rufus's brutality, Leona has a breakdown and returns south. Rufus, meanwhile, 'hits bottom'. Desolate and paranoid, he visits Vivaldo. Such is the fragility of Rufus's mental state – his sanity disintegrating in a world designed to strip him of it – that he threatens to stab his best friend with a knife, before pleading for help. 'They killing me,' he says, referring to the racism he encounters daily. Vivaldo later confides in Eric about this moment:

[Rufus] wanted me to take him in my arms. And not for sex, though maybe sex would have happened. I had the feeling he wanted someone to hold him, to hold him, and that night, it had

to be a man [. . .] I could have saved him if I'd just reached out
that quarter of an inch between us on that bed, and held him.

Rufus is unable to articulate his desperate need, his desire,
for Vivaldo to close the space between them, and Vivaldo,
though he senses this need, is unable to acknowledge it. What
keeps these two men a quarter of an inch from each other?
Why, if Vivaldo senses Rufus's desire, his need for intimacy,
doesn't he reach out? Vivaldo believes that he and Rufus are
equals as men. After all, they frequently 'got drunk together,
balled chicks together': he sees their friendship as a bond
cemented by mutual, casual denigration of women, and
believes this macho camaraderie transcends racial difference.
Rufus, however, knows otherwise: he feels that his masculinity
and sexuality is always under surveillance from Vivaldo. At the
outset of his and Leona's relationship, Rufus chides Vivaldo
about his interest in their coupling: 'I thought all you white
boys had a big thing about how us spooks was making out'.

Rufus's remark is warranted. In another scene, Vivaldo
recalls an interaction that took place while he was in the army.
He and a fellow soldier – a man of colour – exposed themselves to a girl in a bar. This 'by-play', as described by the
narrator, had nothing to do with the girl. The men had used
her as a smokescreen: they wanted to expose themselves to *each
other*, as a kind of dick-measuring contest. The insecure
Vivaldo, though 'relieved by' the results, thereafter had recurrent nightmares in which that same soldier pursued him
through jungly terrain with a knife, a nightmare that catches
up to him, embodied in the very real, blade-wielding Rufus
during his crisis, where he teeters between violence and
vulnerability. Vivaldo is threatened by Rufus's masculinity and
sexuality along lines of racial difference. Vivaldo's inability to
acknowledge this is what prevents him from transcending that

difference, keeping him physically estranged from his friend in his moment of need.

After Rufus's suicide, he becomes a 'phantom protagonist', haunting the other characters from beyond the grave. And their relationships are haunted by the very same forces that Rufus struggled with: misogyny and homophobia, violence, racism, inherited trauma. Forces set in motion and consolidated by that American ideal of masculinity. But what about that evanescent, pluralistic utopia Rufus glimpsed in the jazz bar, at the novel's outset? Was it an adumbration, or a fantasy? Can anything short-circuit or overcome the recursive pain and trauma wrought by that masculinist violence, can anything dissolve those paradigms of difference that keep individuals separated from one another?

Enter Eric, the sexually fluid prodigal son, who returns to New York following Rufus's death, after a lengthy sojourn in Paris. *Another Country* spends a great deal of time exploring Eric's backstory, particularly his privileged childhood in Alabama. Eric's early adolescence was one of 'isolation and strangeness': at school, he sees the other boys as 'creatures in a hierarchy' to be 'adored or feared or despised', while at home, he is perplexed by a burgeoning, proto-sexual desire for Henry, the handyman. This desire leaves Eric 'profoundly and obscurely frightened' because Henry is black, and much older than him. As a child, Eric also experiments with dressing in his mother's clothes. Both these things, he feels, are wrong – at least in the eyes of the world – and therefore must be kept secret. Censuring his queer desires and instinct to manipulate gender norms – keeping them locked in the 'basement of his private life' – causes Eric emotional pain. But he finds temporary salve later in adolescence, through his first sexual experience, which occurs with another teenager, LeRoy.

The two boys were friends. But the difference in their race

and class made their friendship an 'impossible connection' in the eyes of the townsfolk and Eric's family: it was 'indecent' that a white boy should be seen with 'one of his inferiors'. One day, beside a tree-shaded stream, feelings that Eric had been 'unable to allow himself to know' come to the surface. LeRoy reciprocates, and the two lie together, on the banks, the glistening water whispering in their ears. Held tightly in LeRoy's arms – 'under the great weight of his first lover' – Eric finds that an 'eternal, healing transformation' occurs within him. Their intimacy induces a revelation in Eric, a kind of epiphanic transformation: it marks the beginning his life as 'a man'.

This transformation has something to do with Baldwin's notion of manhood as differentiated from broken masculinity: manhood embraces difference and acknowledges complexity, while the predominant state of masculinity is infantile, para-lysed by its need to reject complexity and thereby maintain false innocence. Eric and LeRoy's moment of intimacy – queer interracial intimacy, occurring across class divides – enables Eric to begin that process of maturation. This doesn't mean that all consummated queer desire between men in *Another Country* is de facto epiphanic, or in itself a solution to the prob-lems of masculinity. Indeed, one of the most mesmerising qualities about Baldwin's novel is how it works to resist any such static analysis. He shows how queerness or non-norma-tive expressions of desire do not neatly align with progressiv-ism, or forms of political resistance, simply because queer desire and those who practise it have been oppressed. Queerness between men is also, as Baldwin well knew, structured by power imbalances and redolent of the problems of that broken masculinity. Though Eric has the revelation that he is a 'man' he must still find the 'grace' to bear it. In Baldwinian parlance, he struggles to mature.

Eric's coupling with Rufus, for instance, was not redemptive or transformative simply because it was queer. Eric wonders if his desire for Rufus was merely a 'nostalgia' for the 'bodies of dark men' he had seen labouring in Alabama, glistening with sweat, in a 'garden or clearing, long ago'. In short, he wonders if his pursuit of Rufus was a kind of sex tourism, if his desire was fuelled by racial fetishism. And perhaps Rufus had divined this in Eric, perhaps he had 'looked into his eyes and seen those dark men Eric saw'. Was this *why* Rufus treated him so awfully, was this why he denigrated Eric? Rufus's homophobia was fused with his misogyny and his misogyny with homophobia, and both are diffuse with the effects of racism. As Leona's race and Southernness evoke the lynch mob for Rufus, so does Rufus despise Eric because his desire might be mediated through a racist gaze. Once again, Baldwin's intersectional characterisation shows how different types of inequity galvanise one another.

Queer desire and intimacy troubles Eric elsewhere, too. Eric recalls how he once 'submitted' himself to men whose private desires conflicted with their public masculine identities, men whose 'affections are frozen'. These men are reminiscent of those Baldwin discovered in the Apollo Theater, as a teenager: 'they were husbands, they were fathers, gangsters, football players', and their desires made their limbs heavy as 'drowning bathers'. Eric classifies this clandestine sexual economy as the 'ignorant army' – a phrase which Baldwin has been carrying around in his duffle bag since the Village years. They are ignorant because they have not been 'caressed' with love, they have not been caressed 'with light, with joy'. If they had, they wouldn't pursue their desires with shame.

So queerness in men – desired and consummated – is not figured as some totemic solution to the problems of masculinity, nor is it devoid of power dynamics. Yet, Eric's epiphany with LeRoy did occur, that revelation was instilled in him: something happened during their intimacy which enabled Eric to consider his queerness in concert with being a man rather than something in opposition to it (he is not 'half queer, half man' as Baldwin's friend wrote of the characters in *Giovanni's Room* – there is no discrepancy between these things). It had something to do with love, caress, joy. Eric is eventually able to 'bear' that revelation during *Another Country's* central sex scene, which takes place between him and Vivaldo. It occurs towards the end of the novel, at a time of desperation for Vivaldo, when his and Ida's relationship is breaking down, corroded again by Vivaldo's inability to acknowledge the effects of racism upon and within their coupling. One evening, while Ida is clandestinely with the talent agent Ellis, Eric and Vivaldo spend the evening together in Eric's apartment. Drunk, lying on bed in the gloom, illuminated only by the tiny flares of their cigarettes, Vivaldo confides in Eric about his inability to 'reach out' and touch Rufus, on the night of his suicide. Vivaldo then questions Eric about his sexuality, aware that while his own sexuality appears uncontested, he harbours scarcely acknowledged same-sex desire, too – fantasies 'of the male mouth, male hands' – which he only explored in adolescence.

The sex scene then unfurls, from Vivaldo's perspective. It begins as a dreamscape: Vivaldo is 'running through a country he had always known, but could not now remember'. Much like his nightmares about the soldier, in this dream, Vivaldo is pursued by a threatening Rufus. He begs his friend not to kill him, saying, '*I love you*'. To his 'delight and confusion', Vivaldo's plea for love works, and Rufus 'opened his arms'. Embracing his friend, Vivaldo's dream ends and he emerges into consciousness, discovering that he is – in reality – entangled with Eric. In a torrent of richly descriptive prose stretching over several pages, the two men have sex. It is no less complex than the novel's other sex scenes: Vivaldo is in a 'labyrinth of bewilderment' with Eric – he is afraid, disgusted, uncertain – but he soon feels shielded by Eric's 'love'. Protected thus, he becomes newly aware of his male body and its 'possibilities'. In contrast to that ignorant army, whose benumbed limbs are like those of drowning bathers, Vivaldo feels, in Eric's arms, held in suspension, 'as the salt sea holds the swimmer'. Nearing the scene's climax, Vivaldo and Eric penetrate each other in turn. At this moment, Vivaldo again thinks of his lost friend: '*Rufus. Rufus.* Had it been like this for him? What was it like for Rufus?'

This speculation is not the same kind of paranoid, insecure racialist surveillance of Rufus's masculinity encountered earlier. It is an incantation, an attempt to revivify his friend and embody him both, an impossible task, one born of love, and it occurs at the zenith of Vivaldo and Eric's lovemaking. After climaxing, Eric and Vivaldo declare their love for one another. Even if it never happens again, Vivaldo thinks, he has been transformed by the experience, transformed by the knowledge that there 'was a man in the world who loved him'. And his own feelings of love towards Eric amount to a 'great revelation', one that is 'strange', one which 'made for an unprecedented steadiness and freedom'. The transformation that occurred in Eric through his coupling with LeRoy has now occurred in Vivaldo through his coupling with Eric. If racist, masculinist violence is recursive, coursing through relationships across time, poisoning them and rigidifying those lines of power, then perhaps its opposite could also be true. Baldwin raises the prospect that intimacy between men, an intimacy charged by love, joy and affection, is also recursive. It also ripples through relationships, and has the potential to dissolve – or at least, is not hindered by – those paradigms of difference, and lead to new interpersonal terrain.

Baldwin is not, in *Another Country*, privileging queer sex between men as the only kind of transformative intimacy available for men. Nevertheless, by having the sexually fluid Eric engender a revelation in the macho Vivaldo through sex, Baldwin foregrounds this experience, to make an object lesson of sorts. The broken ideal of masculinity needs to be fixed – it reinforces and organises so many lines of power, those of violence and misogyny – and keeps men in a state of isolation. Repairing masculinity, addressing that isolation, involves closing off the space between men, which may be no more than a quarter of an inch. It means being able to give affirmative intimacy to one another, and this is only possible if *all* kinds of intimacy between men – including the possibility of sexual desire and connection – are ratified. If masculinity is to be fixed, if those infantile 'boys' are to mature into 'manhood', all forms of affirmative male intimacy, wherein love is the propellant, need to be recognised and endorsed.

Growing Pains

Another Country became a national bestseller, its popularity propelled by controversy but tainted by a mixed reaction from critics. Lionel Trilling, who had vouched for Baldwin's artistic talent to the director of Yaddo several years earlier, now paternalistically cautioned that Baldwin's 'extravagant publicness' – a reference to his incipient position as civil rights spokesperson and literary star both – might stymie the 'inwardness' he thought necessary for a writer to access 'truth'. Other critics were less philosophical, critiquing the book's risqué subject matter. The *New Leader* considered the novel pornographic and 'degrading' while taking a potshot at its 'exceptionally bad' writing. A piece in *Freedomways*, a leading African American cultural journal of the time, saw *Another Country* as a great letdown, lamenting that whatever message it attempts to impart about 'America's sexual paranoia' and the country's 'racial dilemmas' fails entirely. 'When [Baldwin] concerns himself,' the reviewer concluded, 'as he has here, so completely with the sexual mores of men uncertain of themselves [. . .] he has come to the end of a road.'

A particularly fierce judgement arrived from Norman Mailer, the stout, hirsute paragon of literary machismo, with whom Baldwin had had an on-again off-again friendship since the mid-1950s. Though perceptively writing that Baldwin's characters 'maim themselves trying to smash through the wall of their imprisonment', Mailer deemed *Another Country* an 'abominably written book' that reads like 'the first draft of a first novelist'. It was a searing criticism, to be sure, but Baldwin may have anticipated such a harsh analysis from Mailer. It was merely the latest salvo in a literary quarrel that had lasted several years.

Norman Mailer's relationships with other writers and contemporaries tended to be lubricated by similar displays of verbal aggression. His steroidal, febrile masculinity wasn't just a writer's persona cut from the Hemingway cloth, so to speak, and certainly wasn't restricted to the page. He was infamous for getting into bar fights, and relished, of all things, head-butting his opponents. Its most horrific manifestation, however, arrived in 1960, when Mailer stabbed and almost murdered his wife, Adele Morales, with a penknife. Baldwin and this physically volatile, cut-and-dried misogynist might seem like an incongru- ous pair. But the two men shared a joint fascination with writing as an act of bearing witness, or truth-telling, and Baldwin felt that Mailer – like him – also had the potential to become a gravedigger of America's collective repression by 'excavat[ing] the buried consciousness of this country' in his work. Baldwin was also fascinated – possibly enamoured – with Mailer's outsized braggadocio. Their friendship, early on, seemed bathed in a fraternal glow. When the two first met in Paris, Baldwin was mesmerised by Mailer's prideful masculinity: he was like a 'glad- iator'. But their connection subsequently petered out.

And then, in 1957, Mailer published 'The White Negro', a long essay in which he offered a speculative survey of the post- war, pre-hippy, Beat-adjacent subculture, the American 'hipster'. The essay is written in prose scattered with superficial references to Freudian psychoanalysis and Marx, and utilises the hipster's argot (itself derived from jive and bop talk, 'the Depression language of deprived Negroes', as Baldwin noted). Mailer argues that under the 'partially totalitarian' society of mid-century America, the white hipsters look to the 'Negro' man as a new

model or hero, and adopt what they believe to be 'black masculinity', an identity they imagine celebrates the body, virility, sex
and pleasure. And these attributes, the hipsters think, might help
them effectively rebel against society. Understandably, Baldwin
was less than impressed by such analysis. It was clear to him that
Mailer's argument relied on an essentialist, fantasy version of
black masculinity. But it wasn't until Mailer published
Advertisements for Myself (1959), a cross-genre collection of autobiographical reflections in which he skewered his literary
contemporaries, that Baldwin retaliated in print. In *Advertisements*,
Mailer remarked that Baldwin's sentences were 'sprayed with
perfume', implying that Baldwin's writing betrays effeminacy
and vanity. These qualities so incensed Mailer that he reached
for a figurative threat of violence, writing that he itched to
'smash the perfumed dome of [Baldwin's] ego'.

Baldwin's counter was 'The Black Boy Looks at the White
Boy', a complex, fascinating essay, published in 1961 in *Esquire*,
on his and Mailer's combative relationship. Baldwin, as though
baiting Mailer, termed the essay a 'love letter'. First brushing
aside 'The White Negro' as an ignorant, unintelligible and
senseless piece of writing, Baldwin then delved into the
complexities of his and Mailer's frictive pairing, complexities
which, Baldwin contested, remain invisible to Mailer. 'I know
something about the American masculinity which most men
of my generation do not know,' Baldwin writes, 'because they
have not been menaced by it the way I have been.' To be an
'American Negro', Baldwin goes on, is to be a 'walking phallic
symbol' and one must pay 'for the sexual insecurity of others'.
Any friendship between a 'black boy and a white boy' is thus
incredibly complex: it plays out on this 'sexual battleground',
in which black masculinity is constantly constructed according
to white fantasy, constantly surveilled by a white gaze (as
explored in *Another Country* in Rufus's and Vivaldo's

friendship.) 'Why malign the sorely menaced sexuality of Negroes,' Baldwin writes, deflating Mailer's argument, 'in order to justify the white man's own sexual panic?'

The American masculinity Baldwin speaks of is also one that presupposes heterosexuality to be the only valid kind of desire. It is Baldwin's queerness, too, which he has been 'menaced' for, and which gives him a unique, outsider's perspective from which to critique: although it is curious that this is only alluded to in the essay. Baldwin didn't explicitly address his sexuality in auto-biographical terms in his extensive nonfiction until the early 1970s, and, even then, he rarely utilises the language of labels or precise orientation. Baldwin was 'out', so to speak, among friends – it was known that he had romantic relationships with men – and he considered the publication of Giovanni's Room a kind of outing-by-art, correctly sensing that it would result in his being labelled in certain circles as a homosexual author. At the same time, Baldwin put a high premium on privacy, believing that what goes on in a bedroom is exclusively a matter for those in the bedroom, not the world.

This partially visible queerness – a slant relationship between his public and private personas – meant public reception of his sexuality was skewed, something conveyed in a 1963 Time magazine profile. The reporter steers clear of explicit sexual classifications, but characterises Baldwin with a raft of adjec-tives – he 'frets', is 'effeminate', 'fragile' and 'slight' – that said implicitly what had not been said explicitly. In the context of Mailer and Baldwin's ongoing dialogue, the former's hit-piece on Another Country might be seen as his attempt at delivering a verbal haymaker, an effort to smash the 'perfumed dome' and knock out a queer man he saw as an opponent on this sexual battleground: two men competing over the terms of interra-cial, homosocial relations, one armed with a love letter, the other with violence.

But *Another Country* and its proto-intersectional exploration of sexuality, gender and race didn't only pique the critical ire of the literati. In 1962, the Washington DC police department flagged the novel as being potentially illegally indecent, and sent a copy to the FBI. There, a special agent was assigned as 'ghost reader' of Baldwin's work. While this particular agent conceded there was nothing illegal about the novel's depictions of sex, the FBI continued to receive complaints. One concerned citizen, writing to the Bureau, said the novel depicted 'sex perversion at its vilest' and asked if there was any federal law that could prevent its sale. He addressed his complaint to the FBI's first director, J. Edgar Hoover, whose tenure had, by the mid-sixties, made him something of a 'national conservative confessor and pen pal' for right-leaning Americans. The FBI's interest in *Another Country* marked the outset of a deep, attritional surveillance campaign waged on Baldwin by the Bureau, one as insidious as it was, at times, comically ineffectual (one agent, attesting to the FBI's occasional incompetence, even reported that Baldwin was married).

This campaign escalated following the publication of Baldwin's next book, *The Fire Next Time*, in 1963, which combines two essays – the short 'Letter to My Nephew on the One Hundredth Anniversary of the Emancipation' and the longer article, 'Down at the Cross, a Letter from a Region of Mind', first published in the *New Yorker*. In *The Fire Next Time*, Baldwin presents a powerful indictment of white hegemony told through a personal, autobiographical perspective, exploring the deleterious effects of white Christianity on the black community, and recounts his experience meeting Elijah Muhammad, leader of the Nation of Islam and mentor of Malcom X. Like *Another Country*, it became a bestseller. And, much like Baldwin's other writings on race relations, it received adulation from white, intellectual readers, albeit in a twisted kind of way. The critic Elizabeth Hardwick described her milieu's reaction to the book: 'Everyone read it. Everyone talked about it and seemed to feel in some way the better for it.' Once again, Baldwin's work was received like an analeptic, administered to assuage collective white liberal guilt.

Even still, the publication of *The Fire Next Time* cemented Baldwin's position as a central name associated with the civil rights movement and its aims. This wasn't ignored by the Bureau. In 1963, Hoover had Baldwin elevated to the FBI's Reserve Index, a covert database listing individuals deemed to be threats to national security, selected at Hoover's discretion. Those on the list were subjected to street-level surveillance. Not long after this, Hoover scribbled on an internal memo: 'Isn't Baldwin a well-known pervert?' Baldwin's status as a threat to national security was viewed through the lens of both his race and his sexuality. It was an analogue to that psychic terrorism Baldwin had experienced as an unknown, aspiring writer almost two decades earlier, where life was like a hall of mirrors, his identity constantly harangued by others. The surveillance had merely escalated in conjunction with his career: Hoover – 'history's most highly paid (and most utterly useless) voyeur', in Baldwin's analysis – marshalled the resources of the US government itself to enact it. Over the years, the FBI amassed a file on Baldwin almost 2,000 pages in length, the longest of any African American writer working during Hoover's tenure.

By the time the FBI tagged Baldwin as a threat to national security, he was known, disparagingly, to some as 'Martin Luther Queen'. His position as a writer-celebrity-spokesperson was increasingly marred by such homophobic and misogynistic attacks. A few months after Mailer's 'perfumed sentences' joust was published, Richard Wright gave a lecture in Paris, in which he referred to Baldwin's work as exhibiting an 'unmanly weeping'. But a more damning, far-ranging and difficult critique came from Eldridge Cleaver, a political activist and senior member of the newly founded Black Panthers, later in the 1960s.

Cleaver had served several years in prison, having been convicted of rape and assault. He considered rape an insurrectionary act: that, by raping white women, he was 'getting revenge' for the 'historical fact' of how the 'white man has used the black woman'. In prison, however, he came to recant, realising that his sense of pride as a 'man' had all but dissolved. While incarcerated, he wrote autobiographical essays and treatises, which were eventually collated and published as a book, *Soul on Ice*, in 1968. These essays sought to blaze 'a new pathfinder's trail through the stymied upbeat brain of the New Left' and reclaim black masculinity and national identity as distinct from that constructed by white hegemony. And in this context, Cleaver had a lot to say about Baldwin. Utilising curious metaphors evoking both sexual desire and pregnancy, Cleaver writes that he once 'lusted' for Baldwin's writing, and would have happily caught each 'newborn' page from the 'womb' of his typewriter. Until he read *Another Country*.

Cleaver took issue with Baldwin's characterisation of Rufus, whom he considered a 'pathetic wretch' who 'let a bisexual homosexual [Eric] fuck him in his ass'. Rufus represents, for Cleaver, the coming to light of a subliminal ideology latent in Baldwin's entire oeuvre: a 'total hatred of the blacks' and a 'sycophantic love of the whites'. In Cleaver's view, Baldwin has bowed and submitted to 'the white man's *power*' and attempts to reclaim a position of masculine dominance by mimesis, aping white supremacy, waging a 'guerrilla war' against 'black masculinity' on paper. The idea of dominance/submission is central to Cleaver's venomous tirade against Baldwin, and finds its most vile expression in a now-infamous passage, in which Cleaver argues that queer men of colour like Baldwin who engage in interracial relationships have a 'racial death wish'. In his homophobic illogic, Cleaver seeks to repudiate queer interracial sex between men by figuring it exclusively as a power struggle in which black men invariably submit to white men. In doing so, he argues, they reveal a secret desire for whiteness, occupying a position synonymous with white femininity: submissive, progenitive, a vessel for, in Cleaver's view, 'the white man's sperm'. It's telling that Cleaver, reading *Another Country*, assumes Rufus is penetrated by Eric: there is no explicit mention of this in the text. And implicit in Cleaver's analysis is the limited, and misogynistic, assumption that men only find hetero sex acts pleasurable because insemination is a speculative outcome; desire quickened by progeny, fucking twinned with futurity.

To support his noxious conclusions, Cleaver looks to the writing of none other than Norman Mailer, citing Mailer's claim that 'one loses a bit of manhood' every time one compromises to the 'authority of any power in which one does not believe'. For Cleaver, the interracial queerness Baldwin depicts in his fiction – and lived – is tantamount to a betrayal of black masculinity, because he sees it as a submission to white masculinity: it is a compromise to an authority, and any such compromise is emasculating. That Cleaver finds alliance with Mailer, and that he is impelled to do so in reaction to Baldwin's *Another Country*, is a bleakly ironic distortion of the radical message contained in that very novel. Where Cleaver finds an interracial homosocial alliance with Mailer because they are both invested in a rigid, inflexible, simplified notion of masculinity, one that repudiates the so-called feminine and the queer, Baldwin's novel depicts the diffusive potentiality of affirmative male intimacy, relations between men that can be repaired across lines of racial difference by joy, caress and love, and by accepting fluidity and complexity.

Baldwin felt 'handicapped' by Cleaver's attack. He felt that Cleaver, in his position at the forefront of the Black Panthers, was priming younger audiences against him. In Baldwin's view, the Panthers posed a genuine, real threat to white supremacy, evidenced by their community orientated initiatives in the 'ghettos' – offering free hot dinners to school children, creating study programmes and the like – which received explicit support from those communities. Such initiatives, Baldwin knew, were designed to allay the demoralisation that attends poverty and stymies self-realisation: they were meant to improve the lives of impoverished people of colour. The efficacy of these initiatives, Baldwin saw, was made evident in the fact that the government was 'absolutely determined to wipe [the Panthers] from the face of the earth'.* Baldwin could not respond to *Soul on Ice* publicly without such a response being interpreted as an attack on Cleaver, which would be an attack on the Panthers, thereby ratifying Cleaver's driving critique: that Baldwin was pro-white. Nevertheless, in private, Baldwin's views on Cleaver's masculinist homophobia were crystal clear. 'All that toy soldier has done is call me gay,' Baldwin told an early biographer, 'all he wants is a gunfight at the OK Corral. He should go and make movies with John Wayne.'†

In 1969, a year after *Soul on Ice* is published, Baldwin is as restless, peripatetic and overworked as ever, writing plays, stories and a fourth non-fiction book, *No Name in the Street*.

---

* Two days after Martin Luther King Jr was assassinated, Eldridge Cleaver and the Black Panther's treasurer, Bobby Hutton, were involved in a shootout with police in Oakland, California. Cleaver was injured. Hutton was murdered.

† It's possible, though, that Baldwin found means for a public response in another way: his fiction. His fourth novel, *Tell Me How Long the Train's Been Gone*, published the same year that Cleaver's essays were collated in *Soul on Ice*, centres on Leo Proudhammer, a famous bisexual black actor, who has a romantic relationship with Barbara, a white actress, and with Christopher, a black activist/militant, modelled on the Panthers.

Temporarily living in Istanbul – the home city of his actor friend Engin Cezzar – Baldwin even tries his hand as a director. Utilising everything he learned under Kazan and Tennessee Williams, he directs a Turkish stage production of *Fortune in Men's Eyes*, a play about prison, homosexuality and sadism, authored by Canadian dramatist and drag performer John Herbert. The play is based on Herbert's own experiences of incarceration: in his twenties, he was mugged, but in court his assailants claimed they attacked him because he had made sexual advances towards them. Under Canada's strict anti-homosexuality laws, Herbert was imprisoned. It's easy to see why Baldwin was attracted to this play: it evokes the ways that men weaponise homophobia to further their own ends; staging it, Baldwin saw another opportunity to expose and therefore undermine the violent structures of patriarchy.

Several months after Baldwin stages *Fortune in Men's Eyes*, the Turkish documentarian Sedat Pakay shoots a short black-and-white film of Baldwin, titled *From Another Place*, which follows the writer through the labyrinthine streets, pigeon-crowded squares and bustling marketplaces of his adopted home. One particularly pleasing shot sees Baldwin rifling through a second-hand book stall, finding a copy of *The F.B.I Story* – a propagandistic history of the Bureau foreworded by none other than J. Edgar Hoover – and holding it up to the camera with a mischievous grin. But the heart of the short film finds us in Baldwin's modest, temporary lodgings: two desks topped with books and papers, and a single bed, upon which a magazine is spread open, showing an article about nineteen Black Panthers murdered in America by police.

At this point in the film, he is asked about his sexuality. He admits that this issue seems to be of importance to his audience. Baldwin wears a corduroy shirt, and twists a lit cigarette between his fingers, on one of which he wears an ancient

Turkish ring that he believes wards off evil. He cogitates, before delivering a staggering truth. 'I've loved a few men; I've loved a few women,' he says, concluding that 'love comes in very strange packages'. It's a profound piece of footage, in which Baldwin reduces the whole issue of sexuality, desire and gender to a simple point that, his studied, casual demeanour suggests, is so self-evident it may as well be a throwaway remark: love trumps difference.

This is the central doctrine of Baldwin's writings on sexuality, desire and gender: that radical intimacy, charged by joy and propelled by love, leads to intersubjectivity and communion with others, between individuals and groups, and across lines of difference; moreover, that to truly accept such intimacy, one must be receptive to the fact that it can come and will arrive from anyone, anywhere, at any time. Applied to the deleterious American ideal of masculinity, the consequences of this philosophy are as local and personal as they are of societal and national importance. True intimacy and love would begin the process of repairing the 'broken' masculinity which perpetuates all those harmful ethics that reinforce lines of difference and inequity, and keep us isolated from one another. But many men are prevented from accepting and embracing such intimacy, in whatever 'strange packages' it might arrive in. It is their infantilism – their reflexive homophobia, misogyny and rejection of complexity – which prevents them from this. Therefore a maturation absolutely must occur. In this respect, maturation becomes synonymous with love: 'Love,' Baldwin wrote, 'is a growing up.'

Epilogue

'I think the great emotional or psychological or effective lack of love and touching is key to the American or even the Western disease,' James Baldwin told cultural anthropologist Margaret Mead in 1972. In the wider gallery of Baldwin's thinking, this is a corollary to his view that the 'failure', and therefore affliction, of American and western life is that of a failed masculinity. Reconstruction must involve touch, intimacy and closeness, of a physical and metaphysical nature, between and among men. These kinds of relations or bonds, however, remain obscured to many because they exist on the same spectrum as, and can and do include, sexual and romantic intimacy between men, which is so repudiated in our culture. The tentacular reach of homophobia and therefore of misogyny indicates how deep set is our culture's affliction.

In his last published interview, Baldwin was unrelenting in his frustrations with those 'macho' men who so vociferously and violently enforce the ideologies of homophobia and misogyny. Such men, he said, are 'far more complex than they want to realise'. This is why he calls them 'infantile' because 'they have needs which, for them, are literally inexpressible'. An infantile masculinity, one in which men are scarcely capable of communication, stems from the fear of 'any human touch, since any human touch can change you'. For men, to allow oneself to be changed through communion and closeness with another is to cede power and control. It is to risk something; to accept that one's image of oneself as a man – dominant, unassailable, solitary – might turn from marble to rubble. The challenge would then be to construct a new sense of self, a stranger masculinity, from that wreckage.

Baldwin died from stomach cancer, in 1987, in his house in Saint-Paul-de-Vence, south-eastern France, where he had eventually settled. In the last years of his life, he hosted an array of artists and musicians, whomever was travelling through the French Riviera, at what he termed his 'welcome table'. There they would sit together for hours, and talk, and eat, and drink. David Leeming, Baldwin's biographer and friend, wrote of the writer's heartrending final days:

> He was insistent on not going to a hospital or having a nurse. He wanted men to take care of him – not, I was sure, because he disliked or mistrusted women, but because it was impor-tant to him that men express the feminine within themselves, that they adopt the kind of tender nurturing usually associ-ated with women. We became 'disciples' of his gospel, 'gentle' men of the 'welcome table'.

Baldwin's legacy, in Colm Tóibín's view, is both 'powerful and fluid [. . .] allowing it to influence each reader in a way that tells us as much about the reader as it does about Baldwin'. And Baldwin's popularity today can tell us as much about our social and political present as it does about his work. In the introduction to *James Baldwin: The FBI File*, which reproduces those documents accrued on the writer by the Bureau (recently obtained under the freedom of information act), editor William Maxwell makes a powerful case for why Baldwin has been held as 'literary conscious, touch-stone, and pin-up' within the broader Black Lives Matter movement. The 'proto-intersectional Baldwinian question of race-and-sex-and-more', he argues, is in greater harmony with current discourses than those of the mid-century, and perhaps 'Baldwin's variously queer misalignment with the social history of his present assures his model alignment with ours.'

In the case of John Cheever, it doesn't seem to be that his 'queer misalignment' with his world has assured an alignment with ours. Despite Blake Bailey's 2009 biography, and Olivia Laing's illuminating exploration into his alcoholism in *The Trip to Echo Spring: Why Writers Drink* (2013), there has been little renewed mainstream interest in traversing 'Cheever country'.* The journals were published in 1991, almost a decade after Cheever's death, in 1982. After publication, it appeared for a time that Cheever's entire life and work would be reduced to the posthumous public revelation of his bisexuality. A comment made by Cheever's daughter Susan, prior to the publication of her 1986 memoir about her father, *Home Before Dark*, reflects the anxiety that Cheever's legacy would be so diminished. She said that she never wanted to see a tabloid headline read: 'JOHN CHEEVER: A FAG'. Hence, she addressed his bisexuality in that memoir, as though to prevent a tabloid getting the scoop and casting Cheever in homophobic terms. 'Faggot', one of the most egregious slurs that can be levelled at queer men, has its roots in a pejorative or abusive term for women. The fear that her father would be labelled a 'fag' is thus a sad echo of Cheever's personal efforts to accept his queerness without modifying his masculinity, without leaving it open to 'feminine' interference: the entire story of homophobia-misogyny in miniature.

But there's every reason why Cheever's work should interest us today. The pressures he faced, and which he funnelled into his fictional haunted men, are arguably more relevant than

---

* Although sales of his works enjoyed a brief spike after *Mad Men* creator Matthew Weiner cited Cheever as a commanding tonal and atmospheric influence on the show.

ever; all those demands society makes on its men to be high earners and effective consumers in the pursuit of progeny, marriage and the 'good life', even as that society sleepwalks into oblivion. And dousing the journals for insights into Cheever's private mind, the many moments of joy, vivid optimism and transcendent self-acceptance – not to mention the rich appreciation of the natural world – is made all the more luminous by the knowledge that he had wrest them free from such all-consuming emotional hardship. While the world and characters of Cheever's stories prefigure and capture something of contemporary masculinity's malaise, the beautiful lyricism and searing honesty of his journals suggest pathways out of it.

For a novelist once hailed as a leading voice of a literary generation and celebrated by peers as one of the greatest writers in America, Carson McCullers is, like Cheever, relatively obscure today. Certainly, she has been eclipsed by those other Southern writers – Truman Capote, Harper Lee, even Flannery O'Connor – upon whom she had an enormous influence. 'Carson McCullers? Never heard of him', a bemused Brentano's bookseller was heard to remark in the late 1960s, by which time her critical reputation was already on the wane. Partially, her descent into the literary doldrums related to her illness, which forced her out of the public eye and drastically slowed her artistic output. But one wonders about a disinclination on behalf of the largely male-led literary establishment to champion or make efforts to canonise a woman whose public persona was very legibly queer. After all, queerness in women also threatens and perturbs the still surface of the prevailing heteronormative culture, though the tactics for disparagement might be different; invalidation brought about by wilful indifference. And McCullers, a woman who said she could, by way of a typewriter ribbon, transform herself into a homosexual man, a woman who consistently reoriented gender expectations of those around her while critiquing – of all things

– the military industrial complex, didn't disturb that still surface so much as detonate it.

A fortnight after McCullers' death in 1967, a film adaptation of *Reflections in a Golden Eye* premiered, directed by Hollywood legend John Huston, and starring a tense, turgid Marlon Brando as Captain Penderton to Elizabeth Taylor's luscious Leonora. It's a faithful adaptation of the text; the whole film is even tinted with a gold filter, staining it with an atmosphere of autumnal resplendence and sepia-toned stasis befitting an 'army fort in peace time'. Despite the star-studded cast, however, the film failed to pull McCullers' work into the pop cultural canon. It generally bemused reviewers and was met with scorn by its audiences. As film critic Roger Ebert recounted, the women in the audience giggled, while the men, their husbands, 'delivered obligatory guffaws in counterpoint. They had never seen anything funnier in their lives, I guess, than Brando nervously brushing down his hair when he thinks a handsome young private is coming to see him.' Maybe, as with Baldwin, this is a similar case of McCullers' 'queer misalignment' with her present. If so, we are surely better prepared to encounter the work today. Indeed, her relative obscurity is one reason why her critiques feel so powerful from our contemporary standpoint, as applied to our present: they feel redolent with possibility.

Tennessee Williams' most famous works and characters are so engrained in the culture – in both the US and UK – that it's difficult to imagine a time in which he won't be a household name. The plays and their film adaptations have, in director Gregory Mosher's estimation, 'reflected and shaped American culture to a degree unmatched by almost any other American writer'. Pop cultural canonisation, however, carries its own perils: the artistry and attendant truths of those famous works have been reduced to bits and parts and resold to us in the pleasant, postmodernist, ultra-processed form of passing intertext and allusion. This is how many millennials first encountered Tennessee's pre-eminent plays – or at any rate, the Hollywood adaptations. In an early episode of *The Simpsons*, both *Cat* and *Streetcar* are satirised in a throwaway skit, which primed millions of nineties kids to approach those stories first and foremost as melodramas that derive their power from a queer subtext so obvious that the very notion there is anything 'subtextual' or ciphered about it is laughable. But Tennessee Williams' canonical work hasn't just been cannibalised by the culture; these plays continue to be staged, and live theatre remains the best, most immediate, unfiltered way to receive Tennessee's transmissions and experience those 'thunderclouds of common crisis' in which his characters are so often embroiled. It's no surprise that the muscular millennial heartthrob of the moment, Paul Mescal, was cast as Stanley Kowalski in a 2022 production of *Streetcar*; even less so that his sexual allure among millennial and Gen-Z audiences helped the production sell out and move to London's West End, thereby broadcasting the play's message of broken masculinity and stalled male relations to a wide new audience.

Beyond those more famous works, Tennessee Williams left a veritable mountain of later, Off-Off Broadway stage plays, in which he continued to stretch the conventions of theatre and taste. Critics often mocked these late-career efforts. 'It is a sad comment on our American culture,' wrote Eve Adamson in the introduction to the posthumously published *Something Cloudy, Something Clear*, 'that to the end of his life we censured the most original poet of our theatre for continuing to explore, whatever the cost or danger, the boundaries of his consciousness'. From *Small Craft Warnings*, in which a gay couple struggle with affection and communication, to *A House Not Meant to Stand*, a grotesque dark comedy set, as theatre critic John Guare described it, in 'a world where the Kowalskis rule', these later plays are just as rich with revelations into masculinity; and they are now beginning to receive due academic and artistic attention. Perhaps the prediction made by the band of carollers at outset of Williams' late one-act play, *The Mutilated*, is finally coming to fruition: 'I think the strange, the crazed, the queer / Will have their holiday this year / And for a while, a little while / There will be pity for the wild.'

Walt Whitman's legacy – his own evergreen effort to explore the outer reaches of himself, to push the very boundaries of masculine self-identity into new, uncharted territory – is just as powerful and fluid as James Baldwin's. Indeed, his call for new affirmative, intimate relations between men as a socially trans-formative force seems to prefigure Baldwin's. And yet, Whitman's 'adhesiveness' so often asserted the putatively masculine over the feminine; in the poems, those loving bonds between men, with all their radical potential, don't so much invite a reconfigured masculinity as redouble traditional notions of manhood. Hence the emphasis on virility, forthrightness, robustness, athleticism, vigour, health and semen besides. It's a closed loop, in which intimacy between men might only trans-form masculinity if it is 'manly' enough.

But there are flashes of something else, something far stran-ger, in Whitman's poems: all those genderless, disembodied, searching and touching hands, those shape-shifting figures with their free-floating desires, deep in the wet woodland. These passages suggest that sexuality and gender are malleable, not fixed but fluid, and they phosphoresce with possibility. And there are those gentler, subtler interludes in his grand and fraught vision of adhesiveness, portals into new, tender, rela-tions between men that do attempt to rework traditional notions of masculinity, that do attempt to be 'relieved of distinctions'. Two men, in 'Calamus', late on a winter night, are glimpsed sitting with each other in a crowded, noisy barroom. They do not imitate the behaviour of the drunken men that surround them, who make 'smutty' jokes, but, rather, sit quietly, holding hands. They find in such intimacy a state of harmony in which they are 'content, happy in being together, speaking little, perhaps not a word'.

Despite arriving to us from well over a century ago, Whitman's enchanting, insistent poems continue to allure, to break boundaries and offer alternative approaches to masculinity, and they will surely continue to do so well into the future. This is the exact role Whitman wrote for himself, right back to that preface to the first, 1855 edition of *Leaves of Grass*. 'Past and present and future are not disjoined but joined,' he wrote, and the poet 'places himself where the future becomes present'. We move through the waterwheel of history, our language and ideas dredged up from the pond waters, exposed to the light and plunged back again, a rotation that produces – one hopes – useful forms of illumination, a rotation that goes on for ever.

Perhaps Tennessee Williams had something like this in mind when he said that the world is like an 'unfinished poem', because 'everything is in flux' and always undergoing a process of creation. And he felt it incumbent upon all of us to finish that poem, together, something only possible through 'understanding and patience and tolerance'. That the creation of more equitable, more beautiful societies and modes of living might be like an artistic collaboration is a remarkable idea. In order to access the connectivity that such a joint effort requires, the diktats of misogyny and homophobia must absolutely be eradicated; male relations transformed; and our broken masculinity repaired and remade. This is a truth that we as a society, and men as individuals, are surely ready to accept; if only we can first recognise it. But perhaps, as Baldwin believed, that future is imminent if not upon us already: 'a day is coming, hopefully, when the shock of recognition will be a joy and not a trauma, a release, and not a constriction: for it is absolutely and eternally true that all men are brothers, and that what happens to one of us happens to all of us.'

Notes

Writing this book, I've relied upon the work of researchers, critics and scholars too numerous to name. The five central writers are each the subject of more than one biography, not to mention scholarly monographs, essay collections, documentary films, and the like. Nevertheless, there is a huge amount of unpublished material still held in archives, and I am indebted to the many generous, knowledgeable and dedicated library staff who helped hunt down particular boxes and folders with nothing but a few cryptic clues to go on, and who facilitated reprography, often with extremely rapid turn-arounds (one batch of Cheever's archived pages even arrived in my inbox on Christmas Eve). I owe particular thanks to those staff at the Beinecke Rare Book and Manuscript Library; the Harry Ransom Centre; the New York Public Library, Henry W. and Albert A. Berg Collection of English and American Literature; the David M. Rubenstein Rare Book & Manuscript Library; the Kinsey Institute Library & Special Collections; and the Houghton Library.

Many of the Whitman texts, including scans and complete transcriptions of every printed edition of *Leaves of Grass*, the letters and the nine volumes of *With Walt Whitman in Camden*, have been accessed in the first instance via The Walt Whitman Archive (whitmanarchive.org), an invaluable resource created and maintained by leading Whitman scholars. Original source texts are cited where possible.

In *Part Two: A Feeling of Estrangement*, I cite and reference the version of *Cat on a Hot Tin Roof* collated in *Tennessee Williams: Plays, 1937–1955* (Library of America, 2000). This reproduces the play's first edition text, published by New Directions in 1955, which contains both Tennessee Williams' preferred ending and the performed ending ('Cat Number One' and the 'Broadway Version'). Referencing the Library of America text helps avoid confusion with subsequent editions of the play, also published by New Directions, especially the 1975 version, which contains an entirely different ending alongside significant revisions.

In *Part Three: What Did I Desire?*, Cheever's published *Journals* are frequently cited. These, however, amount to a mere fraction of the complete journals, which are housed in Harvard University's Houghton Library, in 28 volumes, each containing multiple folders. The archived journals run to over 4,000 pages, or over one million words. The independent scholar, Francis J. Bosha, has created a literary inventory of Cheever's archived journals ('The John Cheever Journals at Harvard University's Houghton Library,' in *Resources for American Literary Study*, Volume 31, 2006). This immensely detailed text – itself well over one hundred pages in length – is an indispensable roadmap for anyone wishing to consult Cheever's archived journals. Folder by folder, it summarises the journal entries, populating these summaries with direct quotations, which I have used at times (in the notes as 'Bosha'). Referring to Bosha's text, researchers can – as I have done – request certain folders from the archive, with a good idea of what will be found in them. In addition, there are several citations here to 'The Bloody Papers', which other biographers have likewise referenced. As far as I can tell, these are a sheaf of pages, containing autobiographical writing, held in Box 5, Folder 7 of the John Cheever Papers at the New York Public Library.

In *Part Four: What About Love?*, I cite the single volume *James Baldwin: Collected Essays* (Library of America), with corresponding essay titles, rather than the original collections in which those essays first appeared. This is for ease of reference, and will, I hope, be of more value to the reader who wishes to consult these texts.

KEY: *Original Works – Commentary*

WALT WHITMAN (WW)
Complete Prose Works	CPW
Leaves of Grass (LG) followed by publication year (18★★)	LG55
Manly Health and Training	WWMH
With Walt Whitman in Camden	WWIC
Walt Whitman: The Correspondence	WWTC

TENNESSEE WILLIAMS (TW)
A Streetcar Named Desire	*Streetcar*
Cat on a Hot Tin Roof	*Cat*
Conversations with Tennessee Williams	*Conversations*
Memoirs	TWM
Notebooks	TWNB
The Selected Letters of Tennessee Williams	*Letters*

CARSON McCULLERS (CMcC)
The Flowering Dream	TFD
The Heart Is a Lonely Hunter	*Hunter*
Illumination & Night Glare: The Unfinished Autobiography	*Illumination*
Reflections in a Golden Eye	*Reflections*
The Lonely Hunter: A Biography of Carson McCullers, Virginia Spencer Carr	TLH

JOHN CHEEVER (JC)
Bloody Papers	JCBP
Conversations with John Cheever	*Conversations*
Glad Tidings: A Friendship in Letters	GT
The Journals of John Cheever	JJC
The Letters of John Cheever	LJC

Home Before Dark, Susan Cheever	HBD
John Cheever: A Life, Blake Bailey	CAL
John Cheever: A Biography, Scott Donaldson	CAB

JAMES BALDWIN (JB)

Another Country	AC
A Rap on Race	*Rap*
Collected Essays	CE
Conversations with James Baldwin	*Conversations*
Giovanni's Room	GR

The Furious Passage of James Baldwin, Fern Marja Eckman	FP
James Baldwin: Artist on Fire, J. W. Weatherby	AOF
James Baldwin: A Biography, David Leeming	BAB
Talking at the Gates: A Life of James Baldwin, James Campbell	TAG

INTRODUCTION

1 '*sexual terrorist*', Arthur Miller, 'Regarding Streetcar', in Tennessee Williams, *A Streetcar Named Desire* (New York: New Directions, 2004), xii.

1 '*I could hardly hold him . . .*', TW in *Conversations* (TW), 216.

1 '*the best-looking young man*', TWM, 164.

2 '*the great problem . . .*', JB, 'The Male Prison', CE, 232.

2 '*masculine sensibility* [. . .] *something broke down*', JB quoted in 'Writers and Writing in America Today', originally recorded by The Poetry Center, San Francisco State College, 22 October 1960. Online at The Poetry Center Digital Archive: diva.sfsu.edu.

2 '*You can't imagine a time . . .*', Ira J. Bilowit, in *Conversations* (TW), 310.

4 '*gracious – full of imaginings*', TW in *Conversations* (TW), 16.

4 '*the war between romanticism . . .*', ibid., 45.

4 '*wandering, dreaming occupation*', '*illuminations*', CMcC, TFD.

5 '*I was born a man*', CMcC, quoted in VSC, TLH, 159.

5 '*divine the motives . . .*', JC quoted in Francis J. Bosha, 'The John Cheever Journals at Harvard University's Houghton Library', *Resources for American Literary Study*, Vol. 31 (2006), 211.

6   *'double life . . .'*, JC, *The Journals of John Cheever* (New York: Alfred A. Knopf, 1991), 200.

7   *'a way of exerting . . .'*, JB quoted in 'Go the Way Your Blood Beats', in *The Village Voice*, 26 June 1984.

8   *'could not cease . . .'*, Eve Kosofsky Sedgwick, *Between Men* (New York: Columbia University Press, 1985), 4.

8   *'residue of terrorist potential . . .'*, ibid., 89.

9   *'Is he? Was he? . . .'*, JJC, 117.

10 *'seismographic shudder* [. . .] *fear of people . . .'*, JB, 'The Devil Finds Work', CE, 529.

10 *'When men can no longer . . .'*, JB, 'The Male Prison', CE, 235.

12 *'sexual iridescence'*, JC quoted in CAL, 480.

12 *'jam'*, CMcC quoted in TLH, 169.

13 *'It doesn't make a goddamn . . .'*, TW in *Conversations* (TW), 230.

13 *'If one's to live at all . . .'*, JB, in *Conversations* (JB), 55.

13 *'homosexuality is just . . .'*, JB quoted in William J. Weatherby, *Squaring Off: Mailer Vs Baldwin* (New York: Mason/Charter, 1977), 13.

13 *'Those terms . . .'*, ibid., 54.

PART ONE: O ADHESIVENESS!

Image: Walt Whitman and Peter Doyle. Photograph by Moses P Rice, c. 1869. Retrieved from the Library of Congress.

THE REBEL SOLDIER FRIEND

19 *'the toppling-off place . . .'*, WWIC, v3, 537.

20 *'books, magazines . . .'*, CPW, 517.

20 *'I am large . . .'*, LG55, 55.

20 *'This poet celebrates himself . . .'*, Walt Whitman [unsigned in original], 'Walt Whitman, a Brooklyn Boy', *Brooklyn Daily Times*, 29 September 1855.

21 *'In his aspect . . .'*, *Conserving Walt Whitman's Fame: Selections from Horace Traubel's Conservator, 1890–1919*, ed. Gary Schmidgall (Iowa City: University of Iowa Press, 2006), 167.

22 *'We felt to each other . . .'*, Peter Doyle, 'Interview With Peter Doyle', interview by Richard Maurice Buck, *Calamus* (Boston: L. Maynard, 1897), 23.

23   '*my darling boy*', WWTC, v2, 83–5.

23   '*my young & loving brother*', ibid.

23   '*Yours for life*', WWTC, v2, 56–8.

23   '*my love for you is indestructible . . .*', ibid., 83–5.

23   '*cant Explain the Pleasure . . .*', Peter Doyle to Walt Whitman [23 September 1868]. Papers of Walt Whitman (MSS 3829), Clifton Waller Barrett Library of American Literature, Albert H. Small Special Collections Library, University of Virginia. Transcribed from digital images. Online.

23   '*I like to look at him . . .*', WWIC, v1, 391.

24   '*I meet new Walt Whitmans every day . . .*', WWIC, v1, 108.

24   '*How much I owe her . . .*', WWIC, v2, 113.

24   '*Doyle should be a girl . . .*', WWIC, v3, 543.

26   '*homosexuality appeared as . . .*', Michel Foucault, *The History of Sexuality*, Vol. I: *An Introduction*, trans. Robert Hurley (New York: Random House, 1980), 42–4.

26   '*superb friendship, exalté . . .*', LG60, 374.

AN ORGY IN ARCADIA

29   '*It was also his object . . .*', Peter Doyle, 'Interview With Peter Doyle'.

29   '*reckless health . . .*', WW, 'Walt Whitman, a Brooklyn Boy'.

30   '*of a live, naive, masculine . . .*', ibid.

30   '*The proof of a poet . . .*' and subsequent, LG55, xii.

31   '*I celebrate myself . . .*' and subsequent, LG55, 13.

32   '*the poet of the body . . .*', LG55, 26.

33   '*every atom . . .*', LG55, 13.

33   '*The bodies of men . . .*', LG55 77.

33   '*so friendly . . .*' and subsequent, LG55, 19–20.

CLAP A CROWN ON TOP OF THE SKULL

38   '*funny . . .*', '*mystery and power . . .*', WWIC, v7, 109.

39   '*has a grand physical constitution . . .*', quoted in Edward Hungerford, 'Walt Whitman and His Chart of Bumps', in *American Literature*, Vol. 2, No. 4 (January, 1931), 360.

40 *'formative stage'*, WWIC, v7, 109.

40 *'extreme caution or prudence . . .'*, LG55, ix.

41 *'Nature is not fixed . . .'*, Ralph Waldo Emerson, 'Nature', in *The Works of Ralph Waldo Emerson*, Vol. 2 (London: G. Bell & Sons, 1904), 443.

41 *'the most extraordinary piece of wit . . .'*, LG56, 345.

42 *'So, then, these rank* Leaves *. . .'*, William Rounseville Alger [unsigned in original], *Christian Examiner*, 60 (November 1856), 471–3.

42 *'It will become a "Household Book" . . .'*, George Hull Shepard [unsigned in original], *Long Islander* 3 (10 December 1858), 2.

42 *'see, talk little, absorb . . .'*, WWIC, v1, 417.

43 *'the great highway . . .'*, WWMH, *New York Atlas*, 26 December 1858.

43 *'healthy manly virility . . .'*, *'best conditions . . .'*, WWMH, *New York* Atlas, 10 October 1858.

43 *'positioned male flesh . . .'*, Eve Kosofsky Sedgwick, *Epistemology of the Closet, Updated with a New Preface* (Berkeley, California: California University Press, 2008), 136.

43 *'without the thoughts irresistibly . . .'* and subsequent, WWMH, *New York Atlas*, 19 September 1858.

44 *'strong, alert, vigorous . . .'*, WWMH, *New York Atlas*, 12 September 1858.

44 *'reckless health . . .'*, Walt Whitman, 'Walt Whitman, a Brooklyn Boy'.

44 *'the development of a superb race . . .'*, WWMH, *New York Atlas*, 19 September 1858.

44 *'the science . . .'* and subsequent, WWMH, *New York Atlas*, 26 September 1858.

45 *'pass forth, in business . . .'*, WWMH, *New York Atlas*, 3 October 1858.

CALAMUS-LEAVES AND WOMAN-LOVE

46 *'The Great Construction . . .'*, LG60 (*Notebooks* 1: 353).

46 *'Free, fresh, savage . . .'*, *'chants inclusive . . .'*, LG60, 5.

46 *'O to be relieved . . .'* LG60, 22.

47   '*Limitless, unloosened*', LG60, 543.

47   '*Profoundly affecting . . .*', LG60, 453.

47   '*to be loved by strangers . . .*', LG60, 320.

47   '*the same to the passion [. . .] the Calamus-Leaves . . .*', WW (*Notebooks* 1: 412).

48   '*the biggest and hardiest . . .*', '*fresh, aquatic . . .*', WWTC, v1, 346−7.

48   '*My brain it shall be . . .*', LG56, 43.

48   '*Who has quenched . . .*', '*thus gave his form . . .*', Nonnos, *Dionysiaca*, trans. W. H. D. Rouse (Cambridge, Mass.: Harvard University Press, 1940), 389−93.

49   '*in paths untrodden . . .*', '*tell the secrets . . .*', '*no longer abashed . . .*', '*silent troop . . .*', '*tomb-leaves . . .*', '*spirits of friends . . .*', '*shall henceforth . . .*', '*It shall be customary . . .*', '*without edifices . . .*', '*new City of friends . . .*', '*invincible to the attacks . . .*', LG60 341−78.

52   '*hours discouraged . . .*', '*out of the like feelings . . .*', '*his / friend . . .*', LG60, 355−6.

52   '*fluid . . .*', '*affectionate . . .*', LG60, 366.

53   '*a friend visiting hospitals . . .*', WWTC, v1, 258−60.

53   '*a fine specimen . . .*', '*handsome, athletic . . .*', '*the heart of the stranger . . .*', *Complete Prose Works* (Philadelphia: David McKay, 1892), 36−7.

54   '*at the foot of the tree . . .*', ibid., 26.

54   '*adhesiveness or love . . .*', ibid., 220.

56   '*transgressively blended role . . .*', Ed Folsom, 'Whitman's Calamus Photographs', in *Breaking Bounds*, eds Betsy Erkkila and Jay Gossman (New York: Oxford University Press, 1996), 196.

56   '*chanter of Adamic songs . . .*', '*the new garden . . .*', LG60, 312−13.

56   '*surrounded by beautiful . . .*', LG60, 294.

56   '*Sex contains all . . .*', '*Without shame . . .*', LG60, 302.

57   '*you women . . .*' and subsequent quotes from 'Children of Adam', LG60, 305−7.

Addendum: see Tom Yingling's generous and expansive 'Homosexuality and Utopian Discourse in American Poetry', in *Breaking Bounds*, for an enlightening discourse on the possibilities and pitfalls of the 'utopian gesture' contained within Whitman's (and Hart Crane's) work.

DISEASED, FEVERISH, DISPROPORTIONATE ADHESIVENESS

60   '*throws against oblivion*', WWIC, v1, 77.

60   '*systematically collecting* . . .', '*I'll be handing you stuff* . . .', WWIC, v1, 66.

61   '*I can hardly find a name* . . .', '*The accomplished languages* . . .', John Addington Symonds, 'A Problem in Modern Ethics', in *John Addington Symonds (1840–1893) and Homosexuality: A Critical Edition of Sources*, ed. Sean Brady (Basingstoke: Palgrave Macmillan, 2012), 128.

61   '*a sort of Bible* . . .', '*desires grew manlier* . . .', '*abnormal inclinations* . . .', John Addington Symonds, *The Memoirs of John Addington Symonds: A Critical Edition*, ed. Amber K. Regis (London: Palgrave Macmillan, 2016), 606. Epub.

62   '*It would hardly be fair* . . .', '*the evolution* . . .', ibid., 24. '*You will be writing something* . . .', '*the forms of what* . . .', '*I have pored for continuous hours* . . .', '*Well, what do you think* . . .', '*I don't see* . . .', '*I often say* . . .', WWIC, v1, 73–7.

63   '*possible intrusion* . . .', John Addington Symonds to Walt Whitman, 3 August 1890. Transcribed from scan of original. Whitman Archive.

63   '*terrible*', '*morbid inferences*', WWTC, v5, 72–73.

64   '*you must not think that* . . .', '*Frankly speaking* . . .', John Addington Symonds to Walt Whitman [5 September 1890]. Whitman Archive.

65   '*I maybe do not know* . . .', '*I say to myself* . . .', WWIC, v1, 77.

66   '*Day by day* . . .', LG60, 311.

66   '*GIVE UP* . . .', '*avoid seeing her* . . .', WW quoted in *Notebooks and Unpublished Prose Manuscripts*, ed. Edward F. Grier (New York: New York University Press, 1984), 888–9.

67   '*Depress the adhesive nature* . . .', ibid., 889–90. The case for the substitution of pronouns in Whitman's notes was first made by scholar and academic Roger Asselineau, in *L'évolution de Walt Whitman* (1955).

PART TWO: A FEELING OF ESTRANGEMENT

Image: Tennessee Williams and Carson McCullers. Photograph by Rollie McKenna, 1954 © The Rosalie Thorne McKenna Foundation, Courtesy Center for Creative Photography, The University of Arizona Foundation.

SEA-SUMMER

71   'such a freakish run . . .', TW, *Notebooks*, 441.

72   'The physical machine . . .', TW to James Laughlin [June 1946], in *The Luck of Friendship: The Letters of Tennessee Williams and James Laughlin*, eds Peggy L. Fox and Thomas Keith (New York: W. W. Norton, 2018). Letter #45. Epub.

72   'blast furnace . . .', TW, *Memoirs* (New York: Bantam Books, 1976), 99.

72   'getting the creative juices . . .', TWM, 214.

73   'so extraordinary . . .', TW quoted in Lyle Leverich, *Tom: The Unknown Tennessee Williams* (New York: Crown Publishers, 1995), 375.

73   'Are you Tennessee and Pancho?', CMcC, quoted in Virginia Spencer Carr, *The Lonely Hunter: A Biography of Carson McCullers* (Garden City, New York: Doubleday, 1975), 272.

75   'victim of . . .', Rex Reed, 'Carson McCullers', 39–43.

76   'My personal trinity . . .', TW, TWNB, 62.

76   'southern degeneracy . . .', TW to Margo Jones [September, 1946], quoted in John Lahr, *Tennessee Williams: Mad Pilgrimage of The Flesh* (New York: W. W. Norton, 2014), 106.

77   'Carson didn't need me . . .', TW, quoted by VSC in 'Exotic Birds of a Feather: Carson McCullers and Tennessee Williams', *Tennessee Williams Annual Review*, 3 (2000).

78   'understanding of another [. . .] affectionate compassion', TW, Saturday Review, 1961, September, Vol 44, Issue 38.

PORTRAIT OF A GIRL

79   'A strange and powerful book . . .', 'I can't understand . . .', Unattributed, [dust jacket], *Hunter*.

79   'round-faced, Dutch-bobbed . . .', Clifton Fadiman, 'Books: Pretty Good for Twenty-two', *New Yorker*, 8 June 1940.

80 *'androgyne'*, Hilton Als, 'Unhappy Endings', *New Yorker*, 25 November 2001.

80 *'lesbian persona'*, Sarah Schulman, 'McCullers: Canon Fodder?' *The Nation*, 8 June 2000. Online.

82 *'blossomed like a sunflower . . .'*, *'I was a bit of a holy terror . . .'*, Rex Reed, 'Carson McCullers', in *Do You Sleep in the Nude?* (New York: New American Library, 1968), 39–43.

82 *'the Archangel Gabriel'*: various sources attribute this quote to the photographer Marianne Breslauer, who shot many portraits of Annemarie.

82 *'bodily resplendent . . .'*, *'a face that will haunt me . . .'*, *Illumination*, 21.

83 *'or it will happen, eventually . . .'*, VSC, TLH, 105.

LOVE AND ESTRANGEMENT

84 *'a projected mood, a state of mind . . .'*, Richard Wright, 'Inner Landscape', *New Republic*, 103, 5 August 1950.

85 *'the words in their heart . . .'*, Hunter, 165, *'whoever [they] wished he would be . . .'*, 173, *'were always together . . .'*, 3, *'A strange feeling . . .'*, *'you cannot do this . . .'*, *'none of your business . . .'*, 7–8, *'he had been left . . .'*, 157, *'the only thing . . .'*, 166, *'wholly to thoughts . . .'*, *'submerged communion . . .'*, *'awe and self abasement . . .'*, *'kaleidoscopic variety . . .'*, *'almost stifled . . .'*, 245–55, *'the placid composure . . .'*, 168, *'sharp, yellow rectangle . . .'*, 11, *'no noise or conversation . . .'*, *'mutual distrust . . .'*, *'special physical part . . .'*, *'new, tender nipples . . .'*, *'as much like . . .'*, 23–5, *'by nature all people . . .'*, 103, *'not only a sundae . . .'*, *'a strange guilt . . .'*, 178.

90 *'consciousness of guilt . . .'* and subsequent, Ralph McGill, *The South and the Southerner* (Boston: Little, Brown, 1963), 217.

THE INVERT

92 *'child-woman'*, *'I gave Carson . . .'*, *'it is a strange love . . .'*, David Diamond quoted in VSC, TLH, 147–50.

92 *'invert'*, VSC, TLH, 168.

93 *'a woman's soul trapped in a man's body'*: this phrase originated with the pioneering sexologist Carl Heinrich Ulrichs.

93 *'one of those strange things . . .'*, Havelock Ellis, *Sexual Inversion* [1897], 3rd edition (1915), in his *Studies in the Psychology of Sex*, Vol. 1 (New York: Random House, 1936), 322.

94 *'somebody of medical . . .'* and subsequent, John Addington Symonds to Edward Carpenter [29 December 1892] in *The Letters of John Addington Symonds*, eds Herbert M. Schueller and Robert L. Peters (Detroit: Wayne State University Press, 1967), viii, 797.

95 *'symbolic castration . . .'*, Wayne Koestenbaum, *Double-Talk: The Erotics of Male Literary Collaboration* (New York: Routledge, 2017), 100. Epub.

95 *'an essential heterosexuality . . .'*, *Epistemology of the Closet*, 87.

96 *'an identity that history had not yet discovered . . .'*, Sarah Schulman, 'White Writer', *New Yorker*, 21 October 2016. Online.

96 *'You're really a little girl . . .'*, CMcC quoted in TLH, 519.

96 *'nothing human is alien to me . . .'*, CMcC, TFD.

Addendum: for more on Ellis, Symonds, and inversion, see 'Havelock Ellis, Sigmund Freud and the State: Discourses of Homosexual Identity in Interwar Britain', and Joseph Bristow, 'Symonds' History, Ellis' Heredity', in *Sexology in Culture: Labelling Bodies and Desires*, eds Lucy Bland and Laura Doan (Chicago: University of Chicago Press, 1998).

A HEALTHY BODY AND PATRIOTISM

98 *'play-writing'*, CMcC, 'Essay on the Creative Process', Box 1, Carson McCullers Collection, Harry Ransom Center, The University of Texas at Austin.

98 *'Grecian purity'*, *'cut like a jewel'*, TW, 'Introduction', in *Reflections in a Golden Eye* (New York: Bantam, 1950), xi.

98 *'Things happen . . .'*, *'all is designed . . .'*, 'There is a fort . . .', *Reflections*, 7.

99 *'neither man, beast . . .'*, *Reflections*, 19, *'obtained within himself . . .'*, 'a sad penchant . . .', 14–15, *'a healthy body . . .'*, 116, 'nearest thing to love . . .', 33, *'something of a mystery . . .'*, 8, *'reconnoiter'*, 'carried in them a deadly . . .', 23, *'soft, urgent whispers'*, 30, 'Flap-fanny', 27, *'miracle of [his] blood . . .'*, *'vague, impersonal eyes'*, 71–3, *'conscious only of the irresistible yearning . . .'*, 118, *'hubbub . . .'*, 'the irresistible shenanigans . . .', 109, *'he is expected only . . .'*, 7.

104 *'eating candy'*, CMcC, 'Essay on the Creative Process'.
104 *'manoeuvres'*, *'the fine looking soldiers . . .'*, *'the best . . .'*, *Reflections*, 49–50.
105 *'categories of handicap'*, *'deviations'*, *'homosexual proclivities'*, quoted in Allan Bérubé, *Coming Out Under Fire* (New York: Free Press, 1990), 12.
106 Quotes on Sexual Perversion sourced in Allan Bérubé, *Coming Out Under Fire*, 18–22. Bérubé's book is essential reading on this subject.
108 *'You mean [. . .] that any fulfilment . . .'*, *Reflections*, 112.
109 *'cool spring water'*, quoted in VSC, TLH, 394.
109 *'he could not always . . .'*, VSC, TLH, 295.
109 *'infant-terrible insight . . .'*, Fred Marsh, 'At an Army Post', *New York Times Book Review*, 2 March 1941.
109 *'offended [. . .] arrogant and pitiless . . .'*, Rose Feld, '[Review of] Reflections in a Golden Eye', *New York Herald Tribune Books*, 16 February 1941.
110 *'if this is a fair sample of army life . . .'*, Edward Weeks, 'First Person Singular', *The Atlantic*, April 1941.
110 *'fairy'*, *'everyone accused me . . .'*, *'I must say . . .'*, CMcC, *Illumination*, 31.
110 *'When I write about a thief . . .'*, CMcC, TFD.

DOWN AND OUT IN NEW ORLEANS

112 *'We ought to be exterminated . . .'* and subsequent text formatted as speech, quoted in TW, 'Sunday, 14 September 1941', TWNB, 233–5.
113 *'Then and there the theatre . . .'*, *'shining blond'*, *'delicacy'*, *'you must do . . .'*, TWM, 52–3.
114 *'fresh and primitive . . .'*, TW, *Orpheus Descending* with *Battle of Angels: Two Plays* (New York: New Directions, 1958), 132.
114 *'a great bronze statue . . .'*, TW to Donald Windham, *Tennessee Williams' Letters to Donald Windham*, ed. Donald Windham (New York: Holt, Rinehart and Winston, 1977), 9.
114 *'I love you'*, TW to Kip Kiernan ([22 or 23 August 1940] Harry Ransom Center), quoted in TWNB, 220.
114 *'seen enough'*, *'being'*, *'violated'*, TWM, 77.
114 *'I shall have to . . .'*, TWNB, 203.

115 'Utterly alone', TWNB, 209.

115 'hover like a bright angel', TWNB, 232.

116 'provide something more clarifying . . .', 'deviation', 'express', TWNB, 233–5.

MEAT!

117 'red stained package', 'Meat!', Streetcar, 4.

117 'one or two exceptions', TWM, 164.

117 'tiger [. . .] roar out . . .', Arthur Miller, 'Regarding Streetcar', Streetcar, xii.

117 'there is one character . . .', TW quoted by Gore Vidal, 'Immortal Bird', in New York Review of Books, 13 June 1985.

118 'jack[ing] off', TW to Donald Windham [20 September 1943], in Tennessee Williams' Letters to Donald Windham, 105.

118 'love affair', TW, Conversations, 108.

118 'the power of a writer . . .', TW to Jim Gaines, 'A Talk About Life and Style with Tennessee Williams', in Conversations, 219.

118 'made to occupy a larger space . . .', TW quoted by Vidal, in 'The Immortal Bird'.

118 'it's got life in it', TW, Battle of Angels, 194.

119 'My heroines [. . .] always express . . .', TW in 'Tennessee Talks to John Calendo', Interview, April 1973.

119 'transsexual self-projection', Camille Paglia, 'Tennessee Williams and A Streetcar Named Desire', in Provocations: Collected Essays (New York: Pantheon Books, 2018), 313. Epub.

120 'It may not be . . .', in The Selected Letters of Elia Kazan, eds Albert J. Devlin and Marlene J. Devlin (New York: Alfred A. Knopf, 2014), 326.

120 'cloudy dreamer type [. . .] objective and dynamic [. . .] vastly provocative', TW to Elia Kazan [May 1947], in Letters, v2, 104.

120 'truthful, faithful [. . .]', Elia Kazan to TW [April 1947], in The Selected Letters of Elia Kazan, 200.

121 'young man', 'Cherry . . .', 'It would be nice . . .', Streetcar, 98, 'the boy, the boy', 28, 'degenerate', 124, 'you disgust me', 115, 'poems a dead boy wrote', 42, 'I hurt him', 42, 'in a house with women', 'at the peak . . .', 'raw colours . . .', 'speak quietly . . .', 46–63.

123 'I couldn't believe . . .', Streetcar, 165, 'the game is seven card stud', 179.

124 *'the subject of sex degeneracy . . .'*, quoted in Kaier Curtin, *We Can Always Call Them Bulgarians: The Emergence of Lesbians and Gay Men on the American Stage* (Boston: Alyson Publications, 1986), 211. See pp. 266–87 for a detailed account on the Wales Law, its impact and challengers, in the years preceding and following *Streetcar*.

124 *'lower the moral standards . . .'*, Motion Picture Association of America, 'The Motion Picture Production Code'.

124 *'sex perversion'*, quoted in R. Barton Palmer and William Robert Bray, *Hollywood's Tennessee: The Williams Films and Postwar America* (Austin: University of Texas Press, 2009), 73. See Palmer and Bray's notes for a more detailed account of *Streetcar's* journey to the silver screen.

WHY DO THEY STRIKE US?

127 *'males do not represent . . .'*, Alfred C. Kinsey, Wardell B. Pomeroy and Clyde E. Martin, *Sexual Behavior in The Human Male* (Philadelphia and London: W. B. Saunders Company, 1948), 639.

127 *'for understanding the futility . . .'*, *'ignorance and superstition'*, ibid., 203.

128 *'American document . . .'*, *'democratic pluralism . . .'*, Lionel Trilling, 'The Kinsey Report, 1948', in Lionel Trilling, *The Moral Obligation to Be Intelligent: Selected Essays*, ed. Leon Wieseltier (New York: Farrar, Straus and Giroux, 2000), 135.

128 *'because homosexuality is prevalent . . .'*, Dr Lawrence S. Kubie, quoted in 'Dr. Kinsey's Misrememberers', *Time* magazine, 14 June 1948.

129 *'sex perverts . . .'*, *'one homosexual can pollute . . .'*, Hoey Committee Report 'Employment of Homosexuals and Other Sex Perverts in Government', US Senate, 15 December 1950, accessed via Stanford University Library, The Digital Stacks. For further analysis of the Hoey Report, and a thorough, detailed historical survey of the Lavender Scare, see David K. Johnson, *The Lavender Scare* (Chicago: University of Chicago Press, 2004).

130 *'put up or shut up'*, FBI files, quoted in James H. Jones, *Alfred C. Kinsey: A Public/Private Life* (New York: W. W. Norton, 1997), 632.

130 *'as dangerous as actual communists'*, Guy George Gabrielson, Republican National Chairman, quoted in 'Perverts Called Government Peril', *New York Times*, 19 April 1950.

130   *'communist or a cocksucker'*, Senator Joseph McCarthy, quoted in K. A. Cuordileone, 'Politics in an Age of Anxiety: Cold War Political Culture and the Crisis in American Masculinity, 1949–1960', *Journal of American History*, Vol. 87:2 (September 2000), 515.

131   *'understanding'*, TW to Alfred Kinsey [18 January 1950], *Letters*, v2, 286.

131   *'should be heterosexual'*, TW, *Conversations*, 245.

132   *'the thing which we all dreaded . . .'*, TW to Jane Lawrence Smith, [8 March 1950], *Letters*, v2, 296.

132   *'unnatural advances'*, John Collins quoted in *Letters*, 297.

132   *'have been prosecuting . . .'*, *'bohemians'*, *'sissy walk'*, TW to CMcC [April 1950], *Letters*, v2, 309.

132   *'Who is Oscar Wilde?'*, TW to Paul Bigelow [11 April 1950], Letters; v2, 296.

132   *'entertainment'*, and subsequent, TWNB, 339.

THE SYSTEM OF MENDACITY

134   *'swats flies in outer space'*, Kenneth Tynan, 'Valentine to Tennessee Williams', *Mademoiselle*, February 1956.

135   *'a black day to begin . . .'*, TWNB, 665.

135   *'a small atom bomb'*, James Laughlin to TW [16 January 1955], in *The Luck of Friendship*, Letter 107. Epub.

135   *'I don't get but one play . . .'*, *'richest creative period . . .'*, Elia Kazan to TW [20 October 1954], in *The Selected Letters of Elia Kazan*, 494.

135   *'many past obstructions'*, *'tremendous wrenching . . .'*, TWNB, 583.

136   *'like lightning in a fair sky'*, *Cat*, 885.

137   *'true quality of experience in a group of people . . .'*, *Cat*, 945.

138   *'unnecessarily repulsive brace'*, Christopher Isherwood, *Diaries*, Vol. 1, *1939–1960*, ed. Katherine Bucknell (London: Vintage, 1997), 479.

138   *'discovered'*, *'homosexual'*, TWM, 310.

139   *'even if* Cat *is not a good play . . .'*, TW to Elia Kazan [October 1954], *Letters*, v2, 549.

139   *'But it's the truth'*, quoted in Jess Gregg, 'Kazan and *Cat'*, *Tennessee Williams Annual Review*, 12 (2011), 68.

139 *'shocking duality'*, TW to Elia Kazan [October 1954], *Letters*, 552.

139 *'no-neck monsters'*, *Cat*, 883, *'naw-mal rid-blooded children'*, 895, *'They're sittin' in the middle . . .'*, 924, *'so goddamn disgustingly poor'*, 907, *'your indifference made you wonderful . . .'*, 892, *'when a marriage goes on the rocks . . .'*, 903, *'this lie true'*, *'that son of a bitch [. . .] that bitch [. . .] five same monkeys'*, *'been able to stand the sight . . .'*, *'I've lived with mendacity . . .'*, 941–2, *'a pair of old bachelors'*, *'the room must evoke some ghosts'*, 880, *'a pair of dirty old men'*, *'sissies? Queers?'*, *'exceptional friendship [. . .] a real real, deep deep friendship [. . .] fairies?'*, *'we gauge the wide and profound reach . . .'*, *'Why did Skipper crack up?'*, 947–9, *'a little bit closer . . .'*, *'We made love . . .'*, 909, *'that ole pair of sisters'*, *'You dug the grave of your friend'*, 949–50.

143 *'hobohemia'*, for more on this interpretation, see Claire Nicolay, 'Hoboes, Sissies, and Breeders: Generations of Discontent in Cat on a Hot Tin Roof' in *Tennessee Williams Annual Review*, 12 (2011). For more on 'hobohemia', see George Chauncey, *Gay New York* (New York: Basic Books, 1995).

145 *'the precise sexual orientation . . .'*, TW in 'George Whitmore interviews Tennessee Williams', in *Gay Sunshine* 33/34 (Summer/Fall 1977), anthologised in *Gay Sunshine Interviews*, ed. Winston Leyland (San Francisco: Gay Sunshine Press, 1978), 310–25.

145 *'Wouldn't it be funny if that was true?'* This line was reinstated by Williams – along with a rewritten third act – in his preferred edition of the play, *Cat on a Hot Tin Roof* (revised edition) (New York: New Directions, 1975). For more information on the *Cat* rewrite debacle, see R. Barton Palmer, 'Elia Kazan and Richard Brooks do Tennessee Williams: Melodramatizing *Cat on a Hot Tin Roof* on Stage and Screen', *Tennessee Williams Annual Review*, 11 (1999).

145 *'the system'*, *Cat*, 953, *'I admire you, Maggie'*, 1005.

148 *'dangerous to the whole art . . .'*, *'a tangential thing . . .'*, *'Revolutionary plays?'*, TW in 'George Whitmore interviews Tennessee Williams'.

CODA

150 *'Next to my sister Rose . . .'* and subsequent, TW in *Conversations*, 89–90.

151 *'sea-summer lit with the glow . . .'* CMcC, 'A Personal Preface', in *The Square Root of Wonderful* (Boston: Houghton Mifflin, 1958), vii.

151 *'The gang is made up of twelve men . . .'*, CMcC, *The Ballad of the Sad Café* (Boston: Houghton Mifflin, 1951), 65–6.

PART THREE: WHAT DID I DESIRE?

Image: John Cheever. Photograph by Ben Martin, 1961 © Ben Martin / Getty.

THE PRISON GUARD AND THE PRISONER

157 *'where there is grass . . .'*, John Cheever to Mary Cheever [1942], *Letters*, 91.

158 *'anything resembling war . . .'*, *'kindness and indigestion . . .'*, JC to E. E. Cummings, Marion Morehouse [October 8, 1942], *Letters*, 81.

158 *'southern boys'*, *'Ain't that pretty?'*, JC, quoted by Benjamin Cheever in *Letters*, 91.

158 *'titanic inefficiency'*, *Letters*, 67.

159 *'mooning over . . .'*, *'chasing a training stick'*, *'Fuck that . . .'*, JC to Bill Maxwell [Undated, 1942], *Letters*, 77.

159 *'like a pack of dogs'*, JC to E. E. Cummings, Marion Morehouse, [Undated, 1942], *Letters*, 82.

159 *'the finest looking group of men [. . .] gullible guard'*, JC to Mary Cheever, [Undated, 1942], *Letters*, 84.

160 *'was a bisexual . . .'*, Benjamin Cheever, 'The Man I Thought I Knew', in *Letters*, 18.

160 *'credentials as a gentleman'*, HBD, 155.

160 *'confinement of traditional values . . .'*, JC, *Conversations with John Cheever*, ed. Scott Donaldson, (Jackson: University Press of Mississippi, 1987), 114.

160 *'flows or should flow . . .'*, JJC, 66.

161 *'the trappings or traps . . .'*, HBD, 155.

161 *'divine the motives . . .'*, Bosha, 211.

161 *'a naked prisoner . . .'*, JJC, 8.

RELICS OF THE PAST

162   'Our lives are not . . .', JC to Elizabeth Ames [April 12, 1935], *Letters*, 36.

162   'crypto-autobiography', JC quoted by Benjamin Cheever in *Letters*, 21.

162   'incongruities', JC quoted in HBD, 199.

162   'verisimilitude', JC, *Conversations*, 97.

162   'to illustrate one's most intimate feelings . . .', JCBP.

163   'lousy with adolescence', JC to Malcolm Cowley [Undated], *Letters*, 30.

163   'boy of summer', JJC, 235, 'centre of [his] world', JJC, 244.

163   'Massachusetts Yankee . . .' JC quoted in Scott Donaldson, *John Cheever: A Biography* (New York: Random House, 1988), 8.

164   'play a little baseball . . .', JJC, 8.

164   'sired a fruit', JJC, 219.

165   'iron woman [. . .] feminine interference', JC quoted in CAL, 116.

166   'devotion to each other is stronger . . .', JC, 'The Brothers', in *The Way Some People Live* (New York: Random House, 1943), 166.

166   'murderous', 'loving', Bosha, 297.

166   'morbidly close', JC, *Conversations*, 156.

167   'relics of the past . . .', JC to Elizabeth Ames [1934, Boston], *Letters*, 33.

167   'twilight world . . .', Joan Didion, 'The Way We Live Now', in *Critical Essays on John Cheever*, ed. R. G. Collins (Boston: G. K. Hall, 1988), 66.

167   'writing, writing, writing', JC, *Conversations*, 5.

168   'rich air . . .', HBD, 25.

168   'peer at the sexual acrobatics', Bosha, 294.

169   'I asked her for a date', JC, *Conversations*, 239.

169   'more important event . . .', Struthers Burt, 'John Cheever's Sense of Drama', in *Saturday Review*, 30 April 1943.

169   'acid accounts . . .', Weldon Kees, 'John Cheever's Stories', in *New Republic*, 19 April 1943.

170   'childlike sense of wonder': this phrase, according to Cheever, originated with Spiegelgass. Apocryphal or not, it became a Cheever truism, which he regularly repeated, as did his family and critics.

170   'to war each morning . . .', John Weaver, GT (New York: HarperCollins, 1993), 2.

MORTAL LOVE

171 '*There was something different* [. . .] *Then I found out* [. . .] *Allan, the Grey boy*', TW, *Streetcar*, 114–15.

172 '*entirely masculine*', Mary Cheever quoted in CAL, 162.

172 '*a torn evening dress* [. . .] *write passionately . . .*', JJC, 12–13.

173 '*good wife*', '*lively children*', JJC, 61.

173 '*everybody in the United States . . .*', JJC, 117.

173 '*stained with desire*', JJC, 61.

173 '*the sexually aberrant male*', US Attorney George Morris Fay, quoted in *The Lavender Scare*, 55.

174 '*aberrant carnality*', JJC, 11.

174 '*young men travelling . . .*', JJC, 14.

174 '*the smell of laurel*', JJC, 17.

174 '*erotic purgatory*', JJC, 61.

175 '*a million dollars*', JC to Josephine Herbst, [September 1948], *Letters*, 135.

175 '*Peter Pan a look . . .*', Mabelle Fullerton, 'Former Quincy Boy Courting Miracle', in *Quincy Patriot-Ledger*, 2 September 1948.

175 '*strain of debt*', JJC, 29.

175 '*windowless chambermaid's cell*', JC, *Letters*, 124.

176 '*army prose*', '*poorly informed snobbism*', JJC, 28.

176 '*shoestring aristocrats*': this is how Cheever characterises the fictional Beers family in 'Just One More Time', first published in the *New Yorker*, 30 September 1955.

176 '*like a cultivated . . .*', George Garrett, 'John Cheever and the Charms of Innocence', in *The Hollins Critic*, April 1964.

176 '*the abrasive loneliness . . .*', James Kelly, 'The Have-Not-Enoughs', in *New York Times Book Review*, 10 May 1953.

177 Quotations from 'The Enormous Radio', first published in the *New Yorker*, 17 May 1947.

178 Quotations from 'Clancy in the Tower of Babel', first published in the *New Yorker*, 24 March 1951.

182 '*old, tender-hearted . . .*', JC quoted in LCJ, 194.

183 '*neurosis*', '*lethal dose*', '*too-sensitive reader*', William DuBois, 'Books of The Times', in *New York Times*, 1 May 1953.

183 '*lovelier-looking ashtray*', JC to John Weaver [May 1953], *Glad Tidings*, 74.

FREUD VERSUS THE EARTH

184   '*a bone, a stone, a stick . . .*', JJC, 219.

185   '*insubstantial as smoke*', '*old WW*', '*excludes Venus*', JCBP.

185   '*deep hue of sexual anxiety*', JCBP.

185   '*repulsive*', '*jumpy and prudish*', Bosha, 219.

185   '*queers and the usual woolgathering . . .*', Bosha, 215.

185   '*divided*', '*paradoxical*', JJC, 217.

186   '*insane, neurotic, queer . . .*', JJC, 57.

187   '*I would like some business . . .*', JCBP.

187   '*a small and dirty fraud . . .*', JJC, 87–8.

187   '*the fragrance of the natural earth*', JCBP.

187   '*vices*', '*masturbating . . .*', JJC, 141.

188   '*heavy succulence [. . .] grass root . . .*', JJC, 50–1.

188   '*pin the tail onto Freud*', JCBP.

xx   '*prolonged psychoanalytical conversations*', *Conversations*, 133.

189   '*terrifying and changeable*', Bosha, 259.

189   '*mirror-person*', CAL, 358.

189   '*doubt[ed] the very existence . . .*', Sigmund Freud, 'Three Essays on Sexuality', in *The Standard Edition of the Complete Works of Sigmund Freud*, v7, ed. James Strachey (London: Hogarth Press, 1953), 114.

190   '*plural history of urges . . .*', Eli Zaretsky, *Secrets of the Soul: A Social and Cultural History of Psychoanalysis* (New York: Alfred A. Knopf, 2004), 52. See Chapter 11 for an engaging overview of U.S psycho-analysis during the Cold War era.

191   '*take themselves as their sexual object [. . .] a young man who resembles . . .*', Freud, 'Three Essays on Sexuality', in *The Standard Edition*, 145. My emphasis.

191   '*Psychoanalytic research . . .*', ibid.

193   '*ploughed the fields [. . .] surveyed the shattered detritus . . .*', Phyllis Grosskurth, *Havelock Ellis: A Biography* (New York: Alfred A. Knopf, 1988), 360.

194   '*rejection of the homosocial . . .*', Zaretsky, 284.

195   '*an* infantile *country . . .*', JJC, 129. My emphasis.

195   '*promise of recaptured youth*', Bosha, 264.

195   '*a lack, a longing . . .*', JC quoted in CAL, 192.

195   '*inalterable, pure*', '*inseminate*', '*demean*', Bosha, 233.

THE LAST SWIMMER OF SUMMER

197   *'unbearable or transcendent'*, HBD, 87.

197   Quotations from 'The Scarlet Moving Van', first published in the *New Yorker*, 21 March 1959.

198   Quotations from 'O Youth and Beauty!', first published in the *New Yorker*, 22 August 1953.

199   Quotations from 'The Swimmer', first published in the *New Yorker*, 18 July 1964.

201   *'persistent clinging . . .'*, *'last swimmer . . .'*, Bosha, 266.

202   *'In the woods . . .'*, Ralph Waldo Emerson, 'Nature', in *The Works of Ralph Waldo Emerson*, Vol. 2, 374.

202   *'transcendentalist'*, John Updike, on *The Dick Cavett Show*, 14 October 1981.

203   *'weird'*, anonymous, in *Newsweek*, 30 November 1964.

203   *'sinister'*, Orville Prescott, in the *New York Times*, 14 October 1964.

203   *'get your trunks on . . .'*, JC in *Conversations*, 63.

THE VALLEY

204   *'freelance writers . . .'*, CAL, 282.

204   *'the colour of artificial lime drink'*, JC to Bill Maxwell [Undated, 1961?], *Letters*, 230.

205   *'our world's inability . . .'*, JC quoted in HBD, 171.

205   *'in making sense . . .'*, JC quoted in GT, 218.

205   *'fucking do-gooder'*, JC quoted in CAL, 519.

206   *'narrative is a synonym for life'*, JC, *Untitled* [Notes, Vignettes, Personal Reflections], The Henry W. and Albert A. Berg Collection of English and American Literature, The New York Public Library.

206   *'cool motherfucker'*, JC to Benjamin Cheever [May 1971], *Letters*, 284.

206   *'faces of exceptional . . .'*, *'comely'*, *'great company'*, Bosha, 268.

206   *'the blasphemy of men creating . . .'*, JC, quoted in Susan Cheever, *Home Before Dark: A Biographical Memoir of John Cheever by His Daughter* (Boston: Houghton Mifflin, 1984), 171.

206   *'balls'*, Donald Lang quoted in CAL, 451.

206   *'dynamism between youth and age . . .'*, JJC, 285.

207 *'writing'*, *'fucking'*, Ned Rorem, *The Later Diaries of Ned Rorem,*
1961–72 (San Francisco: North Point Press, 1988), 195.

208 *'terrifying erotic chaos'*, JJC, 214.

208 *'executioner'*, *'executioner mask . . .'*, JJC, 162.

208 *'strangeness [. . .] sensible strictures [. . .] infections of anxiety'*, JJC, 207.

209 *'in agricultural and maritime societies . . .'*, JC, quoted in HBD, 174.

209 *'enjoyed a forthright robustness'*, ibid.

210 *'unsuitable pastime . . .'*, JJC, 216.

210 *'a series of younger male protégés'*, HBD, 177.

210 *'erotic cult that counts so on beauty'*, JJC, 205.

211 *'back-slapping friendship'*, quoted in CAL.

211 *'irregular'*, JJC, 343.

212 *'How can this man . . .'*, JJC, 312.

212 Quotations from 'The Leaves, The Lion-fish, and The Bear', first
published in *Esquire*, 1 November 1974.

213 *'I'm so glad you ain't a homosexual'*, John Cheever, *Falconer* (New
York: Alfred A. Knopf, 1977), 91.

214 *'grotesque bonding'*, *'so profound a love'*, ibid.

214 *'since Jody was a man [. . .] the danger that Jody . . .'*, JC, *Falconer*, 103.

214 *'a flower seemed to bloom [. . .] wilderness'*, *'become infatuated . . .'*, *'dark
simples'*, *'kiss a man [. . .] unnatural as the rites . . .'*, *'kissing the turf . . .'*,
JC, *Falconer*, 103–5.

214 *'prejudice against faeries [. . .] silly and feebleminded'*, *'like a swimmer . . .'*, *'strange and unnatural'*, JC, *Falconer*, 111–16.

215 *'the Valley'*, *'after chow'*, JC, *Falconer*, 117.

215 *'as I live, homosexuality is not an evil'*, *JJC*, 219.

215 *'What did I desire? . . .'*, JJC, 282.

216 *'bisexual anxieties [. . .] Perhaps I should have said . . .'*, *JJC*, 299.

216 *'I am queer . . .'*, *JJC*, 344.

PART FOUR: WHAT ABOUT LOVE?

Image: James Baldwin. Photograph by Jean-Regis Rouston, 1964 ©
Jean-Regis Rouston / Getty.

THE AMERICAN MADNESS

219 'strange, great and bewildering', JB, 'Freaks and the American Ideal of Manhood', in *James Baldwin: Collected Essays* (New York: The Library of America, 1998), 825.

220 'bottomless, eerie, aimless hostility', JB, 'The Black Boy Looks at the White Boy', CE, 276.

220 'alabaster maze . . .', JB, 'The Price of The Ticket', CE, 832.

220 'wrestling', JB quoted in BAB, 49. Elsewhere, JB refers to 'wrestling' with his typewriter.

221 'hall of mirrors . . .', JB, 'Freaks', CE, 823.

221 'outlaw', JB quoted in BAB, 91.

221 'beautiful ambiguity', JB, 'As Much Truth As One Can Bear', in *The Cross of Redemption: The Uncollected Writings of James Baldwin*, ed. Randall Kenan (New York: Pantheon Books, 2010), 68. Epub.

221 For Baldwin's fears about Paris, see Eckman, FP, Chapter Nine.

222 'It was my season . . .', JB, 'Freaks', CE, 823.

222 'welfare workers . . .', JB, 'Notes of a Native Son', CE, 67.

222 'strange', 'ugliest boy', 'frog eyes', 'the most beautiful woman', JB, 'The Devil Finds Work', CE, 481–3.

223 'sissy', JB, 'Freaks', CE, 823.

223 'like some weird kind of food', JB quoted in AOF, 15.

224 'When I was fourteen . . .', JB, 'Autobiographical Notes', CE, 5.

224 'moustachioed, razortoting . . .', 'shattered', JB, 'Freaks', CE, 818–19.

225 'into Beauford's colours', 'black-blue midnight', 'new confrontation . . .', 'on everything, on everybody', JB, 'On the Painter Beauford Delaney', CE, 721.

225 'absolute integrity', 'living proof', 'a black man could be . . .', JB, 'The Price . . .', CE, 832.

226 'You'd rather write . . .', JB, 'Notes', CE, 80.

226 'conceptions of a good American labourer', JB quoted in AOF, 37.

226 'choking desire . . .', JB quoted in BAB, 42.

226 'a prison', JB, quoted in FP, 113.

226 'monstrous', JB quoted in FP, 96.

227 'reaching towards the world . . .', JB, 'Notes', CE, 66.

227 'decidedly the most improbable', JB, 'Freaks', CE, 823.

227 'monstrously young', JB, 'Memoirs of a Bastard Angel', in *Uncollected*, 334. Epub.

228 '*thought were friends*', JB, quoted in FP, 100.

228 '*beyond the obscenity* . . .', '*sexual proclivities*', JB, 'Freaks', CE, 825.

229 '*by means of what the white man* . . .', JB, 'Stranger in The Village', CE, 123.

229 '*bloody catalogue* . . .', JB, 'The American Dream and The American Negro', 714.

229 '*certain human remove*', JB, 'Stranger', CE, 122.

229 '*appendage*', '*double fear*', JB, 'Freaks', CE, 823–4.

230 '*innocence and terror*', '*beat faggots up*', '*cops, football players* . . .', '*male desire for a male*', JB, 'Freaks', CE, 820–21.

231 '*beautiful cat*', JB quoted in FP, 126.

231 '*both women and men*', '*race truly meant nothing* . . .', JB quoted in AOF, 65.

231 '*all the implications* . . .', JB quoted in FP, 110.

231 '*incandescent boy*' and subsequent on Eugene Worth, JB, 'The New Lost Generation', CE, 660–62.

233 '*desperate moral abdication*', JB, 'Freaks', CE, 826.

233 '*terrifying personal anarchy*', '*dared not discover* . . .', '*lapsed* . . .', JB, 'The New Lost Generation', CE, 662.

233 '*white people were, and are* . . .', JB, 'Down at the Cross', CE, 317.

233 '*split the scene completely*', JB in James Baldwin and Margaret Mead, *A Rap on Race* (Philadelphia: J. B. Lippincott Company, 1971), 49.

234 '*a refuge from the American madness*', '*chilling unpredictability* . . .', JB, 'The New Lost Generation', CE, 665.

INTO THE LAND OF THE LIVING

235 '*I have many responsibilities* . . .', JB, 'Autobiographical Notes', CE, 9.

236 '*one of the best* . . .', Lionel Trilling quoted in 'A Peek at Life in an Artist's Retreat', *New York Times*, 19 July 1999.

236 '*the status of the Negro in America* . . .', Manuscripts and Archives Division, The New York Public Library, 'Report for Committee on Admissions by James Baldwin', New York Public Library Digital Collections.

236 '*Socratic gadfly*', Ernest L. Gibson III, *Salvific Manhood: James Baldwin's Novelisation of Male Intimacy* (Lincoln: University of Nebraska Press, 2019), 34. Epub.

236 '*bear truthful witness*', BAB, 48.

236 '*those airless, labelled cells*', JB, 'The Preservation of Innocence', CE, 600.

237 '*national convulsion*', and subsequent, JB, 'Take Me to the Water', CE, 370–73.

237 '*wild process*', '*failure . . .*', '*American toilet*', 'The New Generation', CE, 665.

239 '*realised he could marry . . .*', JB quoted in BAB, 127. Epub.

242 '*homophobic homoerotic[ism]*', Ellis Amburn, *Subterranean Kerouac: The Hidden Life of Jack Kerouac* (New York: St Martin's Press, 1998), 54.

THE LIGHT OF A SMASHED FLOWER

244 '*the white consciousness . . .*', BAB, 101.

245 '*dead*', JB quoted in FP, 137.

246 '*un film du far west*', James Baldwin, *Giovanni's Room* (New York: The Dial Press, 1956), 52.

246 '*tenderness so painful*' and subsequent, GR, 7–9.

246 '*diseased and undefinable [. . .] smashed flower . . .*', GR, 78.

247 '*regurgitated*' and subsequent, GR, 80.

247 '*I am happy . . .*', GR, 79.

247 '*two grown men . . .*' and subsequent, GR, 74–5.

247 '*insistent possibilities*', GR, 37.

248 '*how profoundly all things . . .*', JB, 'The Preservation . . .', CE, 600.

249 '*stink*', GR, 125.

249 '*an army of boys . . .*' and subsequent, GR, 50.

249 '*grave distrust*' and subsequent, GR, 88–90.

249 '*Please don't shut me out . . .*', GR, 142.

250 '*serious things*', GR, 137.

251 '*harshly bright*' and subsequent scene, GR, 79–80.

251 '*major American ambitions . . .*', '*arrive at man's estate*', '*the most abysmal . . .*', JB, 'The Preservation . . .', CE, 597.

252 '*so paralytically infantile . . .*', JB, 'Freaks', CE, 815.

253 '*half queer, half man*', quoted in TAG, 104.

253 '*instinctive desires [. . .] validity . . .*', Anthony West, 'At Home and Abroad', in the *New Yorker*, November 1956.

THE BOYS

255 '*intolerable nervous strain*', '*like cardboard*', JB, 'Geraldine Page; Bird of Light', *Uncollected*, 68. Epub.

256 '*coming out the faucet*', JB quoted in AOF, 144.

256 '*Elia Kazan is a traitor . . .*', Orson Welles, 'Orson Welles à la Cinémathèque française', 24 February 1982.

257 '*inexplicable transformations*', JB, 'Geraldine Page . . .', *Uncollected*, 70.

257 '*visceral*', '*Tennessee didn't sit . . .*', Elia Kazan, quoted in AOF, 148.

257 '*Relentless caper . . .*', Hart Crane, 'Legend', quoted in TW, *Sweet Bird of Youth* (New York: New Directions, 1959). Epigraph.

259 '*what is happening . . .*', JB, 'A Fly in Buttermilk', CE, 196.

259 '*demand*', JB, 'Nobody Knows My Name', CE, 203.

260 '*one of the most powerful men*' and subsequent, JB, 'Take Me to the Water', CE, 391–2.

261 '*speak on the Death of The Short Story*', John Cheever to Malcolm Cowley [16 September 1960], *Letters*, 226.

261 '*some kind of literary blow-out*', John Cheever to John D. Weaver [24 May 1960], *Letters*, 119.

261 '*much more in common . . .*', JC quoted in AOF, 173.

261 '*relevant*', '*lost suburbanites*', JB in *Conversations with James Baldwin*, ed. Fred L. Stanley; Louis H. Pratt (Jackson: University Press of Mississippi, 1989), 228.

261 '*abrasive and faulty surface*', JC quoted in CAB, 179.

262 '*great cult of nostalgia . . .*' and subsequent, JB quoted in 'Writers and Writing in America Today'.

263 '*when men can no longer love women . . .*', JB, 'The Male Prison', CE, 235.

DO YOU LOVE ME

264 '*strange and frightening*', JB to Mary Painter [Undated], Walter O. Evans Collection of James Baldwin. James Weldon Johnson Collection in the Yale Collection of American Literature, Beinecke Rare Book and Manuscript Library.

264 '*bring to the surface . . .*', JB to Mary Painter [23 December 1957], ibid.

264   *'profound realities'*, *'colour and sex'*, JB quoted in TAG, 134.

264   *'long-playing record . . .'*, Howard Harper, *Desperate Faith: A Study of Bellow, Salinger, Mailer, Baldwin, and Updike* (Chapel Hill: University of North Carolina Press, 1967), 156.

265   *'blues singer'*, TAG, 181.

265   *'universal blues'*, JB quoted in BAB, 206.

265   *'chain of fornication'*, Norman Mailer, *Cannibals and Christians* (New York: The Dial Press, 1966), 114.

266   *'intersectional[ity]'*, Thomas Chatterton Williams, 'I Am Not Your Negro', *Sight and Sound*, May 2017.

266   *'hardest thing'*, JB quoted in AOF, 171.

266   *'my brother . . .'*, AC, 344, *'white and black . . .'* and subsequent, AC, 17–18.

267   *'had expected her to resist'* and subsequent, AC, 30–31.

268   *'same roaring . . .'* and subsequent, AC, 53–4.

268   *'hits bottom'*, *'They killing me'*, AC, 75, *'[Rufus] wanted me . . .'*, 336, *'got drunk together . . .'* and subsequent, AC, 75–7.

269   *'by-play'* and subsequent, AC, 136–7.

270   *'phantom protagonist'*, as described by Gibson in *Salvific Manhood*, 147.

270   *'isolation and strangeness'* and subsequent on Eric, AC, 199–206.

272   *'nostalgia'* and subsequent, AC, 193.

272   *'submitted'* and subsequent, AC, 208–10.

273   *'reach out'* and subsequent sex scene, AC, 377–9.

GROWING PAINS

276   *'extravagant publicness* [. . .] *truth'*, Lionel Trilling, 'On James Baldwin's *Another Country'*, *Mid-Century* 44, September 1962.

276   *'degrading* [. . .] *exceptionally bad'*, Stanley Edgar Hyman, 'No Country for Young Men', in *The New Leader*, 25 June 1962.

276   '"*America's sexual paranoia*" [. . .] *he has come to the end . . .'*, Augusta Strong, 'Another Country', in *Freedomways*, Vol. 2, Issue 4, 1962, 500–503.

276   *'maim themselves* [. . .] *the first draft . . .'*, Mailer, *Cannibals and Christians*, 114–115.

277   *'excavat[ing] the buried consciousness . . .'*, JB quoted in AOF, 167.

277 '*gladiator*', JB, 'The Black Boy Looks at the White Boy', CE, 271.

277 '*the Depression language* . . .', ibid., 277.

277 '*partially totalitarian*' and subsequent quotations from Norman Mailer, 'The White Negro: Superficial Reflections on The Hipster', in *Dissent*, Summer 1957.

278 '*sprayed with perfume* [. . .] *smash the perfumed dome* . . .', Norman Mailer, *Advertisements for Myself* (New York: Putnam, 1959), 471–2.

278 '*love letter*' and subsequent, JB, 'The Black Boy Looks at the White Boy', CE, 269–85.

279 '*frets*' and subsequent, JB, 'At the Root of the Negro Problem', in *Time* magazine, 17 May 1963.

280 '*sex perversion at its vilest*', quoted in *James Baldwin: The FBI File*, ed. William J. Maxwell (New York: Arcade Publishing, 2017), 276. Epub.

280 '*national conservative confessor* . . .', ibid., 139. Epub.

281 '*Everyone read it* . . .', Elizabeth Hardwick, 'Grub Street', in *New York Review of Books*, 1 February 1963.

281 '*Isn't Baldwin a well-known pervert?*', The FBI File, 257. Epub.

281 '*history's most highly paid* . . .', JB, 'The Devil Finds Work', CE, 544.

281 '*unmanly weeping*', quoted in TAG, 124.

282 Introductory passage on Eldridge Cleaver and quotations from *Soul on Ice* (New York: Dell Publishing Co, 1968), 14–17.

282 Cleaver on Baldwin, *Another Country* and Mailer: ibid., 97–110.

283 '*handicapped*', JB quoted in *Conversations*, 252.

284 '*absolutely determined* . . .', JB, 'To Be Baptized', CE, 457.

284 '*all that toy soldier* . . .', JB quoted in AOF, 292.

286 '*I've loved a few men* . . .', JB quoted in Sedat Pakay, *James Baldwin: From Another Place*, 1973, Sedat Pakay, 11:30.

286 '*a growing up*', JB, 'In Search of a Majority', CE, 220.

Addendum: for more on masculinity, Baldwin, Mailer and Cleaver, see Douglas Taylor, 'Three Mean Cats in a Hall of Mirrors', in *Texas Studies in Literature and Language*, Vol. 52, Number 1, Spring 2010. See also Marlon B. Ross, 'Baldwin's Sissy Heroics', in *African American Review*, Winter 2013, Vol. 46, No. 4, Special Issue: James Baldwin, Winter 2013. Likewise, Ross's 'White Fantasies of Desire: Baldwin and the Racial Identities of Sexuality', in *James Baldwin Now*, ed. Dwight A. McBride. (New York: New York University Press, 1999) provided an essential framework for this book's critical approach to *Another Country* and will enrich anybody's reading of Baldwin.

EPILOGUE

287 '*I think the great emotional* . . .', JB, *Rap*, 146.

287 '*far more complex* . . .', JB in 'Go the Way Your Blood Beats', *The Village Voice*, 26 June 1984.

287 '*any human touch* . . .', JB, 'The Devil Finds Work', CE, 529.

288 '*He was insistent* . . .', David Leeming, BAB, 382.

288 '*powerful and fluid* . . .', Colm Tóibín, 'The Last Witness', in *London Review of Books*, Vol. 3; 18, 20 September 2001.

288 '*literary conscious, touchstone* [. . .] *proto-intersectional* . . .', The FBI File, 14–16. Epub.

289 '*JOHN CHEEVER: A FAG*', Susan Cheever quoted in CAL, 666.

290 '*Carson McCullers? Never heard of him*', Rex Reed, 'Carson McCullers', 39.

291 '*delivered obligatory guffaws* . . .', Roger Ebert, 'Reflections in a Golden Eye', 17 October 1967. Online. rogerebert.com.

291 '*reflected and shaped American culture* . . .', Gregory Mosher, 'Foreword', in TW, *A House Not Meant to Stand* (New York: New Directions, 2008), xii.

292 '*It is a sad comment* . . .', Eve Adamson, 'Introduction', in TW, *Something Cloudy, Something Clear* (New York: New Directions, 1995), viii.

292 '*a world where the Kowalskis rule*', John Guare, blurb in TW, *A House.*

293 '*I think the strange, the crazed, the queer* . . .', TW, 'The Mutilated', in *Tennessee Williams: Plays 1957–1980* (New York: The Library of America, 2000), 585.

294 '*content, happy in being together* . . .', LG60, 371.

294 '*Past and present and future* . . .', LG50, vi.

294 '*unfinished poem*' and subsequent, TW in *Conversations*, 90.

294 '*a day is coming* . . .', JB, 'Notes on *Fortune In Men's Eyes*', quoted in Magdalena J. Zaborowska, *James Baldwin's Turkish Decade: Erotics of Exile* (Durham: Duke University Press, 2009), 141.

Selected Bibliography

Bailey, Blake, *Cheever: A Life*, New York: Knopf, 2009.

Baldwin, James, *Giovanni's Room*, New York: The Dial Press, 1956.

——, *Another Country*. New York: The Dial Press, 1962.

——, *Tell Me How Long the Train's Been Gone*, New York: The Dial Press, 1968.

James Baldwin: Collected Essays, New York: The Library of America, 1998.

Baldwin, James, and Margaret Mead, *A Rap on Race*, Philadelphia: J. B. Lippincott Company, 1971.

Berubé, Allan, *Coming Out Under Fire*, New York: Free Press, 1990.

Bosha, Francis J., 'The John Cheever Journals at Harvard University's Houghton Library', *Resources for American Literary Study*, Vol. 31, 2006.

Buck, Richard Maurice, *Calamus*, Boston: L. Maynard, 1897.

Campbell, James, *Talking at the Gates: A Life of James Baldwin*, New York: Viking, 1991.

Carr, Virginia Spencer, *The Lonely Hunter: A Biography of Carson McCullers*, Garden City, New York: Doubleday, 1975.

Cheever, Benjamin, ed., *The Letters of John Cheever*, New York: Simon & Schuster, 1988.

Cheever, John, *The Way Some People Live*, New York: Random House, 1943.

——, *Falconer*, New York: Alfred A. Knopf, 1977.

——, *The Journals of John Cheever*, New York: Alfred A. Knopf, 1991.

Cheever, John, Weaver, John D., *Glad Tidings: A Friendship in Letters. The Correspondence of John Cheever and John D. Weaver, 1945—82*, ed. John D. Weaver, New York: HarperCollins, 1993.

Cleaver, Eldridge, *Soul on Ice*, New York: Dell Publishing Co., 1968.

Collins, R. G., ed., *Critical Essays on John Cheever*, Boston: G. K. Hall, 1988.

Devlin, Albert J., ed., *Conversations with Tennessee Williams*, Jackson: University Press of Mississippi, 1986.

——, ed., *The Selected Letters of Elia Kazan*, New York: Alfred A. Knopf, 2014.

Devlin, Albert J. and Nancy M. Tischler, eds, *The Selected Letters of Tennessee Williams*, New York: New Directions, 2000.

Donaldson, Scott, ed., *Conversations with John Cheever*, Jackson: University Press of Mississippi, 1987.

——, *John Cheever: A Biography*, New York: Random House, 1988.

Eckman, Fern, *The Furious Passage of James Baldwin*, New York: M. Evans, 1966.

Ellis, Havelock, *Studies in the Psychology of Sex*, New York: Random House, 1936.

Erkkila, Betsy and Jay Gossman, eds, *Breaking Bounds*, New York: Oxford University Press, 1996.

Foucault, Michel. *The History of Sexuality*, Vol. I: *An Introduction*, translated by Robert Hurley, New York: Random House, 1980.

Fox, Peggy L. and Thomas Keith, eds, *The Luck of Friendship: The Letters of Tennessee Williams and James Laughlin*, New York: W. W. Norton, 2018.

Gibson III, Ernest L., *Salvific Manhood: James Baldwin's Novelisation of Male Intimacy*, Lincoln: University of Nebraska Press, 2019.

Grosskurth, Phyllis, *Havelock Ellis: A Biography*, New York: Alfred A. Knopf, 1988.

Johnson, David K., *The Lavender Scare*, Chicago: University of Chicago Press, 2004.

Jones, James H., *Alfred C. Kinsey: A Public/Private Life*, New York: W. W. Norton, 1997.

Katz, Jonathan Ned, *The Invention of Heterosexuality*, Chicago: University of Chicago Press, 2007.

Kinsey, Alfred C., Wardell B. Pomeroy and Clyde E. Martin, *Sexual Behavior in the Human Male*, Philadelphia and London: W. B. Saunders Company, 1948.

Koestenbaum, Wayne, *Double-Talk: The Erotics of Male Literary Collaboration*, New York: Routledge, 2017.

Lahr, John, *Tennessee Williams: Mad Pilgrimage of The Flesh*, New York: W. W. Norton, 2014.

Leverich, Lyle, *Tom: The Unknown Tennessee Williams*, New York: Crown Publishers, 1995.

McCullers, Carson, *The Heart Is a Lonely Hunter*, Boston: Houghton Mifflin, 1940.

——, *Reflections in a Golden Eye*, Boston: Houghton Mifflin, 1941.

——, *The Ballad of the Sad Café*, Boston: Houghton Mifflin, 1951.

——, 'The Flowering Dream', *Esquire*, 1 December 1959.

——, *Illumination & Night Glare: The Unfinished Autobiography*, ed. Carlos L. Dews, Madison: University of Wisconsin Press, 1999.

Miller, Edwin Haviland, ed., *Walt Whitman: The Correspondence*, New York: New York University Press, 1961–1977.

Paller, Michael, *Gentlemen Callers: Tennessee Williams, Homosexuality, and Mid-Twentieth-Century Broadway Drama*, London: Palgrave Macmillan, 2010.

Palmer, R. Barton and William Robert Bray, *Hollywood's Tennessee: The Williams Films and Postwar America*, Austin: University of Texas Press, 2009.

Reed, Rex, *Do You Sleep in the Nude?*, New York: New American Library, 1968.

Schmidgall, Gary, ed., *Conserving Walt Whitman's Fame: Selections from Horace Traubel's Conservator, 1890–1919*, Iowa City: University of Iowa Press, 2006.

Schueller, Herbert M. and Robert L. Peters, eds, *The Letters of John Addington Symonds*, Detroit: Wayne State University Press, 1967.

Sedgwick, Eve Kosofsky, *Between Men*, New York: Columbia University Press, 1985.

——, *Epistemology of The Closet,* updated with a new preface, Berkeley, California: California University Press, 2008.

Symonds, John Addington, *The Memoirs of John Addington Symonds: A Critical Edition*, ed. Amber K. Regis, London: Palgrave Macmillan, 2016.

Tippins, Sherill, *February House*, Boston: Houghton Mifflin Harcourt, 2005.

Weatherby, W. J., *James Baldwin: Artist on Fire: A Portrait*, New York: D. I. Fine, 1989.

Whitman, Walt, *Leaves of Grass*, Brooklyn, NY, 1855.

——, *Leaves of Grass*, Brooklyn: Fowler & Wells, 1856.

——, *Leaves of Grass*, Boston: Thayer and Eldridge, 1860–1861.

——, *Leaves of Grass*, Philadelphia: David McKay, 1891–1892.

——, *Complete Prose Works*, Philadelphia: David McKay, 1892.

——, *Notebooks and Unpublished Prose Manuscripts*, ed. Edward F. Grier, New York: New York University Press, 1984.

Williams, Tennessee, *A Streetcar Named Desire*, New York: New Directions, 1947.

——, *The Collected Plays of Tennessee Williams*, New York: The Library of America, 2000.

——, *Notebooks*, ed. Margaret Bradham Thornton, New Haven: Yale University Press, 2006.

Zaretsky, Eli, *Secrets of the Soul: A Social and Cultural History of Psychoanalysis*, New York: Alfred A. Knopf, 2004.

Acknowledgements

I am indebted, first and foremost, to Seren Adams, without whom this book simply would not exist. I wish to extend special thanks to my editor, Charlotte Humphery, for seeing potential in this project in its very early stages, and for helping bring it to fruition; and to Nico Parfitt, whose support has been essential. I also wish to thank the Hawthornden Literary Foundation, for providing a residency where several chapters of this book were written. I am grateful for the enlightening company of my co-residents, Helon, Sarah, Sonia and Sugi, and for the truly unforgettable hospitality of my hosts. Thank you to Cissy, Gabe and Rosa, for your advice, curiosity and infinite generosity; and to my mum, not least for letting me use the garage as writing space during a particularly long winter.

Index